KAZUO ISHIGURO'S GESTURAL POETICS

KAZUO ISHIGURO'S GESTURAL POETICS

Peter Sloane

BLOOMSBURY ACADEMIC
NEW YORK • LONDON • OXFORD • NEW DELHI • SYDNEY

BLOOMSBURY ACADEMIC
Bloomsbury Publishing Inc
1385 Broadway, New York, NY 10018, USA
50 Bedford Square, London, WC1B 3DP, UK
29 Earlsfort Terrace, Dublin 2, Ireland

BLOOMSBURY, BLOOMSBURY ACADEMIC and the Diana logo are trademarks of
Bloomsbury Publishing Plc

First published in the United States of America 2021
This paperback edition published 2023

Copyright © Peter Sloane, 2021

For legal purposes the Acknowledgements on p. viii constitute an extension
of this copyright page.

Cover design by Eleanor Rose
Illustration © Rafael Araujo @rafaelaraujo2222

All rights reserved. No part of this publication may be reproduced or transmitted
in any form or by any means, electronic or mechanical, including photocopying,
recording, or any information storage or retrieval system, without prior permission
in writing from the publishers.

Bloomsbury Publishing Inc does not have any control over, or responsibility for,
any third-party websites referred to or in this book. All internet addresses given
in this book were correct at the time of going to press. The author and publisher
regret any inconvenience caused if addresses have changed or sites have ceased to
exist, but can accept no responsibility for any such changes.

Whilst every effort has been made to locate copyright holders the publishers would be
grateful to hear from any person(s) not here acknowledged.

A catalog record for this book is available from the Library of Congress.

ISBN: HB: 978-1-5013-4799-3
PB: 978-1-5013-7791-4
ePDF: 978-1-5013-4801-3
eBook: 978-1-5013-4800-6

Typeset by Newgen KnowledgeWorks Pvt. Ltd., Chennai, India

To find out more about our authors and books visit www.bloomsbury.com
and sign up for our newsletters.

For Enzo
(Depriver of Sleep, Bringer of Joy)

CONTENTS

Acknowledgements	viii
List of Abbreviations	ix
INTRODUCTION: WHERE THE WORLD WORLDS	1
Chapter 1	
GESTURES	15
Part 1: Realism	18
Part 2: Modernism	31
Chapter 2	
IMAGINATION	47
Part 1: Games	52
Part 2: Childhood arts	62
Chapter 3	
AESTHETICS	75
Chapter 4	
ARCHITEXT	103
Chapter 5	
SPACE	133
CONCLUSION: THE REMAINS OF THE …	161
References	165
Index	177

ACKNOWLEDGEMENTS

This book, imperfect as it remains, has benefitted from much encouragement and advice over the past several years. My gratitude to the University of Lincoln, UK, for giving my research a home and for a generous period of research leave (more so during the various uncertainties of the coronavirus). My sincere thanks to Laurence Publicover (Bristol) for a meticulous reading of the proposal and draft chapters, and for offering suggestions which were instrumental in the formative stages. My thanks also to David James (Birmingham) for supportive readings of draft material. My thanks to the attendees of the wonderful conference *Twenty-First Century Perspectives on Kazuo Ishiguro*, conceived and organized by Sebastian Groes and Max Berghege at the University of Wolverhampton in February 2020. It was a pleasure to speak here with so many fans of Ishiguro, to whom I remain indebted, including but not limited to Andrew Bennett (Bristol), Cynthia Wong (Colorado), Sean Matthews (Nottingham) and Barry Lewis (Sunderland). My thanks to Fanny Bessard (Oxford) for many discussions about Ishiguro and the content of the book, and for reading and commenting on chapters. Thanks also to Haaris Naqvi, Rachel Moore, and Rachel Walker at Bloomsbury for making this project possible and for being generous with deadlines and wordcount. Last, but especially, my gratitude to Sir Kazuo Ishiguro for writing novels of such subtle and profound beauty; I will be thinking, writing and talking about these stories for a lifetime.

ABBREVIATIONS

AFW	*An Artist of the Floating World*
BG	*The Buried Giant*
N	*Nocturnes*
NLMG	*Never Let Me Go*
PVH	*A Pale View of Hills*
RD	*The Remains of the Day*
U	*The Unconsoled*
WWO	*When We Were Orphans*

INTRODUCTION: WHERE THE WORLD WORLDS

After an arduous journey through post-Roman Britain's barren terrain – having participated in the killing of Querig, a sickly dragon cursed by Merlin to breathe a mist of forgetfulness over the land, having encountered Don Quixote-cum-Sir Gawain in his senescence and witnessed (even precipitated) his death – aged Britons Axl and Beatrice find themselves having to prove their love to a Charon/Morgan le Fay-like boatman who will ferry them across their lives' journey's final threshold to 'dwell together' for eternity on a sacred island, perhaps Avalon (*BG* 342).[1] Such a fate would require a rare and generous dispensation; most cross alone to live in solitude, only very 'occasionally a couple may be permitted to cross to the island together', but only if they 'have an unusually strong bond of love between them' (*BG* 43). However, it is for the boatman to 'perceive if their bond is strong enough to cross together', by asking questions about their shared past (*BG* 43). Axl and Beatrice worry that Querig's vaporous nepenthe will have veiled the memories needed to demonstrate the depth of their love, that 'without our memories, there's nothing for it but for our love to fade and die' (*BG* 49). Their more urgent fear is that Querig's death and the lifting of that veil will uncover memories of conflict, infidelity and shared bereavement. Axl solicits his wife's reassurance that she will remember their love 'no matter what you see once the mist's gone', before Beatrice seeks assurance that Axl will not abandon her on the bare mountain because of the 'dark things I did to you once, husband' (*BG* 280, 307). Naturally, the course of a lifelong relationship has witnessed numerous petty and profound hurts, and the now-evaporating mist (nothing more than age, passing time manifest) obscures kindnesses and harms.

Having left Gawain, Querig, Wistan and Edwin on the mountainside, once again escaping a deluge, they re-encounter the boatman met earlier as they sought refuge from rain in a ruined villa. About which moment of trauma or triumph does he question them? Perhaps Axl's participation in brokering (a subsequently betrayed) peace between the warring Saxons and Britons on behalf of King Arthur? After all, as Robert Eaglestone remarks, Axl 'played a crucial role in Arthur's genocide', whether wittingly or, like Stevens, unwittingly serving the wrong master (2018: 312). Maybe Beatrice's infidelity? Or their now forgotten mourning and recriminations for a dead son? Even the many hardships jointly surmounted during their recent pursuit of Querig? No; the boatman asks 'no searching question', but rather one about 'the day the two of you carried eggs back from a market':

> 'She said she held them in a basket before her, and you walked beside her, peering into the basket all the way for fear her steps would injure the eggs. She recalled the time with happiness.'
> 'I think I do too, boatman', he says, and looks at me with a smile. 'I was anxious for the eggs because she'd stumbled on a previous errand, breaking one or two. A small walk, but we were well contented that day.'
> 'It's as she remembers it,' I say. (*BG* 338)

For Ivan Stacy, this 'seems an unlikely means of determining the nature of their bond', certainly less effective than the boatman's subsequent query to Axl about a moment in 'their time together that brought him "particular pain" (355)' (2019: 16). Yet, after Axl offers an honest and moving admission that he 'kept locked through long years some small chamber in [his] heart that yearned for vengeance' over Beatrice's brief affair, the boatman insists on carrying a progressively more fragile Beatrice to the boat, remarking tellingly to Axl that 'it will be like when she carried those eggs and you went anxiously beside her' (*BG* 340–1). Any ambiguity about the sinister implication of the apparently casual comment disappears when the boatman observes that on this comparison 'the fear returns to [Axl's] face' (*BG* 341). Axl, clearly, has failed the test before he is encouraged to speak about the ostensibly more profound harms. Shortly after reassuring Axl that they will remain together, the boatman dissembles, telling Axl that the boat is too small to accommodate two, despite twice very clearly mentioning that couples could '*cross to* the island *together*', that in cases of 'abiding love' boatmen are 'only too happy to *ferry* the couple *together*' (*BG* 47, my italics). Beatrice pleads with Axl to trust the boatman will 'hasten back to fetch' Axl after she has been safely conveyed. Inevitably, like the old woman at the villa tricked into waiting as her husband was ferried to the island, Axl will not be carried across, but will remain alone, on shore, waiting and, like most of Ishiguro's narrators, recalling the past in order to discover some moment, some turning point at which their paths diverged.[2]

What precisely was the boatman's test designed to uncover? Beatrice recalls this day as one of mutual cares when they were equally invested in the careful carrying of the eggs which were entrusted by both to Beatrice. In this scenario, the memory is joyful because the task unites them in shared goals: both were anxious to preserve the eggs, imagining together the delicious uses to which they will be put on their return to the warren's domestic sanctuary. But, Axl's anxiety was not aligned with Beatrice's, or he with her sense that their concerns intersected; Axl is deeply anxious *about* Beatrice carrying the eggs, having lost faith in her simply because she had 'stumbled', once, 'on a previous errand'. Perhaps on this prior occasion she had shopped alone; now, Axl no longer trusts in her ability to perform so small a task but escorts her on her chore. Seemingly 'pretty innocuous' (to borrow a phrase from Kathy H. in an equally mundane scenario about a pencil case), the anecdote gestures towards a series of trivial yet ultimately fatal tensions that emerge in a scenario that involves Beatrice being entrusted with something fragile (like love, or trust, or memories) (*NLMG* 56). If, as Alain Badiou suggests, 'real love is one that triumphs lastingly, sometimes painfully, over the hurdles erected by time, space and the world', then Axl and Beatrice's love, which falters at such trifling obstacles, seems not to meet these requirements (2012: 32). Indeed, in this moment, Axl is forced to confront a possibility that has surfaced for both he and his wife: that their love perished long ago and that they remain together 'for fear of loneliness and nothing more' (*BG* 47). In this reading, one wonders whether Beatrice truly believes the boatman would return for her husband, or whether either even wants such a reward/deferral, finally. The Socratic boatman attempts through a somewhat indirect method to tease out from a seemingly unremarkable moment some certainty about the nature of their bond. Unfortunately, but inevitably, even Axl cannot have such certainty, a fact revealed by his confession that he merely 'thinks' he recalls the day in the same way.

What emerges from this mundane, even absurd interrogation about eggs is that the essence of 'love' or the 'true nature' of romantic bonds, for example, are not themselves amenable to apprehension, as an object might be. We can make an inference here, about the fate of Klara from Ishiguro's upcoming novel *Klara and the Sun* (2021), attempting to answer the abiding question, 'what does it mean to love?' Love is not an object as such, neither is the intangible yet often lifelong bond which it forges between persons. These things cannot be seen, sensed, handled. We might think of *Never Let Me Go*'s clones, hopelessly lost in the belief that a few childish artworks crafted from society's 'trash' (as are they according to Ruth) might reveal the presence of souls (in a soulless world), that two pictures might somehow manifest when a couple were 'deeply in love' (*NLMG* 247). Like Tommy and Kathy, Axl and Beatrice seek a deferral for the end of their relationship based on the apprehension or demonstration of the essence of a shared feeling and its possible manifestation in the everyday. Madame and the boatman are assumed to be able to perceive the ineffable and to grant such a reward: but deferrals, it transpires, are mere fantasy, partially because these essences are definitionally undisclosable. The soul is that ineffable essence upon which so much philosophy and theology rests, love the invisible tie that binds people and therefore communities together. If Tommy, Kathy and Ruth are betrayed by such a fantasy, their error is inherited from Hailsham; like them, Miss Emily and Marie-Claude naïvely believe that through the students' artworks they might 'prove' the clones 'had souls at all', that they were more than the 'shadowy objects in test tubes' as 'most people' thought 'in the early days, after the war'.[3]

War is Ishiguro's most persistent and pervasive subject, although he has no interest in the dramatic guns and tanks and bombs of battles themselves, but in the radiating political, historical, social and personal scars of conflicts' aftermath. Those scars are signifiers, of sorts, traces in personal and national memory. In the context of these fictions, one might consider the knotted skein of memories as a dense, layered complex network of interwoven neural scars. Ishiguro's novels unfold against backdrops of momentous post-war events: the end of the British Empire (*RD*); the bombing of Nagasaki (*PVH*, *AFW*); the formation of the idea of Britain after the collapse of the Western Roman Empire (*BG*), organ harvesting/genocide (*NLMG*). Although these seem to be the novels' contexts, their 'historical truth' in Ishiguro's words, he pays them little attention, despite his narrators' desire to place their lives in and to benefit from their socio-historic significance (Gaby Wood 2017). As Eaglestone has commented on *Never Let Me Go*, the novel 'focuses less on the genocide itself and more on the public secrecy that both hides and empowers it' (2017: 17). Moments of genuine gravity, however, are seldom spectacular, often banal. Persons' lives are defined, Ishiguro seems to suggest, not by those occasional incidents in which we try to make or imagine that we have made 'a contribution to the course of history' – Banks recovering 'stolen jewels', Ono painting a provocative poster, Stevens serving brandy to the great names of interwar European politics – but by the slow synthetic accretion of the stratified minutia that constitute the geology of our unremarkable, undocumented private lives. As he recalls of his memories of his first five years in Japan, 'nothing monumental' comes to mind, just 'ordinary things' like 'cutting [his] thumb with a pair of scissors' (leaving scars both material and mental): 'these very little things have somehow stayed', he goes on, but he has a 'vast array of such memories' (Bigsby 2008: 15). Ishiguro's decision to conclude *The Buried Giant* with its grand literary, historical and political themes with so prosaic a moment comes as no surprise in the context of an oeuvre in which crayon drawings of superman (*U*), childhood memories of 'luscious' pencil cases (*NLMG*), polished silver (*RD*), juvenile detective games (*WWO*) and many such paltry events are presented in retrospection to have been decisive 'turning points' in which or from which the essence of a life might be distilled (I will (re)turn to turning points below). It is only through such inconsequential details that we can approach asymptotically, like the boatman, what Martin Heidegger calls the elusive 'thingness' of our world(s).

Unfortunately, it is in the nature of *the* and *our* worlds to remain beyond introspection's grasp, to recede from attempts at distillation, because, as Heidegger remarks, the essence of world is simply not to be found in things that 'stand before us':

World is not the mere collection of countable or uncountable, familiar and unfamiliar things that are at hand. But neither is it a merely imagined framework added by our representation to the sum of such given things. The *world worlds*, and is more fully in being than the tangible and perceptible realm in which we believe ourselves to be at home. World is never an object that stands before us and can be seen. World is the ever nonobjective to which we are subject as long as the paths of birth and death, blessing and curse, keep us transported into Being. (2011: 108)

Ishiguro has a recurring interest in such 'paths'. Our sensory perception of the 'tangible' contributes to our experience of the world. But, as William Shakespeare famously poeticizes in *Hamlet* (1601–2), 'there are more things in heaven and Earth ... Than are dreamt of in our philosophy' (2008: 195). Philosophy, like fiction, or science, is one 'imagined framework' that endeavours to find knowledge of or impose knowledge on the 'ever nonobjective' thingness of the world to which we remain irredeemably subject. Our senses may enable us to apprehend the phenomenal world, facilitating what Bertrand Russell calls 'knowledge by description'; yet, although things in the world cause 'such-and-such sense-data', the 'Thing Itself', whether that be a chair or an emotion, a memory or a reverie, is 'not, strictly speaking, known to us at all' (2009: 192). In *Hard Times* (1854), Charles Dickens, playfully parodying scientific 'knowledge', offers such an example in defining a horse as 'Quadruped. Graminivorous. Forty teeth, namely twenty-four grinders, four eye-teeth, and twelve incisive' (2003: 12). For the positivist Thomas Gradgrind, these are the facts with which one must be acquainted in order to 'know what a horse is' (2003: 12). Yukio Mishima gestures towards the more profound ontological nature of beings' being in an enigmatic and disturbing scene in *The Sailor Who Fell from Grace with the Sea* (1963). After his young protagonists kill and skin a cat, they meditate that the flayed non-objective entity before them 'seemed to be wearing a cat mask. The cat was only an exterior; life had posed as a cat' (1977: 49).[4] Life is the ineffable essence which merely takes the physical form of the cat or horse which 'stands before us', but which is not contained in or disclosed by description, or even brutal dissection of its various parts. The thing itself with which we are acquainted through our senses remains little more than an echo of and a gesture back towards its own ineffable thingness, an essence (like the clones' missing souls, Axl and Beatrice's love, Stevens's dignity) which evades metaphysical, scientific or linguistic reduction. If, as Russell concludes, 'all our knowledge ... rests upon acquaintance', our apperception of objects, of truths, even oneself is proximate, mediated, gestural (2009: 192). In Kantian terms, we can apprehend the material phenomena presented to our senses, but the noumena that lies behind the mask must be inferred.

The things that 'stand before us' to be judged, as it were, are merely emanations (the shadows cast on the wall of Plato's cave) of the things in themselves. Troublingly, the noumenal world is not amenable to any form of interrogation.

Indeed, it is definitionally of a different order to any of the available means of experiment; it is pre- and super-linguistic, immaterial and imperceptible:

> A stone presses downwards and manifests its heaviness. But while this heaviness exerts an opposing pressure upon us it denies us any penetration into it. If we attempt such penetration by breaking open the rock, it still does not display in its fragments anything inward that has been opened up. The stone has instantly withdrawn again into the same dull pressure and bulk of its fragments ... Earth thus shatters every attempt to penetrate it ... The earth appears openly cleared as itself only where it is perceived and preserved as that which is essentially undisclosable, as that which shrinks from every disclosure and constantly keeps itself closed up. (Heidegger 2011: 110)

Oddly, Decca Aitkenhead commented after interviewing Ishiguro that 'there is an opacity about him that eludes description, giving no glimpse of what might lie within' (2009). In Heidegger's understanding, even if Aitkenhead were to 'break open' the object that is Sir Kazuo Ishiguro, or to flay him like Mishima's cat, aside from being bad manners, the thingness of his being would withdraw more deeply into the 'non-objective'. Wondering whether he might have achieved enough in his faultless service to the disgraced Lord Darlington to be considered a 'great butler' (the book is his plea for such a judgement from a reader assumed to be a fellow butler, as Kathy's is a final submission to we, the human gallery, in support of her deferral), Stevens asks 'what precisely is this "greatness"? Just where, or in what, does it lie?' (*RD* 28). He manages to break it open but reveals only fragments from which arise further questions; to be a 'great butler' is to have 'dignity in keeping with [one's] position' (*RD* 35). Perplexingly, as Stevens recognizes, 'this merely begs the further question: of what is "dignity" comprised?' (*RD* 33).[5] Indeed, Stevens identifies the category error of attempting to approach the intangible through the tangible, observing that it is no use 'trying to put our fingers on the constitution of this "dignity"' (*RD* 34). Kant argued too, perhaps first (unless we consider Platonic 'Ideals') that 'objects of sense [are] mere appearances', that they 'are based upon a thing in itself [ding an sich], though we know not this thing as it is in itself but only know its appearances' (2001: 53). Superficial attributes that are presented to the senses are acquainted with and acquaint us with an essence not situated in the parts, but which supervenes upon them while 'shattering every attempt to penetrate'. *Hamlet* expresses a similar conception with great eloquence, philosophizing that certain things such as grief may manifest in 'customary suits of solemn black', or 'windy suspiration of forced breath', but they 'have that within which passeth show' (2008: 159). Stevens too is sensitive to the fact that it is all too easy to take 'the superficial for the essence', while the 'thing-in-itself' remains unknown (*RD* 34). While for Hans-Georg Gadamer the 'continuous transition from one aspect of a thing to another' gives rise to the 'unified matrix of our experience', the world nevertheless remains, returning to

Heidegger, more than the 'sum of such given things', beyond show (1977: 73). The atopic noumenal world must be encountered as a perpetual immanence, tantalizingly beyond the grasp because it does not 'lie in' anything that is 'openly cleared' (as we reach, so it recedes). Stevens pre-empts the readers' suspicion that there 'will always be, I realize, those who would claim that any attempt to analyse greatness as I have been doing is quite futile' (*RD* 30). Nonetheless, he along with Madame, Ono, Ogata and the boatman endeavour philosophically to grasp the essence of being, usually by identifying what Ishiguro posits as 'turning points'.

The worlding of the world in its 'essentially undisclosable' nature reveals its presence, or perhaps absence, in 'turning points', seemingly irrelevant or trivial non-events that at first 'go unrecognized' but which are often 'rediscovered by new enquiry' (Heidegger 2011: 108). As Yugin Teo comments, for Ishiguro's characters, 'Pivotal events or incidents that have taken place in the past (and some may appear to be deceptively insignificant at the time) often prove to have significantly shaped the unconscious later on' (2014: 1). Stevens, for example, thinks back to an argument with Miss Kenton before he peevishly ended their ritual cocoa evenings, recalling that he 'was perhaps not entirely aware of the full implications of what I was doing' at the time, but that 'it might even be said that this small decision of mine constituted something of a key turning point [which] set things on an inevitable course towards what eventually happened' (*RD* 175). Christopher Banks thinks back to an unremarkable meeting with Sarah Hemmings, which 'in hindsight ... could well be viewed as some sort of important turning point' (*WWO* 208). Kathy, thinking of a conversation with Tommy, recalls that 'I think of it now as a kind of marker between the two eras. Not that anything significant started to happen immediately afterwards; but for me at least, that conversation was a turning point. I definitely started to look at everything differently' (*NLMG* 76). Several turning points occur in *The Unconsoled*, usually involving moments that seem objectively trivial, but which are of great importance to the characters. Fiona, an old friend of Ryder expecting a simple favour, talks with her colleagues from 'The Women's Arts and Cultural Foundation', who recall proudly their 'bunting for the Peking people' alongside 'all the effort we put into the sandwiches for the Henri Ledoux lunch' as being a 'real turning point' for their organization (*U* 232). Gustav asks Ryder to speak for the porters in what he expects to be 'an historic turning point for our profession' (*U* 296). Ryder too wonders, in a rare moment of doubt about the concert planned for his final evening, whether it would in fact 'prove a turning point for the community after all?' (*U* 482). Gustav and Ryder try and fail to create, to pre-empt turning points, but Ishiguro shows us that these attempts to control fate are futile, that, as Heidegger remarks, they can emerge only on subsequent enquiry and usually when it is too late to change their 'inevitable course'. In failed lives, simple events dredged from unremarkable pasts find themselves subsequently overloaded with significance, because they appear to characters despairing of finding meaning to manifest something profoundly true about their essential natures. But, as Stevens thinks, 'with the benefit of hindsight one begins to search one's past for such "turning points", one is apt to start seeing them everywhere' (*RD* 175). Though not as such things in themselves, turning points are ontological rifts through which the noumenal essence of world ruptures the phenomenal world and is glimpsed, momentarily. These fleeting encounters reveal the world worlding, something shifting, an opening or closing off of certain paths. These flashes of the noumenal ground of their phenomenal being cannot be seen immediately, but manifest only in retrospect, through recall, and even then remain speculative, hypothetical, indicative.

Memory has proven to be the single most pervasive thread of Ishiguro scholarship, a theme explored most fully in Teo's important *Kazuo Ishiguro and Memory* (2014). As Teo notes, the 'work of memory is an aspect of [Ishiguro's] writing that makes him unique among his contemporaries' (2014: 151). Each of Ishiguro's fictions sketches characters in the iterative process of trying to identify the ineffable essence of their lives, the decisive moments which, to return once more to Hamlet, 'can denote [them] truly' (2008: 159). His characters' desperation to fix some objective semblance of a self from the details of lives through recollection is, inevitably, fruitless, partially because that essence does not inhere or lie within these things (if it lies anywhere at all), but also because of the fragility and manipulability of the means of recovery: memory. Memory is Protean, wrestling with it like Menelaus or Aristaeus simply forces it to explore its repertoire of metamorphoses in the (misguided) hope that, with eventual exhaustion, it must assume its true form. Memory is a contortionist, adeptly accommodating itself to new spaces. Recall and its susceptibility to interference and error certainly is central to each of Ishiguro's works, although characters do not so often accidentally misremember as intentionally recall and alter past moments as they attempt to edit in real time their life stories (like Beckett's Krapp). As Carlo Sini and Thomas Behr suggest, such (decisions and) revisions are a fundamental aspect of our compulsion to rewrite our autobiographical narratives:

> Living persons retell their origin to themselves always starting afresh: one keeps revising versions of oneself while going on living ... The significance of that which one has lived depends instead on one's uncertain memories and on one's ever-changing interpretations: at ten one has one version, at twenty, another, and so forth. The significance of one's life reveals itself as a moveable threshold that defies a permanent setting, that is, that defies confining itself within merely empirical facts. To put it in other words: someone's life continually meets the limit of its significance, right up to the final fact of death. (2011: 126–7)

Death (a final barrier or merely another border?) itself births altogether more troubling questions about the limits of knowledge. As Derrida asks, 'Is my death possible? Can we understand this question? Can I, myself, pose it? Am I allowed to talk about my death?' (1993: 21). Lives, like the objects of sense perception, exceed signification, defy 'permanent setting', are not reducible to the 'countable' 'empirical facts' that present themselves. Another explanation for this is that lives are plural and do not have a single origin: each new stage of life requires a new autobiographical narrative, which we see eminently in *The Remains of the Day* after the arrival of Mr Farraday, *Never Let Me Go* on the collapse of Hailsham, *A Pale View of Hills* after the suicide of Keiko, *An Artist of the Floating World* as Ono tries to negotiate a new political present. The Delphic maxim to 'know thyself', implicitly endorsing a single life perspective, is troubled by such a conception of the plurality of lives (Louis MacNeice's 'drunkenness of things being various' ('Snow')), more so if one can merely be acquainted with the self that is oneself at any given point as a little more than another of the world's elusive non-objects.

Despite the fact that autobiographical memory is 'critical to self', that it may 'constitute the knowledge base of the self', it remains 'nebulous, intangible, and intrinsically slippery' (Conway 1996: 295). Self's moveable threshold, like the withdrawal of thingness, makes self-perception radically impossible because the self also exists atopically. We might think of Mrs Dalloway attempting to remember something about her lifelong friend Peter Walsh, meditating on the fact that 'when millions of things had utterly vanished' all that remains is 'a few sayings like this about cabbages' (Woolf 2003: 5–6).[6] What emerges however, organically, gesturally, is the radical impossibility of not only grasping but of representing, expressing selfhood, because, no matter the details gathered for inspection, they remain mere attributes for essences that are not and cannot be contained by signification: Etsuko, Ono, Stevens, Banks, Kathy, Axl and Beatrice's lives encounter repeatedly the 'limit of [their] significance'. Their stories are little more than accounts of things that remain themselves ineffable, inexpressible. Moreover, memory is not in fact the subject of Ishiguro's fictions at all, but merely a metonym for the ineffable. Though exploring the failures of memory and the manipulation of recollection, he employs memory as a convenient symbol for the intangibility of life's essential nature. Memory, in this sense, is for Ishiguro the ineffable bridge to the ineffable essence of characters' lives. What they are searching for is not in the memory, but the memory is positioned as an attribute of something that remains beneath the surface as they refashion their autobiography to suit circumstances. Perhaps this is inevitable, given that, as Conway remarks, 'the function of autobiographical memory is [itself] ineffable' (1996: 295). Although the ineffable is perhaps the only available and appropriate means to approach the ineffable, the ineffable results would be, ironically yet suitably, ineffable.

Such ineffability is, in the end, inevitable, simply because the human mind is mechanically incapable of apprehending and/or representing certain things. In his intriguing study, *Ignorance: Agnoiology and Literature* (2009), Andrew Bennett identifies the fact that 'the human is a kind of ignorance machine, since its "apparatus for acquiring knowledge"' is, as Friedrich Nietzsche explains *contra* John Locke and others, not 'designed for "knowledge"' (2009: 9). Thomas Hofweber describes this design flaw as 'structural ineffability':

> Our minds are such that they can represent some of the facts, but other facts are completely alien to our conceptual thought. Our minds and reality are not in harmony overall, they only harmonize for a part of reality, the part we can represent, but not for reality in general. And structural ineffability would mean a deep disharmony obtains. We don't even have the kinds of representations available to represent certain facts. (2017: 131)

Fundamentally, the thing in itself exists within or constitutes a 'reality' to which our faculties do not and cannot have access. Our experience of the world, in this understanding, is predicated on an irreconcilable disharmony. While the mind remains alienated from the non-objective, language provides another veil. As Jean-Luc Nancy remarks, using Heidegger's image of the stone, '"This stone" is the stone that my statement designates *and* before which my statement disappears. Or, instead of inscribing this stone in a lexicon, my statement comes to *exscribe itself* in this stone. At the heart of things, there is no language' (1993: 175). Language cannot penetrate but is merely penetrated by its ostensible referent. Derrida once said of certain writers, most notably Beckett, that they write 'texts which make the limits of our language tremble' (Kearney 1984: 112). Here Derrida alights upon what Nancy has referred to as 'the external limit of deixis': the world can be indicated, but only so far (1993: 175). Language is merely a construct which rests upon its subject. As such, it cannot be used to reflect on its own being; to expect language to disclose itself is to expect it to uncover the very possibility, the pre-linguistic ground of its being. Language, that is to say, cannot be used to harmonize us and our realities because language is perched on top of but not rooted in its pre-linguistic, pre-symbolic ground. But, as Asja Szafraniac comments, according to Derrida, the 'metonymy that allows us to speak about what is otherwise ineffable is as much a way of "speaking" as of "keeping silent"' (2007: 61). Thomas Gould finds a similar contradiction, arguing that 'to describe an object as "ineffable" is at the very same time to refute that object's ineffability [and] is thus an emptying of language' (2018: 107). The word ineffable is, however, little more than the placeholder for an aporia, a significance beyond signification. Ishiguro makes a virtue of the ineffable in texts and characters that are fundamentally irreducible, uncountable, but which in so being motion towards the profound thingness of lives, which is, paradoxically, to be unknowable.

This concern with the undisclosable thingness of lives is not simply a comment on the ontologically ineffable. Ishiguro is also interested in the form of literature which is, as Bennett remarks, inherently 'bound up with the question of not knowing' (2009: 1). Reading and writing necessarily involve uncertainty and the desire for certainty. The aesthetic experience itself is ineffable, giving rise to what Roman Ingarden describes as the 'quasi-oblivion of the real world' (1961: 298). For Heidegger, even if the production of a 'work [of art] means to set up a world', still 'the essence of world can only be indicated' (2011: 108). A work of art indicates, points towards world's elusive essence. What is a novel but a series of scenarios (about eggs, for example, or memories of tea and games of chess) from which the reader is invited to draw conclusions about characters, to infer, to disclose the essence; in this sense, we are Madame, the boatman, attempting through such trivia to discern, to perceive the important in the mundane. That is to say, in the final analysis, each narrative is an extraliterary plea, a request for dispensation that manages to emerge from the page into the real world which must remain undisclosed to the characters. As Maurice Blanchot comments on the 'Thing Itself' that is literature:

> No matter that it has so many different meanings: it is the art which is above the work, the ideal that the work seeks to represent, the World as it is sketched out in the work, the values at stake in the creative effort, the authenticity of this effort; it is everything which, above the work that is constantly being dissolved in things, maintains the model, the essence, and the spiritual truth of that work. (1995: 308)

Like the object, like love, like remorse, the work 'sets up a world' while remaining itself undisclosed. The work of fiction has an essence that cannot be spoken of directly, which 'shatters every attempt to penetrate it'. We see that Ishiguro's sketching of lives that resist empirical reduction corresponds to a poetics of obscurity, aware of the failures of language. As he has commented, he enjoys 'language that suppresses meaning rather than language that goes groping after something that's slightly beyond the words. I'm interested in speech that kind of conceals and covers up' (Elysha Chang 2015). As Brian W. Shaffer remarks, this trend is found in several narrators who 'tell stories that characteristically mask rather than uncover the true essence of their tales' (2001: 161). The boatman's question about 'pain' seems designed to penetrate to the essence of something that cannot be approached frontally, because the emotions that constellate around a hurt so pervasive withdraw at the approach. Perhaps, as Raymond Carver writes, 'it ought to make us feel ashamed when we talk like we know what we're talking about when we talk about love' (2003: 122). Love is only one of many feelings, such as regret, concern, pride, envy, which are central to life but whose precise nature retreats from signification.

Ishiguro's novels, as objects, are profoundly unknowable to us. In this attempt to 'break open' Ishiguro's fictions, I reformulate Heidegger's suggestion that the 'essence of world can only be indicated' as 'the essence of world can only be *gestured towards*' (2011: 108). Ishiguro's fictions point towards the ineffable essence of their characters' worlds which, much to their dismay, remains 'slightly beyond' the language and which vanishes on too close inspection (under the absurd scrutiny of Banks's magnifying glass, Stevens's

Socratic analyses of greatness and dignity). All literary criticism is an attempt to eff the ineffable, to locate, uncover, bring into the open the undisclosed essence of fiction, that which perpetually withdraws from the anatomizing clinical scrutiny of critical reading. However, Ishiguro's works not only invite but even demand such an approach precisely because of their gestural poetics, their use of a language that does not go 'groping after something that's slightly beyond the words': his works are deeply attuned to the profound and necessary absence of their subject, as are his narrator's profoundly aware that they can do little more than offer anecdotes and scenarios to us, their judge, that we might grant them some variety of dispensatory consolation. Ishiguro's fictions constellate around gravitational points (the hub of Stevens's great wheel) that emit no light, as it were, but which can be apprehended merely by virtue of their measurable effects on the text-space around them. In a way, a reading of Ishiguro is little more than a detection of wave patterns of distortions, ruptures that emanate from a point that lies not simply behind, but in another order, both parallel and alternate, but which nevertheless send ripples through the texts' sensitive, labile fabric. In a less optimistic reading, this point from which the sense of some evasive meaning radiates may be little more than an infinitely dense aporia, an ontological black hole.

These gestures towards the essence of the world and worlds take several forms in Ishiguro's writing, some of which I attempt to limn here. In Chapter 1 (divided into two parts: (1) Realism and (2) Modernism), I situate Ishiguro's fictions in the traditions of realism and modernism, suggesting that he takes the definitive elements of each of these modes of engaging with the 'real' and from these produces a synthesis that is deeply sensitive to the failures of literary form and fundamentally language itself. What is at stake is understanding, communication and, in its absence, a profound isolation arising from the inability to express. As a result, Ishiguro's characters develop 'unspoken' understandings which gesture towards those things that lie beyond words. In Chapter 2, I extend this discussion into his fascination with childhood imagination and childhood sketching. Ishiguro's children are eminent fantasists, deploying the imagination in both solo and shared play to counter the traumatic circumstances of their lives. Sketching also plays an important role in coming to terms with the world while also making manifest Ishiguro's own compositional techniques. Ishiguro's exploration of these two aspects of the childhood imaginary contributes to his evanescent gestural poetics, illustrating a recurring interest in ideational constructs which develops from his interrogations of realist and modernist poetics. Necessarily, this creative urge continues into adulthood. Chapter 3 grapples with Ishiguro's interest in the arts and his attempt to convey other forms in the form of fiction. His works often portray artists, painters and musicians struggling to negotiate, in past and present, the demands of aesthetic purity and the ideological and political implications of the arts. Ishiguro poses and responds to a range of salient and pressing questions about the relationship between aural and visual aesthetics and ethics. I argue that Ishiguro sees the arts as relational, or at least having the capacity to form communities, but that the individual producer often stands in the way of her own art. Chapter 4, through a reading of Gaston Bachelard, focuses on the art of architecture, uncovering Ishiguro's interest in the oneiric home and the state of homelessness that has come to typify each of Ishiguro's forlorn narrators. I draw out the symbolic resonance of Ishiguro's most iconic architectural spaces, Darlington, Hailsham, Masuji Ono's house, the warren, Ryder's hotel and the ruined or dilapidated buildings that linger in decay, to argue that these material and metaphoric structures play fundamental roles both in their specific narrative occurrence and in Ishiguro's gestural poetics. Finally, Chapter 5 moves into the open country, exploring Ishiguro's use of landscapes, from the domestic garden to the sea. Each of these things constitutes a gesture towards his characters' lives, their emotional and psychological states while also performing a reflection on the possibilities of literary fiction. The text/landscapes explored by Ishiguro's characters can exist only for them; they manifest and represent not objective space but rather subjective emotional place.

Like its introduction, this book gestures obliquely towards Ishiguro's gestures towards the ineffable, in the full awareness that too direct a critical glance will shatter the object into its literary fragments that will necessarily resist further scrutiny: What do we gain by suggesting that his characters are often misguided? That they live in the regret of turning points missed? That Hailsham's residents do not or cannot try to escape their brutal fates? That Axl and Beatrice betrayed one another? The non-object behind these superficial observations is not and cannot be sought in the text, in the language, because, as Sini and Behr comment, 'the being of a thing cannot be reduced to an event of language' (2011: 126). Ishiguro remarked in an interview that the aim of fiction is to 'make the projector come on inside a reader's head, you can't afford to have too much detail [in a novel]. You give just enough detail' to enable the reader to bring 'all these other images that are floating around in his or her head' to the novel (quoted in Teo 2014: 20). The writer's role, in Ishiguro's own estimation, is merely to gesture, to indicate, but always partially. Heidegger comments that the 'earth is the essentially self-secluding', and producing a work of art 'means to bring [world] into the open region as the self-secluding' (2011: 110). In other words, to produce a work of literary fiction means simply setting up a world that indicates its own absence, because that absence is the ineffable proxy signifier of an essence beyond the work: 'literature presents itself as a nullity, or more precisely, as its own absence' (Rodolphe Gasché 2005: 35). Literature's nullity also gestures towards language's multiple failures, and the fact that, as Walton writes forlornly to his sister in Mary Shelley's *Frankenstein* (1818), 'paper ... is a poor medium for the communication of feeling' (2008: 8). Ludwig Wittgenstein famously proposes in the preface to his most renowned and later recanted work that 'what can be said at all can be said clearly; and whereof one cannot speak thereof one must be silent' (1922: 23). It is exactly those things which cannot be spoken of clearly or confidently or unambiguously that occupy Ishiguro, and which form the subject of the arts. Fiction, in many ways, is an attempt to create a space for that which cannot be spoken of, or at least to indicate where that space might be, to roughly limn an outline (with a worn crayon, perhaps). Ishiguro's fictions, while making the edge of language tremble and testing the external limits of deixis, try to provide a shape for something to emerge, create an opening through which 'the earth appears openly cleared' in its nature as 'essentially undisclosable'. Although he places his characters in a multitude of different situations, genres, times, he is asking one question in the knowledge that no single answer is available: what does it mean to be a human being among other human beings? Ishiguro's gestural poetics is an acknowledgement of the unavailability of the essence of world; his works merely sketch, point towards world and self's moveable threshold which always exceeds and, in so doing, recedes from signification.

Notes

1. Ishiguro borrows this idea of national amnesia from Gabriel Garcia Marquez's *One Hundred Years of Solitude* (1967), in which the town of Macondo is beset by insomnia and related memory loss.
2. A case might be made that the old woman in the first example was Beatrice in an alternate narrative, and that Axl had in that instance been the one carried across. A hint is offered when the boatman tells them that they 'shouldn't by rights have met today, but some curious chance brought is together' (*BG* 46).
3. Indeed, their house itself is in the process of 'donating' furniture during Kathy and Tommy's visit.
4. Mariko's cats play a prominent role in Ishiguro's gothic debut.
5. It is unclear whether Stevens or Ishiguro misuses the term 'begs the question', which is an act of rhetoric that takes for given that which is to be demonstrated, as opposed to merely prompting further questions.
6. This is a very complex scene. Clarissa remembers standing in the gardens of Bourton when Peter Walsh approaches and says: '"Musing among the vegetables?" – was that it? – "I prefer men to cauliflowers" – was that it? ... it was his sayings one remembered ... a few sayings like this about cabbages' (2003: 6). Clarissa offers two possibilities for Peter's witticism – one about cauliflowers, the other about vegetables – and then seemingly without irony tells us that the one thing she remembers is his sayings 'about cabbages'. Woolf could quite easily have remedied this if it were an oversight, simply by having 'musing among the cabbages' and referring in the end, correctly, to 'sayings about vegetables' as a category which includes both cauliflower and cabbage. Her memory approximates the past, or at least her sense of it. More, she lacks recourse to the textual evidence, the written record of her failure to recall, to which we the reader have access.

Chapter 1

GESTURES

Prose fiction has always been either unwittingly but constitutionally resistant to formal classification or knowingly antagonistic towards it. For Michael McKeon, this intransigence is endemic; 'categorical instability', he argues, is 'central to the rise of the novel' (1985: 161). For Georg Lukacs ('in process of turning from Kant [Transcendence] to Hegel [Immanence]'), the novel is 'the most hazardous genre' precisely because it is always 'in the process of becoming' (1971: 12, 72–3). The same typological ambiguity surrounds short fiction, which, as Viorica Patea remarks, has its origin in a range of apparently disparate forms, from 'myth and biblical verse narratives, medieval sermons and romance' to 'fables, folktales, [and] ballads' (2012: 1). Ishiguro himself is reluctant to define *Nocturnes*, his only collection of short things, referring to it as 'just a fictional book that happens to be divided into these five movements' (Aitkenhead 2009).[1] All fiction, all writing even, is necessarily experimental, a series of arbitrary conventional gestures towards capturing what Virginia Woolf describes, in a language textured by advances in physics in the early part of the twentieth century, as the 'incessant shower of innumerable atoms' that 'shape themselves into' daily life (1986: 160). The mass-printed (mechanically reproduced, cloned) novel or collection of short fiction is little more than a practical concession to the formlessness of experience and the infelicity of expression, on the one hand, and the pragmatics of the modern publishing industry, on the other.[2] In *The Rise of the Novel*, Watt speculates that it 'is perhaps the only literary genre which is essentially connected with the medium of print' (1983: 223). For some Marxist critics, this connection with and dependence upon the means of production is particularly problematic, certainly for the realist novel, which 'overlooks or conceals its own uncritical acceptance of an ideologically derived reality', thereby performing, according to Pierre Bourdieu, 'a *denegation* of what it expresses' (Tallis 1988: 50; Bourdieu 1996: 4). Prose fiction represents a series of aesthetic and material negotiations always knowingly or unknowingly attuned to the critical and political efficacy of language and form.

Ishiguro's deceptively 'conventional' novels and short stories cultivate and manipulate finely wrought tensions between lexical precision and semantic ambiguity on the level of form, and the ostensibly 'objective reality' of history and the 'subjective realities' of lived experience on the thematic level. As Cynthia Wong remarks, regardless of changing settings and characters, Ishiguro's fictions endeavour always 'to capture the elusiveness of human consciousness' (2005: 23). Ishiguro is not a metaphysician but more of an existentialist (he has much in common with Kafka, Thomas Bernhard and Kobo Abe), and his interest is not in consciousness abstracted from historical circumstance. Rather, he shares with the great realists a penchant for creating characters that are complexly intertwined with dynamic social and political reality. His protagonists, always at the mercy of changing winds, are often overtaken and overwhelmed by history's fickleness. Another feature of Ishiguro's repurposing of realism is the search for unity, and with it the sense of an ending so typical of the form. His characters gather and attempt to order 'all the details' of their often 'misguided' pasts and, from these, to salvage some meaning, or evasive certainty's fragile solace. Kathy, Stevens, Ono and Banks move towards what they naively (informed by their readings of 'Victorian novels' and 'sentimental romance' in the first two cases) imagine will be dénouements, moments of euphoric revelation which will somehow retroactively confer meaning to *their* lives along with what Frank Kermode might call a 'regressive pleasure' for the reader (2000: 55). Alongside his various realist borrowings (which I'll discuss in more detail later), Ishiguro adopts and adapts modernism's privileging of the 'fleeting', 'contingent', 'ineffable' nature of experience and the slippages between perspectives so typical of the subjective turn in the arts at the turn of the twentieth century (Nicholls 1995: 6; Walkowitz 2006: 20). Indeed, as I will argue here, it is the fine balance that Ishiguro exploits between the most characteristic elements of realism (unity, certainty, closure) and modernism (disunity, uncertainty, irresolution) that invests his sentences and their aggregated yet always imminent wholes with their uniquely peculiar effect of ambiguity-through-precision.[3] As James Wood remarked of *The Buried Giant*, in a phrase which neatly summarizes Ishiguro's gestural poetics, it is 'at once too literal and too vague' (2015).

Often labelled a realist, Pico Iyer speculates that Ishiguro wrote *The Unconsoled*, his most intentionally experimental work, to 'prevent him from ever being taken as a realist again' (1995). Matthew Beedham makes the same point, suggesting that Ishiguro wrote the novel because he was frustrated 'by critics who attempted to categorise him as a realist' (2010: 4). Despite being viewed as predominantly realist, he has always been an elegantly but pragmatically innovative writer or, as James writes, an 'inconspicuous stylist' (2009: 61). *The Unconsoled* is almost aggressively experimental, 'something close to exhibitionism' as Ryder thinks of Brodsky's ill-fated return to conducting (and suffered the same fate as those avant-garde musical performances it parodies), seeming for all intents and purposes to be the work of an author revelling in difficulty, despite his assurances to Charlie Rose that he did not 'mean deliberately to be difficult' because it would be 'bad manners to just deliberately be difficult' (1995). Viet Thanh Nguyen's description of Ishiguro as 'both a popular and accessible writer, and yet also one who is smart, sophisticated, inventive, and experimental' seems wholly accurate (Kellogg 2017). In this sense, he shares with Maggie Gee a desire to 'conceal complexity under a surface ease', giving rise to what James describes as an 'artful' 'self-effacing' 'authorial modesty' on the level of book and narration (quoted in James 2012: 11, 2009: 55). Nevertheless, after the success but misunderstanding of his early novels which led to what he describes as the 'issue of people taking [him] literally', Ishiguro has spoken of a desire to 'get away from a straight social realist way of writing' (Gaby Wood 2017). Perhaps realism forecloses interpretative possibility because its methodology encourages faith in the 'reality' of the subject, stifling meaning's ambiguous freeplay. In moving away from realism, he attempts to regain a form of authorial control, 'to announce how I want my novels to be read', pleading that readers 'don't take historical truth too seriously; try to look for something else' (Gaby Wood 2017). What emerges here is Ishiguro's loss of faith in the reader's willingness, or even ability, to seek more than mere verisimilitude. His appropriation of intentionality is a proscription not for closure, however, but polysemy.

Making an initial exploratory pass at aligning Ishiguro's fictions with several key stylistic and thematic elements of realism and modernism (both will run into the following chapters), and his repurposing of these, this chapter examines his play with detail, order, unity and the varieties of ambiguity of expression and communication which preoccupy Ishiguro's characters and make his writing so beguilingly distinctive. While situating Ishiguro in a wider tradition of experimental fictions, I suggest that his own prose takes recourse to a gestural poetics, one that is aware both of the failure of the form of the novel and the failure of language to communicate meaningfully, or with sufficient precision to enable authentic expression of 'selves'. His novels gesture towards space, history, the literary, towards shared experiences of love and regret, to war, betrayal and disappointment, but always in an awareness that the object itself remains ineffable, unconducive to linguistic transfiguration. Mimetic and communicative failures inflect the narratives with uncertainty, doubt, his characters attempting to form or simply maintain meaningful relationships but taking recourse to 'understandings' in the absence of adequate language, or because of what Salman Rushdie has eloquently termed 'an inarticulacy of the emotions' (*The Guardian*, 2012). It is in this way, I argue, that Ishiguro engages with the traditions of realism and modernism, highlighting the failures of both and synthesizing from these a philosophically, epistemologically sceptical late modernist aesthetic which is invested with meaning by its situation in a compromised rationalist realist narrative frame. Ultimately, what is at stake for his characters, and by implication the reader, is understanding, communication and, in its absence, a profound isolation arising from the failures of language which is itself, ironically, beyond expression.

Part 1: Realism

I

In a friendly but not overly positive review of *The Buried Giant*, James Wood highlights what he describes as the 'dizzying dullness' of Ishiguro's novels, which often involve 'episodes as bland as milk' (or even eggs) (2015). However, as he goes on, the peculiar power of Ishiguro's writing derives from this apparent triviality, because the author's

> banality has always been a rhetoric in search of a form. He doesn't need the pressure of realism (though his best work is powerful surely because it exerts its own pressure on the real) ... But he does need the pressure of form, a narrative shape that forces his bland fictional representations to muster their significance. (2015)

Ishiguro has referred to his own work as realist, at least those novels before, and one can surmise by similarity after but not including *The Unconsoled*; 'although they're interior monologues', he comments, 'basically they're realistic books' (Rose 1995).[4] For Wood, when style is employed artfully (but inconspicuously), it can imbue the 'bland' with 'significance' (we might think here of Williams's 'The Red Wheelbarrow' (1923) or Herbert's 'Easter Wings' (1633)). Ishiguro's works, in this understanding, are emergent, their significant totality supervening upon disjointed fragments of closely studied insignificance. Form, then, more particularly realism, orders and privileges the disordered and unprivileged, producing a dynamic and meaningful 'whole'.

Fittingly, realism is itself an ongoing and incomplete experiment in the ordered narrativization of experience, one that, much like later experimental movements, was written against a precursor perceived in some sense to have become 'exhausted', to use John Barth's term, or 'moribund', in Ishiguro's (1984: 62; *The Geek's Guide to the Galaxy*, 2015). Writing in the late nineteenth century of the shift from romance to realism and later naturalism, Émile Zola noted 'that all the conditions of the novel have changed. Imagination is no longer the predominating quality of the novelist'; in the new novel, the 'great thing is to set up living creatures, playing before the readers the human comedy in the most natural manner possible. All the efforts of the writer tend to hide the imaginary under the real' (1893: 209, 210). Ishiguro's early success as a novelist (his debut *PVH* won the Winifred Holtby Memorial Prize; *AFW*, the Whitbread; *RD*, the Booker) evidences his mastery of this technique, as does his evident frustration at readers taking the 'historical truth [of his works] too seriously'. The 'human comedy' is a singularly apt description of Stevens, Ono and Banks, three buffoons caught up in the mechanics of world affairs, but 'not remarkable enough to stand outside of that generation and moment' (Ishiguro and Sean Matthews 2009: 115). Kenzaburo Oe complimented Ishiguro, who left

Japan aged five and wrote his Japanese novels without revisiting, that he 'was struck by the excellent descriptions of life in Japan, of Japanese buildings and landscapes' in *An Artist of the Floating World*, to which Ishiguro replied that 'the Japan that exists in that book is very much my own personal, imaginary Japan' (1991: 110). Here, we see precisely the 'pressure' applied to the real and realism by the effect of verisimilitude achieved by Ishiguro's realistic rendering of an imaginary Japan, and the reason that his work has often, much to his displeasure, been taken 'literally'.

In some ways, Oe's comment seems unsupported by the text; aside from the repeated refrain of 'tatami' in Ishiguro's first two novels, and the use of traditional Japanese names and suffixes (-san), there is very little specificity to his literary portrait of his estranged country of birth. In Ishiguro's second novel, Masuji Ono, a retired artist, recalls of his acquaintance's apartment that it was 'small, and like many of these modern affairs, had no entryway as such, the tatami starting a little way inside the front door' (*AFW* 109). The post-war Japan that Ishiguro conjures is textured by the influence of the West (and filtration through Western media): 'each apartment identical; the floors were tatami, the bathrooms and kitchens of Western design' (*PVH* 12). Tatami functions as a lexical, atomistic detail, at once vague and idiosyncratic, communicating an understanding that the novel is set in Japan (under Western, essentially US administration). Niki, the daughter of *A Pale View of Hill*'s Etsuko, is named as a 'compromise' with her English father; 'it was he who wanted to give her a Japanese name, and I – perhaps out of some selfish desire not to be reminded of the past – insisted on an English one. He finally agreed to Niki, thinking it had some vague echo of the East about it' (*PVH* 9). Possibly influenced by this interview and Ishiguro's own description, Barry Lewis sees in *A Pale View of Hills* a 'displaced Japan, a recreation of an original that probably never existed' (2000: 23). Perhaps this is because the 'Japanese' novel was originally conceived to be set in a 'Cornish town', until Ishiguro 'realized that if [he] told this story in terms of Japan, everything that looked parochial and small would reverberate' (Hunnewell 2008). A political decision, then, reflecting the post-war reconstitution of global politics which had, as Ishiguro remarked, led to a feeling among young British authors that 'England is not an important enough country anymore' to garner international interest (Oe 1991: 119). Ishiguro's choice of Japan as a less 'parochial' setting than England could not have been coincidental, but also works from an association of the name 'Kazuo Ishiguro' with the traditionally Japanese (one character in *PVH* is, after all, named Kazuo). Perhaps it is here, the accumulation of period-specific cultural details, that for Zola, and presumably for Oe, gives the successful novel the 'sense of reality' which if achieved is 'very easy to detect', because it creates what Roland Barthes has called 'the reality effect' (Zola 1893: 214). But these details are no more than gestures towards or 'vague echoes' of an always imaginary Japan which bring us no closer to the 'real'.

If the 'real' is constructed (imaginary/unreal) and subject to ongoing radical ideological revisioning (much to the consternation of Ogata, Stevens, Ono and Kathy as they renegotiate their relationship with *the* and *their* pasts), then the material from which the real is modelled must be equally plastic. Writing against the idea that 'twentieth-century reality is peculiarly "unreal"' (Eliot's 'Unreal city' has a lot to answer for), Tallis argues that, even were this to be the case, it would be 'no reason why a novelist should not attempt to deal realistically with the sense of unreality', that 'it is precisely those most concerned to address reality with maximum fidelity who are required to be most *daring* in their experiments' (1988: 9, 3, my italics). Alain Robbe-Grillet, with whom Ishiguro shares a great deal, is ample evidence for Tallis's claim. Coincidentally, James Wood finds Ishiguro's fictions '*daring* in the way that they seem almost to invent their own gauges of verisimilitude' (2015, my italics). Reductively but helpfully, one might agree with Lukacs that the realist novel, despite being 'the epic of an age in which the extensive totality of life is no longer directly given' (because presumably *it* is peculiarly unreal), 'still thinks in terms of totality'; 'however violent its critique of reality', he writes elsewhere, the realist novel 'had always assumed the unity of the world it described' (1971: 56, 1969: 39). Unity in this reading is a necessary condition of realism's being and is usually reinforced at novel's end.

Unpicking William Makepeace Thackeray's struggles with endings, Ina Ferris argues that, although 'realist fiction [has a] generic resistance to the idea of ending', in the conclusion to a realist novel 'both readers and writers surrender themselves (with more or less embarrassment) to gratification, more specifically to gratification of the desire for control over time, for knowing what happened "ever after"' (1983: 289–91). As Henry James once remarked, ends are the occasion for 'a distribution at the last of prizes, pensions, husbands, wives, babies, millions, appended paragraphs, and cheerful remarks' (quoted in Kermode 2000: 22). Such desire may be for the gestural consolation that seems inevitably to elude the grasp (Stevens would very much like Miss Kenton to be his wife; Kathy would like to find herself miraculously with the baby she imagines embracing; Axl and Beatrice would like to be reunited with a lost son in a welcoming village). It might be that this literary phenomenon produces what Tallis sees as misunderstandings, including Lukacs's, of past reality as 'organically whole in the way that contemporary reality is not', or at least of the 'extensive totality' of reality being 'directly given' (1988: 15). Suffering from this misunderstanding, Ishiguro's characters seek consolatory certainty in the illusory, 'directly given' totality of the past in the face of a much less organically whole present, always in the expectation that their struggles will be rewarded at story's end.

Desire for elusive 'extensive totality', 'control over time' and its consolations motivate Ishiguro's hyperrational narrators, retroactively as they revisit and reconfigure 'pivotal' moments from their pasts (often with an eye on legacy, future), and reactively in the present, or multiple heterogeneous presences of narration. In her record of life at Hailsham and the subsequent experience of guiding her donors towards 'completion' (another finality/totality), Kathy H. writes in response to an 'urge to order all these old memories', 'to get straight all the things that happened' after the people to whom they have happened have died (*NLMG* 37). Unfortunately, for our absurd heroes and heroines, they have a tendency to react too late to their circumstances and to respond to the past in the present (and by implication the present in the future). An adult Banks raids the house where he believes his kidnapped parents are held long after any possibility of rescue had vanished (Banks is Ishiguro's most explicit nod towards the realist novel, his narrative borrowing its finale from *Great Expectations*, 1861); Ryder awaits and prepares for a concert that he never plays (or which he plays and takes for practice as Brodsky buries his dog) for parents who do not attend (or who have been and left many years previous); Stevens (like Brodsky and Sophie) belatedly attempts to rekindle a past relationship only to realize that he has profoundly misunderstood Miss Kenton's/Mrs Benn's letters just as he had previously misread Lord Darlington's political interference in the interwar period (and by extension his own vicarious complicity); and, perhaps most movingly, Axl and Beatrice finally travel to visit a long dead son, before Axl says farewell to his 'one true love' Beatrice (Dante's guide now guided) with such profound ambiguity that closure comes at the cost of ignorance, Ferris's 'surrender' to the desire for a gesture towards consolatory closure. As Ishiguro mentioned in conversation with Brian W. Shaffer, he is interested in 'the ways in which we try to repair something from the past when it's actually far too late – a kind of absurd, unrealistic ambition to try and put back something that fragmented a long time ago' (2001: 3). If the modernist tradition within which these unreliable characters are situated depends upon fragmentation, Ishiguro draws our attention here to the futility of their (un)realist(ic) project of unification.

Ishiguro's careful intra- and extradiegetic manipulation of the realist fascination with closure allows for the peculiarly unsatisfying conclusions to his novels which unfold *as if* they lead towards a dramatic moment that both reader and character 'retrospectively sees to have been perfect and practically inevitable', as often happens in the realist mode according to Mary Francis Slattery (1972: 60). Unfortunately, for both reader and narrator, this moment has been and passed unnoticed, or hovers somewhere behind, between, outside (on the periphery as I'll suggest later) of Ishiguro's texts' many digressions (the fragments that never coalesce), tantalizingly close yet always out of reach. His works are what Barthes calls 'writerly' texts, in that 'everything signifies ceaselessly and several times, but without being delegated to a great final ensemble, to an ultimate structure' (2002: 12). Ishiguro's novels are not nihilistically devoid of meaning, in the way that a postmodernist novel might be. We might think here of Thomas Pynchon's *The Crying of Lot 49* (1965) which ends at the precise moment that meaning becomes a possibility on the revelation of the grand signifier which should unite the disparate narrative threads in an 'ultimate structure'. Rather, meaning is diffuse, vagrant (homeless like the characters that dwell therein), suffusing the text on myriad levels which are variously accessible and inaccessible. The emotional power of Stevens's and Kenton's final encounter, Axl and Beatrice's bittersweet farewell, Banks's discovery of the truth of his father abandoning the family, comes not because these represent the novels' denouements but because the protagonists each recognize, with an irrevocable finality, that the denouement came and went unobserved many decades prior, and that what remains of the day is likely to be solitary precisely because they let someone go (Axl must very literally let Beatrice go, alone): as Stevens foreshadows, life is an 'expedition ... which I will undertake alone' (*RD* 3).

Paradoxically, past moments are invested with meaning in the present because their immediate significance was missed. Or, perhaps, the moment had no significance in the context of its original occurrence but has meaning *only* in a present that cannot (and *because* it cannot) permit the reoccurrence of that very moment. Lukacs agrees with Aristotle that 'Man is *zoon politikon*, a social animal [which] cannot be distinguished from their social and historical environment. Their human significance, their specific individuality, cannot be separated from the context in which they were created' (1969: 19). Problematically for Ono, Ogata and Stevens, 'the context in which they were created' can be and is aggressively separated from them: it is this fact that the passing of time decontextualizes his narrators and renders them and their ideas anachronistic that invests Ishiguro's *as if* memoirs with their insistently recurrent intergenerational tension. That is to say, Etsuko, Ono, Ogata, Stevens, Axl and Gawain find themselves in altogether different narrative and sociopolitical spaces which necessitate reappraisals of past actions. If Darlington was successful, Stevens could not have regretted neglecting his personal life (would Stevens recall leaving Miss Kenton sobbing behind a door?); if the war was won, Ogata and Ono would not need to revisit now ambiguous moments and trivial conversations from unremarkable pasts; if Beatrice and Axl had not betrayed one another, there would be no need in the present to try to find meaning in ostensibly mundane misunderstandings about the carrying of eggs. Yet, as Stevens remarks, 'one can surely only recognize such moments in retrospect. Naturally, when one looks back to such instances today, they may indeed take the appearance of being crucial, precious moments in one's life; but of course, at the time, this was not the impression one had' (*RD* 179). These are all examples of Heidegger's 'world worlding': 'Wherever those utterly essential decisions of our history are made, are taken up or abandoned by us, go unrecognized and are rediscovered by new enquiry, there the world worlds' (2011: 108). In *The Unconsoled*, Mrs Hoffman forlornly expresses hope, 'that all it will take will be one moment, even a *tiny* moment, provided it's the correct one. Like a cord suddenly snapping and a thick curtain dropping to the floor to reveal a whole new world, a world full of sunlight and warmth' (*U* 418). Characters act as realist readers, attempting to read their own pasts *as if* they were building towards a missed moment of dispensatory consolations *as if* it were yet to come. Such humble yet futile hope, as Mrs Hoffman will come to realize, too late, engenders the subtle tragedies of Ishiguro's worlds.

II

Ishiguro's stories then are related by narrators who think and act *as if* they inhabit the traditional realist/rationalist space, and so their subjunctive and often counterfactual narratives adopt something approaching a mock historiographic methodology designed to assure the reader, and themselves, of their recollections' reliability (while also sustaining a fragile hope for the future). Lodge identifies a close affinity between realism's quasi-sociological methodology and other sociohistorically situated discursive forms, defining realism as 'the representation of experience in a manner which approximates closely to descriptions of similar experiences in nonliterary texts of the same culture' (2015: 31–2). Works of realist fiction re-create non-fictional modes of representation, and in so doing gesture towards other kinds of communicative gestures which more or less approximate the real. George Eliot's proto-sociological fascination with the expansion of English socioeconomic and civic life in *Middlemarch* (1871) and Charles Dickens's career-long ethnographic interest in the inherent social inequalities of expanding urban industrial spaces are good examples.[5] We might think here of the faux oral narrative of *The Buried Giant*, the memoir of *Never Let Me Go*, Christopher Banks's exaggerated and absurd Victorian detective drama, or Stevens's perpetually backgrounded and wilfully digressive travel narrative (which evokes similar techniques to those deployed by W. G. Sebald's mock travel work *The Rings of Saturn*, 1995), in which Stevens himself 'impersonates a diction' (Lewis 2000: 94).

Zola too recognizes that the changing epistemological paradigm that emerged in the nineteenth century necessitated an 'experimental' approach to literature:

> The metaphysical man is dead; our whole territory is transformed by the advent of the physiological man … In short, everything is summed up in this great fact: the experimental method in letters, as in the sciences, is in the way to explain the natural phenomena, both individual and social, of which metaphysics, until now, has given only irrational and supernatural explanations. (1893: 54)

Zola's naturalist project is predicated on a belief that, by adopting a scientific approach, literature can move beyond the irrational and supernatural to the rational and natural (a comment here on the function and efficacy of art, which will recur throughout this study). Oddly, if the non-literary aspires to objectivity and unadorned data (the results of experimentation represented unexperimentally), the realist writer must experiment with representation to achieve meta-verisimilitude (to represent and to re-present representation). In the age of scientific method, the novelist becomes a sociologist of both real and imaginary phenomena, compiling and analysing fictional data which replicates real-world data: 'The plan of the work is brought to [the fiction writer] by the data themselves, because the facts always classify themselves logically', much in the way that, for Woolf, they 'shape *themselves* into' life (Zola 1893: 210). Where Woolf later employs the term 'atom', Zola borrows the notions of 'classification' and 'data' (a word which became popular around the turn of the nineteenth and twentieth centuries). This literary appropriation of the credibility of scientific methodology might be achieved by giving, as Flaubert wrote to Louise Colet, 'the humble detail as much emphasis as the grandiose' (Allott 1959: 51). Stevenson too remarks that 'the great change [in literature] of the past century has been effected by the admission of detail' (Allott 1959: 72). Barthes also sees 'data, descriptive details' as the hallmark of realism (1982: 12). The Unconsoled's Hoffman, as professional a hotel manager as Stevens is a butler, 'goes over every detail in his head, over and over' and has, as Ryder notes, a 'fanatical attention to detail' (*TU* 67). This intention to elevate the ordinary, to privilege the mundane to the point of 'dizzying dullness', to impose a form on the humble detail to produce a composite whole which is grandiose is precisely what we see in Ishiguro's fictions.

Ishiguro's narrators are concerned with the attempt to order details from the past, confounded by repeated retrieval distortion and the often-unwelcome intrusion of other voices, and more widely the fluidity of the global political landscape. As Daniel Bedggood comments, Ishiguro juxtaposes 'well-observed attention to detail [with] the accounts of often wildly unreliable narrators' (2017: 110). Indeed, where Masuji Ono, coming to terms with his 'separation from the context' of pre-war imperialist Japan in which he was created and negotiating anti-imperial post-war Japan, attempts to 'recall … the details' in order to re-evaluate the facts of his and his nation's past, Stevens in the same situation digresses from his travel narrative, his motoring trip, to repeatedly return to the details of events and conversations at Darlington Hall and their modified significance (*AFW* 28). The details they manage to recall are frequently irrelevant; astute observers all, they atomize and anatomize the past while remaining oblivious to the equally fraught ambiguities of the present. If they do aspire to gather all relevant data, their projects are undermined because they cannot grasp the objective but must rely rather on the subjective, the intensely personal details and, from these inappropriate materials, reconstruct the wider canvas (these ripples in the fabric of their life that shape an absent centre).

Of course, their misguided faith that their trivial preoccupations are of global importance (Stevens's silver polishing, Ono's painting, Ryder's piano recital, Banks's sleuthing) is both comedic and tragic while also once more gesturing towards their efforts to disclose the undisclosable noumenal ground of their being. Christopher Banks, a perpetually anachronistic 'celebrated detective', relishes and revels in facts. Everywhere he goes he takes a magnifying glass (his transitional object), allowing him to scrutinize the smallest detail but excluding wider frames of reference. Looking in the material realm for evidence of the ineffable essence of his Shanghai childhood, his peculiar habit leads him to believe, or is predicated on his necessary belief, that those traumatic and life-changing personal events which occupy his limited field of vision continue into the world at large. Resolving his monomania, somehow reversing his parents' disappearance, will, he *must* believe, solve the issues of the war-torn world in which he sleuths. In some ways his utter conviction inspires confidence, because, as Hélène Machinal remarks, the 'aura and esteem of Sherlock Holmes' which Banks borrows establishes the 'narrator's credentials' (2009: 81). We trust, that is to say, that Banks is neither mislead nor misleading. In borrowing from this tradition, as Frederick M. Holmes has commented, Ishiguro creates the expectation that Banks' deeds will have heroic potential' (2005: 15). Bedggood sensibly cautions us that Ishiguro revels in 'manipulations of generic expectation' (2017: 109). Each of Ishiguro's narrators wields a magnifying glass of sorts, yet they unwittingly neglect the world beyond the glass's rim, and so cannot contextualize revealed details in such a way as to see their implications (local over the general, national over the international, personal over the public). Such practised and wilful myopia may be intentional, as James argues – a way to forestall 'descent into periods of graver contemplation' about the less laudable or more sinister realities of their lives (2009: 57). Absurdly, they try to mine from the tangible world some certainty about the intangible.

Ironically, in obsessively, iteratively (mis)recalling the minutiae of their lost pasts, Ishiguro's narrators sacrifice attention to the ambiguous details of their equally contentious present. In so doing, under the scrutiny of the reader, Kathy, Stevens and Banks each re-create the conditions for the missed moment that so preoccupies them, betraying a constitutional inability to be in the present which necessarily brings into question their recollection of presence in the past. Their greatest tragedy is that, in focusing on hazy and ambiguous images of moments past, they disregard the present, misty memories of which will inevitably come to preoccupy them in the future (the death of Stevens's father, his decision to allow Miss Kenton to close his dead father's eyes). Turning points with the potential to be of great significance arise during narration (Banks's failure to act as a parent to Jennifer, for example, Ryder's unwillingness to offer affection to Boris) but appear insignificant to narrators focused on futile recuperative quests to correct past turning points that are, once more, paradoxically so profound only because they were missed. While living outside of time, Ishiguro's narrators all share a selective inattention, their narratives 'filled with blind spots' (Molino 2012: 326). Presence is perpetually deferred, characters always, like Tristram Shandy, trying to catch up with themselves but always a step behind the lived moment: as Tristram Shandy remarks, astutely, 'In short, there is no end of it' (1760: 35). The act of relating their stories acts as a blind, distracting them from the present, which is backgrounded until its significance inevitably emerges in a future beyond the text's boundaries, inspiring the 'absurd, unrealistic ambition to try and put back something that fragmented a long time ago' that typifies each of his works (Shaffer and Ishiguro 2001).

In a list of dream techniques now in the Harry Ransom Center archive, Ishiguro refers to 'tunnel memory' in an insightful rhetorical conflation of memory and vision. He mentions in these notes what he calls 'The Dim Torch Narrative Mode', which is beautifully descriptive of all of his works. Mr Ryder, the fugue-like and haunted/haunting subject of *The Unconsoled*, Ishiguro's extended 'anxiety dream' is the clearest example (Rose 1995). Ryder suffers from an extraordinary lack of awareness throughout, but most notably on two occasions. First, failing to notice Miss Hilde in the tiny space of the hotel elevator: 'Turning, I saw with a start that we were not alone in the elevator' (*U* 9); and, failing to notice during a long conversation with Sophie that she was carrying a large parcel: 'Turning [once more this odd sense of repositioning while also retaining the linguistic trace of turning points], I noticed for the first time that Sophie was carrying on one arm a large shapeless package' (*U* 91). So preoccupied is Ryder with his diplomatic role and his piano recital that he fails to notice that Sophie is his wife, Boris his son. Drifting through surreally mundane, or mundanely surreal scenarios which defy comprehension, unable to manage time or space, Ryder commends himself with unwitting irony that he has over the years been associated with 'attention to detail, precision in performance, and control of dynamics' (*U* 136). We could take this as a definition of the realist novel; as Zola, Lodge, Stevenson and many others have suggested, it is the 'attention to detail', the control of the various emergent dynamics, ordering and precision that characterize the mode. Clearly, Ishiguro plays with these while not being 'a straightforward realist' because he is 'trying to make a universal statement' (Cain 2015). That universal statement might have something to do with missing the bigger picture, ironically through paying too much attention to the details assumed to constitute that picture.

III

Some things are not simply on the periphery of personal and political awareness but are rather beyond expression (in theology we would call these apophatic). Philip Roth, the great American realist of the unreal American postmodern, famously commented that American reality 'is a kind of embarrassment to one's own meagre imagination. The actuality is continually outdoing our talents' (1961). It is not simply 'American reality' (as if, in the twentieth century, there were any other reality): Certain atrocities too exceed, overwhelm, even explode language's expressive potential. If we agree with Theodor Adorno that 'to write poetry after Auschwitz is barbaric', the other defining event of the Second World War, the unleashing of the world's first atomic weapons against civilians, evokes only the silence that Wittgenstein recommends when confronted with 'that whereof we cannot speak': Ishiguro gestures towards the events in *A Pale View of Hills* and *An Artist of the Floating World*, but always obliquely, looking rather at the 'nuclear shadows' than their atomized subjects (Adorno 1997a: 34; Wittgenstein 1922: 90). *A Pale View of Hills* has two time signatures: the calm English present of the narrator Etsuko, and her past in a post-war Nagasaki undergoing modernization. Her faux memoir is so beguiling because it takes the form of an emotionally honest attempt to reckon with and to give voice to the silent anguish of loss in a seemingly realist mode that is haunted by a gothic imaginary of which the narrator seems largely unaware. Shortly after the war, Etsuko left her husband Jiro to emigrate to the United Kingdom with their daughter Keiko, who had subsequently 'hung herself in her room' in Manchester. The novel documents Etsuko's moving yet often cryptic reflections on her traumatic past and her perceived responsibility for this personal tragedy, a narrative (sometimes uncannily) seamlessly interwoven with that of Sachiko, a neglectful mother dreaming, with a hopeless, despairing optimism, of moving to America with her unreliable American lover. In the background, Ishiguro introduces a theme that will come to define his novels – intergenerational responsibility for national and global tragedy (the burying of giants). Etsuko's memoir approaches the brutal realities of the loss of a child and the carnage wrought by the nuclear blasts. However, the ineffable essence of these realities necessarily evades language and can only be gestured towards in a series of often-ambiguous and confused anecdotes.

Etsuko reminisces fondly about the times she spent with her grandfather Ogata-san, a retired pre-war teacher who, like Masuji Ono, has found his once-eminent social position challenged because of the changing ideological landscape of the US occupation and the lost war, and the implicated failure of Japanese Imperial ideology that both he and Ono proudly perpetuated. Like Ono and Stevens, Ogata tries to justify decisions made in a past that bears little resemblance to the political present of narration. In one ekphrastic scene, Etsuko and Ogata visit Nagasaki's 'Peace Park', which boasts a 'massive white statue in memory of those killed by the atomic bomb', sculpted by the otherwise little known Seibo Kitamura in 1955 (*PVH* 137). Hiroshima and Nagasaki (city names now metonyms for the devastation of war that have had their original denotation detonated) linger in the periphery of Ishiguro's first two novels. This real-world monument is as close to a direct address to the atrocities as we find in Ishiguro's works, because he avoids any description of the events themselves (we are permitted only sideways glances, peripheral awareness). Ogata recalls that the statue

> resembled some muscular Greek god, seated with both arms outstretched. With his right hand, he pointed to the sky from where the bomb had fallen; with his other arm – stretched out to his left – the figure was supposedly holding back the forces of evil. His eyes were closed in prayer. (*PVH* 137)

The 'Greek god' is radically plural: a pagan idol from a polytheist tradition, incongruously praying as if to a single Christian deity in a predominantly Buddhist country. According to the sculptor, the 'right hand points to the atomic bomb, the left hand points to peace, and the face prays deeply for the victims of war. Transcending the barriers of race and evoking the qualities of Buddha and God'. The statue is a composite of not entirely integrated (only the face prays) gestural details. Explicitly in a nation rethinking its global position after the lost war and the collapse of the imperial ideal, the statue intermixes Western and Eastern theology. Pointing is another kind of gesture towards the external but directly given 'real'. The statue, however, points to a past event, its moment of signification eternally and absurdly anachronistic, ineffectual. Interestingly, we find in the statue's indexical failure further evidence that Ishiguro's characters respond in the present to a past that cannot be changed, that they have missed the pivotal moment (the 'turning point'). If, for Kitamura, one hand points to the 'bomb' and the other to 'peace', the statue represents an attempt to position an intermediary point between the material and abstract (matter and spirit); further, if the material past bomb becomes de-reified, abstracted, transcending the spatiotemporal, peace becomes reified, subject to the spatiotemporal, 'present'.

Ogata reflects further on the various infelicities of the statue:

> It was always my feeling that the statue had a rather cumbersome appearance, and I was never able to associate it with what had occurred that day the bomb had fallen, and those terrible days which followed. Seen from a distance, the figure looked almost comical, resembling a policeman conducting traffic. It remained for me nothing more than a statue, and while most people in Nagasaki seemed to appreciate it as some form of gesture, I suspect the general feeling was much like mine. (*PVH* 138)

The statue acts as a critique of verisimilitude, of art's capacity to approach, capture, manifest 'reality'. Ogata notes various failures of expression in this piece of art which is in fact an act of political rhetoric. He has a vague 'feeling' not that the statue *is* cumbersome but that it has a (rather) cumbersome 'appearance' (back to resemblances). Crucially, if the statue is intended to point towards (to index) something, it is a profoundly failed act of signification, one which cannot be 'associated' with the real event that it is designed to commemorate, both because the bomb fell long before and, more importantly, because the 'cumbersome' 'comic' 'form' is radically incompatible with the magnitude of an event which itself is composed of innumerable distinct but related (atomic/atomistic) 'horrors'. The atomic chain reaction that *is* the explosion gives rise to a chain reaction of suffering, the repercussions of which linger like radiation in the background of the novel as a 'vague echo'. Tellingly, especially for chapter 3, Ogata remarks that it remains 'nothing more than a statue', one that has little aesthetic merit and fails to perform the role of memorial. There is, however, a secondary level of signification, a meta-message that has to do not with the statue but with the fact of the statue's being, acting not as a gesture towards the bomb but a 'form of gesture' towards gesturing, as Ogata suggests. As Henri Lefebvre remarks of the work of art, 'If you take it for what it is (a paint-daubed or coloured scrap of paper [statue]), it falls short of its goal. If you take it for what it seeks to evoke, it accomplishes it' (2019: 32). Crucially, the event itself is beyond expression, beyond the capacity of artistic re-presentation; the statue is incommensurate with the horrors unleashed by the weapon, yet it stands as a gestural attempt to offer some form of consolatory memorial.

Another degree of mimetic difficulty arises when Ogata tries to gesture towards that gesture (towards, etc.). If the statue attempts to translate a past and temporally finite event into a simultaneously present and timeless memorial, Ogata confronts the difficulty of translating this translation from the sculptural to the textual, via the pictorial. Holding a postcard (a very specific mode of communication) of the statue which he intends to send to a friend, Etsuko, 'became curious when [she] noticed him staring at the blank side of the card, his pen poised, but not writing. Once or twice, [she] saw him glance up towards the statue, as if for inspiration' (*PVH* 138). This 'as if' mood is pervasive. If the statue fails to express, to represent, then this explains Ogata's inability to say something about that statue: the event is beyond language, this commemoration offensively 'comic', and the postcard, a trinket from a tourist attraction, not simply inadequate but trivial in the extreme. If the statue is inspired by the atomic bomb, that statue itself inspires no further act of writing, but rather evokes the silence that might have been the only valid response to so inhumane an act of violence. Here we have a comment on language's ability to apprehend 'the real', Ono's failure that of the form of realism itself. Ishiguro and Ogata's ekphrastic intrusion provokes more fundamental questions about the limits of expression. This, as Zeitlin remarks, is typical: 'ekphrases call forth interpretation in broader terms of the relationship between word and image, as between content and context, and they inevitably raise issues of representation, with all the ambiguities, tensions, and contradictions that the notion entails' (2013: 21). On the level of the novel, the failure becomes its own comment on the communicative and memorial possibilities of sculpture, photograph and writing, which in turn jeopardize the very narrative acts of which they form a part. One might also suggest that Kitamura's explicatory plaque, a poetic ekphrastic supplement, indicates the pre-empted failure of that statue to signify, an awareness that art is always ambiguous, interpretative and so inept to communicate certain, or any, 'truths'.

The critique of the communicative and expressive possibilities of representation recurs later, this time in England. While visiting from London shortly after Keiko's funeral, Niki tells Etsuko that one of her friends is writing a poem about Etsuko's life in Nagasaki during and after the war, and that she'd like some material artefact to help. To assuage any concerns Etsuko might have that an English teenager might struggle to capture the tenor of so difficult a period, Niki assures her mother that her friend has really 'been through a lot' (how might one read this in a novel that asymptotically approaches yet evades atomic trauma and the suicide of one's child?) and would like Niki 'to bring back a photo or something. Of Nagasaki ... Just an old *postcard*, anything like that. Just so she can see what everything was like' (*AFW* 177, my italics). This moment is contextualized by the failure of the postcard, the statue and of language itself that occurs earlier in the novel. It is a deeply meaningless suggestion, the casualness of the language demonstrating Niki's disinterest and lack of curiosity in Etsuko's experiences (she tries many times to engage Niki in conversation about her life in Japan). The vagueness and haste of her question betrays an indifference to her mother, but a desire to somehow please or impress her friend, who either (a) is genuinely interested in her friend's mother or (b) appropriates her suffering for her 'art'. Molino, however, offers another reading, suggesting that 'Niki has even gone so far as to seek others, such as her poet friend, who might reveal something of her mother's past life to her' because of a failure to communicate that 'one or the other fails to respond' when conversation turns to the past (2012: 326). There is an implication in Niki's request (however unwitting) that a single picture might capture and reveal the totality of the suffering of the Japanese during and after the most destructive human act in history. A further supposition is that poetry is possible after Nagasaki, yet further still that a young English poet might capture something of the unspeakable horror euphemized by the statue, a horror avoided by both Etsuko and Ishiguro. Etsuko replies a little sarcastically that she is 'not so sure. It has to show what everything was like, does it?' (*PVH* 178). Here we are reminded of Kathy, approximately Niki's age, trying 'to get straight *all the things that happened*' (my italics), trying herself to see how 'everything was'. Sophie too, hinting at a betrayal of Ryder, offers despairingly to 'tell you everything. Everything you want to know. Every detail' (*U* 88). The problem for Ogata and Etsuko, Ono, Stevens, Sophie and many of Ishiguro's characters struggling to impose reason and order onto their stories is that there is no 'everything', no 'all the things', or 'every detail', and even if there were, these 'things' would not amount to anything approximating 'truth' or 'objectivity' because the emergent composite narrative would be irreducibly polysemic and would do little more than indicate the aporia beneath the superficial. In a realist universe, we might expect these events to accrue some significance, for some semblance of profound closure to condense from these symbolic moments. However, each is attuned instead to the failures of expression, of communication, of art, of realism and verisimilitude, in the same way that the ludicrously eclectic statue fails to cohere. Ogata's refusal to write about the statue represents a comment on the failure of a symbol that might, in an earlier form, have signified.

Part 2: Modernism

I

For José Ortega y Gasset, the popularity of much nineteenth-century art, more particularly the realist novel, derives from the fact that it was 'made for the masses', from which he infers that it 'is not art but an extract from life' (1972: 12). He argues that in any society there are always two 'types of art', one for the cultured enjoyment of the educated minority and one for the consumption of the uneducated majority (so it is an art after all), 'the latter has always been realistic' (Ortega y Gasset 1972: 12). Ortega y Gasset somewhat simplistically implies that life is amenable both to 'extraction' and subsequent representation (begging at least two questions that modernism poses to the earlier form) and, further, that only the minority can appreciate or understand 'art' that aspires to more than mere mimesis. The twentieth and twenty-first centuries have witnessed an ongoing exploration of long- and short-form fiction's expressive and representational potential, bound to questions of recall and unreliability, but also, as Ortega y Gasset suggests, the nature of art and its intended audience (I return to these questions in Chapter 3). Andre Brink writes of the arts' developing disillusionment in realism's certainties, arguing that, 'in a turmoil of uncertainty', the 'Age of Realism, in many ways the last great affirmation of the Enlightenment with its impressively self-confident faith in reason and reason's access to the real, drew to an end as the nineteenth century began to spill in to the twentieth' (1998: 1). Modernism is not the beginning of literary experimentation but rather, as James proposes, 'the scene of an unfinished argument about the novel's formal and critical potentiality' that was instigated in and through the Victorian realist novel (2012: 3).

In apparent agreement with Ortega y Gasset, Lukacs suggests that, at the turn of the century, the novel as a form ran the risk of 'sinking to the level of mere entertainment literature', a danger which could be avoided only if it attempted to gesture towards 'the fragile and incomplete nature of the world as ultimate reality' (1971: 71). Something of Heidegger's 'essentially undisclosable' world, here. In this sense, Lukacs seems to take issue with Zola's earlier contention about the teleological 'inevitably' of the realist novel:

> The story builds itself up from all the observations gathered together, from all the notes taken, one leading to the other, through the linking of the lives of the characters, and the climax is nothing more than a natural and inevitable consequence. (Zola 1893: 210–11)

Necessarily, the world must remain incomplete (immanent), in the absence of an applied or imposed schema. That is to say, there is nothing inevitable or natural about the 'lives of characters' because 'this order or structure [that typifies the realist novel] is alien to reality itself' (Tallis 1988: 21). Modernism's various formal and epistemological disjunctions and discontinuities disrupt the realist foundation of ordered totality, demonstrating that not all data is either absolute or collectible, that reality rarely has climaxes as such, and that language may not be entirely adequate to the mimetic challenge. Order's profound absence poses catastrophic interpersonal and existential problems for Ishiguro's ontologically precarious characters, trying desperately, valiantly to patch together a harmonious canvas imbued with absolute truth from the partial matter of their own subjective memory, or to apprehend world's evasive essence as it manifests in the superficial, the often comically trivial. Kathy, once again, trying poignantly to get all the 'things in order' as her own death, and with it her memories of Hailsham, approaches. Of course, most typical of modernism is the shift from outside (the omnipotent hyperrational narrator of realism) to inside, introducing the variously unreliable and often irrational first-person narrative. Ishiguro works only in the first person, with the exception of *The Buried Giant*, which borrows from the oral tradition. Again, he himself comments on the conflation of forms in his works, noting that 'although they're interior monologues [a predominantly modernist form], basically they're realistic books' (Rose 1995).

Where the realist novel found its subject in 'the social experiences of persons', Ortega y Gasset's 'extract of life', modernism, while still retaining an interest in social experience, begins to draw the readers' attention to the individual sensory perceptions that coalesce to constitute these more expansive social experiences (Tallis 1988: 45). Seemingly an aesthetic and epistemological response, modernism is a politically attuned reaction to the changing nature of social reality at the turn of the century, acting as a 'medium for connecting interiority and accountability, braiding the description of characters' innermost reflections into the fabric of worldly situations' (James 2012: 9). For Woolf, the change in art's response to 'worldly situations' at the turn of the century was abrupt, a fact recorded in her diaries. Referring to her visit to the exhibition 'Manet and the Post-Impressionists', organized by Roger Fry at the Grafton Gallery, she wrote, 'On or about December 1910 human nature changed' (1971: 320). The ostensibly unified realist movement fractures into a series of aesthetic experiments at responding to the changing reality of 'modern' life and its mimetic representation, which in turn inflected the nature of experience itself, in Woolf's understanding. Perhaps this shift arises due to the perception that modernism is interested in the peculiarly modern fragmentation of consciousness and experience, that there is no longer *a* real(ity), as such. Tallis sensibly argues that 'human consciousness has always been riven by discontinuities', and that the 'invention of the motor car or the micro-computer has not cut deeper into the continuity and the uniformity of an agreed-upon reality than do sleep or coma' (we might add memory to this list, too; 1988: 12). Presumably Plato, Descartes, Locke, Berkeley, Wittgenstein and even Ryder would agree.

Modernism took many forms and was, as Woolf herself shows, inspired by the techniques employed by visual artists to offer impressions as opposed to realistic representations of the burgeoning modern world (in the advent of photography's birth). Woolf was highly attuned to the interrelation of writing and painting; as Jack F. Stewart has commented, she 'accepted the challenge of designing a literary art closer to the plastic values of painting' (1985: 438). This is eminently demonstrated in *The Waves* (1931), which also evidences a growing fascination with sense data, the phenomenal matrices that give rise to our illusory experience of the world as unified:

> 'I hear a sound,' said Rhoda, 'cheep, chirp; cheep chirp; going up and down.'
> 'I see a globe,' said Neville, 'hanging down in a drop against the enormous flanks of some hill.'
> ...
> 'Stones are cold to my feet,' said Neville. 'I feel each one, round or pointed, separately.'
> ...
> 'The back of my hand burns,' said Jinny, 'but the palm is clammy and damp with dew.' (2015: 4)

Sound, sight and feeling. We are reminded of the 'unified matrix of our experience' that, for Hans-Georg Gadamer, coalesces from apprehension of such uncoordinated datum (1977: 73). These are merely the superficial gestures towards an undisclosable ground. No one voice is privileged, or even one sensation; the picture presented is a composite of the available perceptions, with the implication that: (a) infinite other perspectives are available; (b) that no two perspectives can coincide; and (c) they do little more than indicate the possibility of an underlying but undisclosed reality. Woolf's sensory details are more than reflections; in her works, we see the beginning of the turn to qualia in literature, and to the idea of contingency, perspective, heteroglossia. These apparently neutral observations are also tinged with figurative language, metaphor, simile; birdsong going 'up and down', the hill's 'enormous flanks'. Nothing in this imagistic scene can be said to provide Brink's 'access to the real', but the scene nonetheless conveys authentic experiential realities. Language crudely externalizes the shape of the internal perception of the viewing subject, but all that's accomplished is a limning of the unbridgeable divide between subject and object. Lukacs sees this 'rift between "inside" and "outside"' that typifies modernism as elemental to both philosophy and to 'literary creation', a sign of the essential difference between self and world, 'the incongruence of soul and deed' (1971: 29). Earlier, he writes that modernist literature 'has its emotional origin in the experience of a disintegrating society. But it attains its effects by evoking the disintegration of the world of man' ([sic] 1969: 39–40). Crucially for Ishiguro, individual parallel experiential worlds are alternate, often misaligned, irreconcilably out of sync, and even threatening.

Memory is to the modernists what industrialization was for the realists, certainly for Beckett, most explicitly in *Krapp's Last Tape* (1958), and Marcel

Proust in *À La Recherche Du Temps Perdu* (1913–27). Proust epitomizes modernism's struggle with the 'shifting and confused gusts of memory', unearthing the past and re-encountering it in a present which it conditioned. Krapp suffers from a faulty memory but has, over a long life, curated a library of diary-like recordings. However, he repeatedly takes recourse to a dictionary to find the meaning of words which he himself once used but has since forgotten. As Miki Iwata notes, his 'estrangement from his younger self is most acutely shown in the scene about the word "viduity"' (2008: 36). Exasperated by his own past persona(s), he concludes: 'just been listening to that stupid bastard I took myself for thirty years ago, hard to believe I was ever as bad as that. Thank God that's all done with anyway' (2006: 222). Aged and deeply alone, Krapp listens to a younger Krapp recalling with pride his refusal to sacrifice his undefined ambitions for the sake of love: 'Perhaps my best years are gone. When there was a chance of happiness. But I wouldn't want them back. Not with the fire in me now. No, I wouldn't want them back' (2006: 223–5). This version of Krapp is a stark contrast to Ogata, Stevens and Ono, who must each hold on to, rather than renounce, their past selves or risk acknowledging that their past deeds and their reciprocal sacrifices were not in fact 'worthwhile'. Even Stevens, who tries to recapture a moment in which a 'chance of happiness' presented itself, does so only after the failures of Darlington (someone else's 'fire'). Krapp searches his technology-augmented memories for a turning point, the pivotal decision that led to his present isolated circumstances. But the text tells us that, even were he to 'lay there without moving' (as he does in his self-imposed hermitage), the world continues to world: 'under us all moved, and moved us'. Working with her donors through their completion, Kathy notices in speaking with one about her past that 'the line would blur between what were my memories and what were his' (*NLMG* 5). Her only consolation for her brutal life is that whatever happens 'I'll have Hailsham with me, safely in my head, and that'll be something no one can take away' (*NLMG* 281). Ishiguro sees this as evidence that Kathy's 'memories are more benevolent. They're principally a source of consolation. As her time runs out, as her world empties one by one of the things she holds dear, what she clings to are her memories of them' (*Readers Read*, 2005). As the Peace Park episode contextualizes Niki's fatuous request for a postcard that 'shows how everything was' in post-bomb Nagasaki, Tommy's theory that Hailsham's residents are 'told and not told' about the realities of their fates, that 'all this stuff was there in our heads without us ever having examined it properly' problematizes Kathy's claim to ownership over the arbitrary and uncertain contents of her malleable psyche, as does the porousness of neural borders, the bleeding of memories across minds. Kathy relies on a distinction, perhaps even a dualist one, between the material organs which can be removed from her body and the part of her that is 'safe' because it is immaterial, ungraspable. She believes in the sanctity of thought, selfhood, the quasi-spiritual intangible aura that supervenes upon the vulnerable material body; tragically, the clones' existential predicament involves a collective social denial that they have such things as souls. Ishiguro's poetics relies upon the painful and repeated fact that nothing remains safe or unchanged in one's head, and that what is in one's head is simply a function of contingency, positionality: where one sees duty, sacrifice, another sees self-interest, 'meddling'. Even had Kathy, Ono, Stevens, Axl and Beatrice their own written or spoken records (history), these would still offer no more certainty about the past, or more confidence in their decisions.

Woolf's Rhoda, Neville and Jinny simply report sense data; Krapp is isolated and the only other persona that intrudes into his diminished world is his own. Although each is aware of other conflicting voices, it is in Ishiguro that memory is most susceptible not simply to retrieval's distortion but to the threatening recall of others and the challenges posed by these to self-narration. It is this phenomenon that creates the tension we see in Ishiguro's narratives which strive to be monologic but find themselves undermined by the subtle but insistent intrusion of contradictory perspectives. We might think of Axl and Beatrice trying to remember shared moments in case they should have to prove their love with two perfectly harmonious pictures. One day they remember walking 'arm in arm' through a village when confronted by a man Axl recalls as paying Beatrice a harmless compliment, 'like he was beholding a goddess' (*BG* 84). Disagreeing with Axl's remembrance, Beatrice recalls that the man was drunk, that Axl 'grew jealous and quarrelled with him' (*BG* 84). Unharmonized memories have an even deeper resonance in this novel, in which Axl and Beatrice's future together depends on their sharing affectionate memories, their harmonious proofs of love (like Tommy and Kathy's artworks). Sometimes characters become aware that they have unwittingly misattributed speech, or particular phrases. Ono, recalling an argument with Jiro Miyake, his daughter's previous fiancée who had abruptly pulled out of marriage negotiations (prompting Ono's memoir), remembers Miyake using the phrase 'the greatest cowardice of all' (*AFW* 56). However, a moment later, he wonders 'did Miyake really say all this to me that afternoon?', speculating that it sounds more like 'the sort of thing Suichi [his son in law] will come out and say' (*AFW* 56). The same thing happens later, when Ono attributes the phrase 'exploring curious avenues' to his sensei, Mori-san, before once more thinking that 'he may well not have used that precise phrase', that in fact he may have been 'remembering my own words to Koruda on that later occasion on the same pavilion' (*AFW* 177). Stevens has a similar moment with Miss Kenton, after recalling her words he confesses that he is 'not sure she could actually have gone so far as to say things like: "these errors may be trivial in themselves, but you must yourself realize their larger significance". In fact, now that I come to think of it, I have a feeling it may have been Lord Darlington himself who made that particular remark to me' (*RD* 60). As Ono reflects, 'It is inevitable that with repeated telling, such accounts begin to take on a life of their own' (*AFW* 72). Seemingly innocuous, the phenomenon of misattribution occurs just often enough to cast significant doubt on the reliability of narrator and narrative, and to shift the novels from a realist to a modernist paradigm.

Banks's defining feature is his fear of being portrayed or remembered in a way that does not fit his carefully crafted self-narrative. The trait arises early in the novel, when his friend Osbourne visits and recalls light-heartedly how Banks used to 'quiz me about my being "well connected"' (*WWO* 5). Harmless, likely even correct, yet Banks confides in us that his 'annoyance grew' because he 'cannot imagine' that he '"mercilessly interrogated" [Osbourne] as he had claimed' (*WWO* 5). Later, the 'Colonel' who accompanied Banks to England after his parents' disappearance reminisces fondly about Banks the child on a long sea journey:

> Gradually, from behind his cheerful anecdotes, there was emerging a picture of myself on that voyage to which I took exception. His repeated insinuation was that I had gone about the ship withdrawn and moody, liable to burst into tears at the slightest thing ... according to my own, quite clear memory, I adapted very ably to the changed realities of my circumstances. I remember very well that, far from being miserable on that voyage, I was positively excited about life aboard the ship. (*WWO* 27)

This impression, this sketch of Banks as a 'miserable loner' is repeated later by Morgan, much to Banks's growing 'annoyance' (*WWO* 182). Yet, despite Banks's assurance to us, a reader assumed to be sympathetic, that Morgan 'keep[s] muddling things up', an alternative, less flattering but perhaps more human picture of Banks emerges from the repeated intrusion of these other voices which tangentially present a coherent image of a traumatized and withdrawn child attempting to negotiate the world under radically altered circumstances, in the same way that alternate Krapps emerge from the tapes he tries so valiantly to edit under the scrutiny of the theatre audience. *When We Were Orphans* is interested in things being mistaken and misgiven (the assumption of his benefactor's identity, for example): In a rather Dickensian (or Wodehousian) manner, one character is named 'Miss Givens' (*WWO* 127). Banks is a consummate storyteller, his narrative a tale of an independent, confident, self-assured, celebrated detective endeavouring to right global wrongs. This 'picture' of Banks works only if it is not undermined by conflicting perspectives. Problematically, with communication comes the possibility of alternate realities, events remembered in other ways, not always conducive to a singular, unified picture. As Banks struggles to forge for himself a character based on images of his pop culture heroes, he is assailed by other narratives that slip through the spaces but which nevertheless reveal the profound degree of his traumatic self-dissociation. It is from these interstitial spaces themselves that the 'real' Banks emerges in negative; it is not simply one or the other picture that is 'real', but rather the tension itself that gestures back towards Banks's essential and essentially undisclosable nature in a way that cannot be stated explicitly. Banks's pride is threatened by these other versions; but more troublingly, if Banks is not the dignified, self-assured, precocious detective he takes himself to be, he must give up the consolatory, sustaining hope of reuniting his family (and his wilder associated ambition of ridding the world of evil).

Kathy H. has the same foible; her memoir is an attempt to inscribe Hailsham and herself in written form, to give the definitive authoritative version for posterity, one that often struggles against the disruption of others', more specifically Ruth's, memories. Like the rest of her species, Kathy has what appears to be an abbreviated surname that seems to mimic a technique for implying tact in the Victorian novel's meta-verisimilitude (pretending to protect the identity of its subjects, *as if* they were real persons). Her initial, H., also gestures towards Hailsham, with which she alone in the text shares an initial. However, the H is not abbreviated because she has no family, no family name, no lineage; she is simply the eighth Kathy in a series of presumably identical Kathy's.[6] As Robert Eaglestone comments, the trick 'summons up the idea of a "batch" number' (2017: 17). Our version of Kathy is not interested in making an objective record, getting 'straight all the things that happened' in an unbiased documentary; that is to say, she is not concerned with History, but rather *a* history. In one scene, Kathy recalls trying to make a point to Ruth about their juvenile lack of understanding about poetry, getting frustrated because Ruth 'was determined to remember us all as more sophisticated than we were' (*NLMG* 18). Later Kathy thinks about the 'secret guard business' which arose around the arrival of Miss Lucy; '[Ruth] claimed it had been just a matter of two or three weeks – but that was almost certainly wrong' (*NLMG* 49). Kathy is repeatedly and deeply aggravated by 'the way Ruth kept pretending to forget things about Hailsham', admitting that although 'these were mostly trivial things [she] got more and more irritated with her' (*NLMG* 186–7). What else is there in Ishiguro's fictions but 'trivial things'?

Kathy has two motives for drawing up what will likely be her final testament as she heads towards her own completion: to ensure, like Banks, that her picture of herself is the one that sticks; another, more sinister, is to undermine and avenge herself on Ruth, who exerted such power over her, and who prevented her from having time to experience love with Tommy. Marc Farrant describes the novel's style as 'post-literary esthetics of estrangement', arguing that the work's novelty is its subversion of 'the novel's conventional modes of emotional and empathic solicitation' (2020: 152). In fact, it is immediately after Ruth tells Kathy that, even if Tommy were free and available, he is too 'fussy' to be with girls 'who've been with … well, you know' (the implication remains unsaid), that Kathy announces her decision to become a carer, a decision about which she 'never wavered' (*NLMG* 198). To avoid any suggestion that her decision (which leads to her overseeing Tommy and Ruth's deaths) is coincidence, Kathy lets slip a resentment that lingers below the surface of the text: 'Maybe Ruth thought … she'd have a big influence on whether or not I changed my mind. But I kept a certain distance from her, just as I did from Tommy' (*NLMG* 199). The narrative is Kathy's carefully orchestrated attack on Ruth, one which Ruth has been anticipating, as Kathy comments as she visits Ruth in her recovery centre: 'It was like she'd been waiting and waiting for me to do something to her, and she thought the time had now come' (*NLMG* 211). Indeed, despite the fact that Kathy and Tommy do get together as Tommy approaches completion, it is, as they recognize, 'a pity we left it so late' (*NLMG* 235). Of course, they were manipulated by Ruth. Kathy's only regret is that she could not take revenge on Ruth while Ruth lived. As she admits, 'maybe it would have made [Ruth] feel bad' to see that the 'damage she'd once done to us couldn't be repaired' easily, a part of her wishes that Ruth 'knew it all before she completed' (*NLMG* 279). Her narrative masquerades as a realist document but is troubled repeatedly by the intrusions of others' memories which are aggressively challenged in the way that Banks challenges the colonel, Osbourne and Morgan.

Stevens, Ogata, Ono, Kathy, Axl, Beatrice and Banks each recall moments where they have somehow misunderstood or been misunderstood in ways which, although seemingly 'pretty innocuous', turned out to have great importance. This is most poignant for Stevens, who lets the possibility for love and family slip by for a misguided duty, recalling at the end of the day that 'I *trusted*. I trusted in his lordship's wisdom. All those years I served him, I trusted I was doing something worthwhile' (*RD* 243). When other perspectives intrude, Ishiguro's realist narratives are jeopardized by the heteroglossia of a modernist aesthetic which refuses to privilege, to grant omniscience to one voice, one picture. Ishiguro's defining mood is ambiguity, richly wrought, delicately interweaved with the narratological and rational certainty of his narrators undermined by the intrusion of contrary recollections. Ishiguro borrows from the modernists a concern with unreliability in the traditional sense, with narrators who are repeatedly shown to be untrustworthy both because they lack knowledge and awareness and because they hope to convey not objective reality but a carefully edited version of *a* history. Multiple often conflicting perspectives produce a composite image over which the narrator struggles to exert editorial control, to ensure that we do not get a 'slightly misleading picture' (*RD* 124). Oddly, the narrators themselves allow these alternative positions into their texts. Ishiguro perpetrates countless brutalities against his characters, none more than forcing them to confront unflattering pictures of themselves and their actions sketched by less sympathetic others. Sometimes, then, labile language is so liable to be misremembered or misgiven that communication is better served with silence. In a world suffused with divergent perspectives and the failures of language, communication relies on faith and mutual 'understandings' which form in the absence of genuine understanding.

II

Each of Ishiguro's novels has at its centre a fact that is unuttered, and unutterable, but which gradually seeps through his narrators' tightly knit prose. Silences, then, are central, as Wong has written, 'if Ishiguro's narrators both lie and comfort themselves in the same breath, what they do not tell us is as dynamic as what they reveal' (2005: 17). Language plays only a small role in communication, much of which is tonal, gestural. Seemingly aware of the multiple failures and limitations of spoken language, many of Ishiguro's characters develop 'understandings', communicating, or at least believing they are communicating, through a series of subtle unspoken codes. Indeed, Lewis remarks that the world of *The Unconsoled* is 'governed by an unspoken set of quirks' (2000: 125). It is precisely because so much of what transpires between Ishiguro's characters occurs without language that they find themselves imaginatively revisiting the past in order to reinterpret moments of ambiguity which appeared at the time to be unambiguous. Perhaps, as Søren Kierkegaard enigmatically remarks, 'Life can only be understood backwards; but it must be lived forwards' (1967: 306). Troublingly, if the immediate event provides something like details to interpret, the present of recall offers only distorted (misty in *BG*) shadows, Etsuko's 'vague echoes'.

Never Let Me Go exploits non-verbal 'understandings' to best effect, as the children of Hailsham attempt to navigate life in a group (with a terrible unspoken truth lingering like the foreboding woods on the periphery of their awareness). Indeed, such understandings help to foster the illusion that their institution is something like a family, as Vincent Descombes remarks, 'The sign of being at home is the ability to make oneself understood without too much difficulty' (quoted in Augé 2008: 87). A particularly resonant instance of communication happening without words involves a disagreement between Kathy and Ruth after they have fallen out over another equally trivial matter (Wood's 'banality'). Ruth produces a pencil case and gives a rather provocative response to questions of its provenance: '"Let's just agree. Let's *agree* I got it in the sale." Then she gave us all a knowing smile' (*NLMG* 56). Kathy is aggravated by Ruth's insinuation: although a 'pretty innocuous sort of response ... I knew exactly what she'd meant by her answer and smile: she was claiming the pencil case was a gift from Miss Geraldine' (*NLMG* 56). Kathy's narrative details her search for various kinds of certainty, confirmation, 'extensive totality', and here she pre-empts questions of misinterpretation by letting us know that 'there could be no mistake' about her reading of Ruth's ambiguous answer that 'it had been building up for weeks', and there was a 'certain smile, a certain voice Ruth would use' in these situations where she wanted to imply some special bond between her and the students' favourite guardian. We can either trust that Kathy is a reliable witness, or question her motivations in a narrative which frequently betrays a sinister purpose. Sensitive to the possibility that we may find her an unreliable narrator, Kathy forestalls such an accusation, assuring us that she is not mistaken and is therefore invested with the variety of certainty we might associate with a traditional, pre-modernist narrator. Importantly, nothing is stated as such, but simply insinuated, mimed, gestured.

In order to redress this perceived wrong, Kathy decides to prove that she knows that the pencil case in question, evocatively described by Midge A. as 'luscious', has come from one of the sales that play an important role in the students' cloistered lives; she pretends that she had spent some time looking through the sales registers. Ruth responds that it's a 'boring sort of thing to look at', to which Kathy replies, 'No, it was quite interesting really. You can see all the things the people have bought' (*NLMG* 59). Once more we see Kathy's fascination with 'all the things'. Kathy intuits from Ruth's nonchalance that her friend 'now knew exactly what this was about' (*NLMG* 59). Immediately assuming that her plan has worked and that she has communicated to Ruth that she knows that Ruth was lying about the pencil case, Kathy repents, feeling 'awful' and 'confused' (*NLMG* 60). To assuage her guilt, Kathy adds to the enigmatic aura of the pencil case when Midge A. later asks Ruth where she got it, referring to its provenance as a 'big mystery' (*NLMG* 63). Kathy and Ruth, or perhaps just Kathy, establish an unspoken economy of mutual support. In this exchange, Kathy intuits from behavioural cues that Ruth feels indebted to her:

> Now, for much the same reasons I'd not been able to talk openly to Ruth about what I'd done to her over the Sales Register business, she of course wasn't able to thank me for the way I'd intervened with Midge. But it was obvious from her manner towards me, not just over the next few days, but over the weeks that followed, how pleased she was with me … it was easy to recognise the signs of her looking around for some opportunity to do something nice, something really special for me. (*NLMG* 63)

In Kathy's understanding, the sequence of events, of exchanges, is entirely logical and 'easy to recognise': she and Ruth fall out; Kathy oversteps some important line; she feels remorse; she offers support to Ruth; Ruth (in Kathy's expectations derived from this fragile economy) is trying to find a way to repay her. Nothing here, as Kathy tells us, has been discussed 'openly'; there is and cannot be any objective or verifiable proof that Ruth has been an active or even aware participant in these extensive transactions in the economy of resentment and repayment which evokes B. S. Johnson's *Christie Malry's Own Double Entry* (1973), and David Foster Wallace's later repurposing of the 'double entry' in the character Toni Ware from *The Pale King* (2011). Indeed, when Kathy is so passionately defending Ruth's acquisition of the pencil case, 'Ruth herself had on a vague expression, like she'd suddenly become preoccupied with something else entirely' (*NLMG* 63). This may be Ruth signalling to Kathy that she understands the effort that Kathy has made to redeem the previous fault, and that now she has inherited the burden of debt. On the other hand, Ruth may be completely unaware of the complex, almost paranoid series of associations and inferences that Kathy has made over her original enigmatic claim about the pencil case. Crucially, narratologically, certainty is essential for Kathy; in its absence, *her* narrative about her relationships is undermined by the variety of radical uncertainty she seeks to preclude because it poses risks to the image she has 'safely in [her] head'. Like Banks, the integrity of her self-image is of utmost importance because so much rests upon it. If much communication is unspoken, paralinguistic, then much may also be entirely fictitious, or 'imaginary' to come back to Ishiguro's own word.

Kathy might be forgiven for her creeping paranoia, an entirely appropriate response to her situation as a clone being prepared for a short and brutal life, a fact that the 'students' and the reader have been 'told and not told' (*NLMG* 79). As Miss Lucy, a passionate but not entirely professional (Stevens would argue that she lacked a certain 'dignity') guardian, one day tells them, 'Your lives are all set out for you. You'll become adults, and then before you are old, before you're even middle-aged, you'll start to donate your vital organs' (*NLMG* 80). Kathy once again takes the opportunity to make assumptions about the unspoken (Ryder perfects this skill for reading minds):

> Then she went silent, but my impression was that she was continuing to say things inside her head, because for some time her gaze kept roving over us, going from face to face as if she were still speaking to us. (*NLMG* 80)

We have seen throughout the novel that Kathy is preoccupied with the thoughts of others, with the sense that something is being conveyed through gesture alone. Or, once more, we may assume that the thing being conveyed by Miss Lucy's attentive silence is so utterly beyond reason that it too places too much pressure on language. Returning to Jacques Derrida and Jean-Luc Nancy, we see here that the reality of Hailsham makes 'the limits of our language tremble', pushes against 'the external limit of deixis' (Kearney 1984: 112, 1993: 175). Further, Miss Lucy is preparing the students for a horror to which she herself is immune, and there is a terrible sanctity in a shared future which she cannot penetrate. Where language fails, words simply stop, her gestural gaze gives some sense, enabling 'understandings' to form. This is peculiarly resonant in Kathy's narrative; to a degree, she becomes complicit in the programme, and her narrative too withholds key information. As Patrick R. Query comments, some critics have remarked on Kathy's 'excruciatingly slow disclosure of information' (2015: 156). However, he argues that this is precisely the purpose: the novel is a 'metaphor for the way novels make meaning', 'an elucidation of the experience of novel reading itself' (Query 2015: 157). Kathy mimics the realist mode of the novels she reads in the cottages and at Hailsham, but in the process of recording her past in this mode, she encounters the polysemy of others' memories, which pose a challenge to her record, and her self-positioning as the all-knowing narrator.

Ruth and Kathy develop an evening ritual in the 'cottages', refurbished farm outbuildings, which act as a kind of halfway house between Hailsham and their final destinations in 'recovery centres'. They get together over a hot drink (remarkably like Stevens and Kenton) and talk about their usually uneventful days. For Kathy,

> what made these heart-to-hearts possible – you might even say what made the whole friendship possible during that time – was this understanding we

had that anything we told each other during these moments would be treated with careful respect, that we'd honour confidences ... this had never been spelt out exactly, but it was definitely, as I say, an understanding. (*NLMG* 124)

Gustav, proud porter at Ryder's hotel, also develops an understanding with his now-estranged daughter. As he tells Ryder while trying to convince him to intervene on his behalf, they 'had this ... *understanding* now for many years', after a small misunderstanding, so that they have not spoken to one another without an intermediary, usually Boris, for a long time (*U* 82). 'Incidentally,' Gustav tells Ryder, 'this understanding of ours, it wasn't something I originally imagined going on for very long' (*U* 82). As Kathy assumes with Ruth, Gustave is certain that 'Sophie understood our arrangement and respected it' (*U* 85). In a further tragedy, Ryder is in the process of developing just this kind of understanding with his own son, Boris, calibrating him for a life defined by the kind of regrets that preoccupy those characters in middle and old age: Ryder, unwittingly politically manipulated, is Stevens, Ogata and Ono in the making. Another understanding forms between Axl and Beatrice, to do with their journey to visit a lost son: 'before long an understanding had grown between them, in the silent way understandings do between husband and wife of many years, to avoid the subject as much as possible' (*BG* 20). There is here and in the many instances of 'understandings' between Ishiguro's characters an irony, one involving the tension between the desperation to communicate something on a level that transcends the mere verbal, and the recurring failure of these idiosyncratic and often unilateral semiotic systems which enacts a deeper degree of isolation and aloneness than mere verbal misunderstanding. Confronted with the failure of language, or as a result of an initial misunderstanding, mutual 'respected' silence usurps language, in so doing erecting a barrier (Ryder's wall) in the tense interpersonal vacuum between characters. Stevens reminisces about the 'fine professional understanding' between he and Kenton while being, to various degrees, knowingly and unknowingly blind to his stubborn resistance to the deeper, more meaningfully intimate personal understanding which Kenton seeks to establish between them. Understandings can themselves be subject to misunderstanding, as Ryder suggests to Gustav in an untypically sympathetic insight: 'this matter of your understanding. Isn't it possible that this might itself be at the heart of what's bothering her?' (*U* 85).

Ishiguro works in precisely this way, providing apparently 'banal' details before we have the context to interpret their concealed immanent significance. In Tommy's words (too conspiratorial for Kathy), we cannot 'understand properly the latest piece of information', although we 'take it in on some level, so that before long all this stuff was there in our heads without us ever having examined it properly' (*NLMG* 81). We the reader are 'told and not told'. The details we are offered are those that are significant and relevant to the immediate interests of the narrators, and something like a picture (a sketch), an understanding, emerges organically from the texture, the background, the silences of the characters and the silences which occupy the spaces between the heterogenous voices. Ishiguro's writing manipulates negative space; sparsely populated, the narratives emerge mistily on the periphery of the visual field (from 'behind' as Banks imagines), replicating with striking fidelity the vagueness of recalled images. One challenge that arises when writing about Ishiguro is that very little of import is stated explicitly, and that which is stated explicitly tends to be so trivial as to seem either digressive or irrelevant.[7] There are rare moments of emotional honesty, sincere vulnerability, which in the context of subterfuge and self-protection feel incongruous, sometimes even false. When Mrs Benn tells Stevens of those 'desolate occasions' during which she imagines the life that they may have shared, completely uncharacteristically, Stevens declares, 'Indeed – why should I not admit it? – at that moment, my heart was breaking' (*RD* 239). Generally, like Banks and Ryder, his most typical narrators, there is a feeling that the world into which we are thrown is only partially formed, hazy, replete with a meaning that lingers behind the speech, the text, the confessions, the details, and that we are in this sense both told and not told. It is as if then the world emerges, perhaps from those innumerable atoms which Woolf speaks of, only that world is partial, contingent, subjective. An understanding forms between reader and text, but one that is always ambivalent: it's as if Ishiguro borrows Ruth's enigmatic plea: 'let's just *agree*' he asks.

Highly respected as a carer (she informs us several times), Kathy gets to choose her own wards, a privilege in which she takes great professional pride. Towards the end of the novel, she sees both Ruth and Tommy through to 'completion' (a euphemism which she borrows from her abusers). Like each of Ishiguro's narrators, Kathy has a remarkably acute awareness of her physical surroundings, most notably the décor of rooms. Here, she describes Ruth's 'recovery centre':

> Everything – the walls, the floor – has been done in gleaming white tiles, which the centre keeps so clean when you first go in it's almost like entering a hall of mirrors. Of course, you don't exactly see yourself reflected back loads of times, but you almost think you do. When you lift an arm, or when someone sits up in bed, you can feel this pale, shadowy movement all around you in the tiles. (*NLMG* 17)

Just like the wonderful use of the word 'luscious' above, Kathy's 'has been done' (and we come back to 'everything') evokes so much more than can be expressed about her character by description alone. This passage is symbolically rich, (almost) capturing the world of the novel (clones are oneself but not quite) and the essence of writing, of literature, of verisimilitude itself. The gleaming white tiles act *as if* they were mirrors (of nature), fleetingly capturing and gesturally representing something while simultaneously veiling and distorting the subject. We might see these tiles as pages, Kathy's perhaps, showing or at least appearing to show a facsimile of Kathy and the misty memories that she attempts to reify. We return here to Plato's analogy of the cave; Kathy indicates that her story shows little more than reflections of an always ambiguous past traced hazily in a medium which further distorts the already distorted. The tiles capture the shadows of the phenomenal world in a way that does little more than gesture towards their noumenal ground. Importantly, if we take these as pages, whether wittingly or unwittingly, Kathy informs us that they and those of her memoir show nothing more than refracted shadows, Etsuko's 'vague echoes' of herself; ostensibly a record of Hailsham, it is nothing more than an impression, a sketch derived from a series of often-challenged memories of a time that itself was always ambiguous. Again, the periphery is hazy, unfocused. There is also here in these vague mirror selves, a kind of polytemporal self-haunting which we see in each of Ishiguro's works, peopled with doubles and spectral selves from other times (Etsuko seeing herself in or as Sachiko, and seeing Mariko as Keiko before Keiko's birth; Ryder is both Boris and Stefan, he is Brodsky in making). Kathy's description of the tiles is a peculiarly apposite metaphor for Ishiguro's gestural poetics, and his borrowings from the modernists.

A similar moment occurs towards novel's end, when Tommy and Kathy notice a sketch of a house that might be Hailsham in Madame's hallway. Kathy is unsure because 'the table lamp beneath it had a crooked shade covered with cobweb traces, and instead of lighting up the picture, it just put a shine over the murky glass, so you could hardly make it out at all' (*NLMG* 244). Even here Kathy insists on contradicting Tommy, who is persuasively confident that the picture shows 'the bit round the back of the duck pond', to which Kathy replies impatiently, 'What do you mean? … There's no pond. It's just a bit of countryside' (*NLMG* 224). Interestingly, the cobwebs bring us back to earlier in the novel, when the clones realize that Madame is afraid of them 'as someone might be afraid of spiders' (*NLMG* 35). The picture is a subtle rendition of memory itself; the light cast over the image is murky, imprecise, tinged with emotions (of 'being the spiders'), penetrated by other memories, and others' memories, the subject once so familiar now obscured and even unrecognizable. The disagreement forcefully illustrates that, even so soon after leaving Hailsham, its memory has faded to the degree that what remains of its structure is imaginary, individual to each clone's memory, and that there is not now, nor has there ever been, a single Hailsham, as there can be no single record of it despite Kathy's aggressive insistence on the validity of her singular vision. It is, after all, simply a representation. As with the Peace Park Statue, and the white tiles, this simple image condenses the novel's concerns and Ishiguro's own concern with both memory and verisimilitude with subtle economy. These then are the deceptive 'details' that so fascinate Ishiguro's narrators.

III

If realism offered meticulously crafted line drawings, modernism's canvas is more impressionistic, sketch-like, despite, perhaps even because of its attention to the finer details of sensory perception. Stevens makes an observation that we might also see as typical of Ishiguro. Planning his motoring trip, he looks through a travel book by Mrs Jane Symons, called *The Wonder of England*, which 'describes to readers the delights of Devon and Cornwall, complete with photographs and – to my mind even more evocative – a variety of artists' sketches of the region' (*RD* 11). What additional quality do sketches have that Stevens finds absent in photographs? Perhaps it is exactly the mediation, the moment of subjective interpretation that intercedes between world and image that interests Stevens. Perhaps too sketches are evocative precisely because they are impressionistic, partial, often with areas of great detail vanishing into an edgeless and undefined canvas. Sketches, like the worlds evoked by and through the single perspective of Ishiguro's characters, are suggestive, gestural, 'immanent' even as Lukacs argues of the novel form. Later, Stevens is showing one of Mr Farraday's guests, Mrs Wakefield, around Darlington Hall, after Farraday has assured her that the house, and Stevens, are 'genuine'. Mrs Wakefiled, looking at an archway, suggests that it is a 'mock period piece done only a few years ago', 'very skilful, but mock' (*RD* 123). We might here come back to Oe's response to the authenticity of Ishiguro's imaginary Japan, to suggest that that too, while skilful, is merely mock.

The effectiveness of Ishiguro's poetics of uncertainty relies on his unique ability to foreground local detail at the expense of global insight; the more information we have about the minutiae of his narrators' lives, the less able are we, and they, to place that information into anything like an objective context. This results from those various failures that Ishiguro enacts between his characters, the fact that communication always in some vital sense provides an inadequate picture of reality: the data that Zola speaks of, the innumerable atoms preferred by Woolf, never cohere, fail to coalesce. Lukacs's sense that the novel as a form is perpetually immanent seems apposite, here, in a poetics of uncertainty, of becomings that never quite become. A feeling pervades that, while on some diffuse preconscious level, information is being imparted, that we are being 'told and not told', this takes the form of the shadowy reflections of self that Kathy detects in those tiles/pages of the recovery centre. For Ishiguro, there is a careful blending of the fascination with detail and unity, order and completion that, according to Lodge, Lukacs, Tallis and many other critics, typifies the realist work with the rejection of certainty and the turn to the subjective that has come to be seen as definitional of modernism. However, his characters are ironically out of step, politically and aesthetically. They act *as if* some certainty were available, and the novels act *as if* there were such things as conclusions, but they inhabit amorphous textual, political, aesthetic spaces, ones in which the idea of certainty, of knowing the crucial moment, is absurd. In aesthetic terms, this amounts to a poetics as radical as that of Robbe-Grillet, Barth, Laurence Sterne, Christine Brooke-Rose or any more overt stylist. As Ishiguro has noted, his works manage somehow to be realist, in a broad sense, while also sustaining interior monologues for the duration. These contribute to what James Wood has eloquently called Ishiguro's 'gauges of verisimilitude'. Ambiguity is the key mood, one oddly but powerfully counterpointed with the certainty, the self-assurance of narrators wrangling with their own and others' memories to produce some variety of definite history. Here, I have tried to place Ishiguro in the context of realism and modernism, and to make sense of the manner in which he adopts and adapts these modes, forming a synthesis that works precisely because of its awareness of and resistance to formal definition in both senses. Of course, Ishiguro's novels are fascinated by the political, aesthetic and communicative possibilities and failures of the arts. They are, in the end, gestural, working around and with an awareness of the failures of language.

Notes

1. One might place a *sic* after 'fictional', but for Ishiguro, this is possibly an intentional conflation of ontologies.
2. In an interview with Cody Delistraty, Ishiguro explained that genre is 'basically a marketing label that's put on retrospectively by the book industry to help market books to certain demographics' (2015).
3. This does not mean that Ishiguro is a postmodernist, his works are far too humanist in their concerns to warrant this epithet. Even his most ostensibly postmodern novel, *The Unconsoled*, is fundamentally an exploration not of form but of the form of human emotion.
4. A terminological anomaly once more; where he uses 'fictional' for fiction above, here it is 'realistic' for realist.
5. Ishiguro '[grew] up reading Western fiction: Dostoevsky, Chekhov, Charlotte Bronte, Dickens' (Mason 1989: 336).
6. A similar technique appears in Michel Houellebecq in *La Possibilité d'une île* (2003), which features the clone Daniel24. Cf. P. Sloane (forthcoming), 'Empathy and the Ethics of Posthuman Reading', in Sloane and Shaw (eds), *Kazuo Ishiguro* (Manchester: Manchester University Press).
7. In Chapter 4 I discuss this in relation to the reading theory known as 'ideational scaffolding'.

Chapter 2

IMAGINATION

Ishiguro's gestural poetics operates through the precise diffusion of atomistic details into partially formed space, giving rise to fictional worlds which manage to be replete with trivial significance while simultaneously attuned to but unable to do more than indicate the occluded presence of wider contexts of meaning (sociopolitical, personal and world's undisclosable essence). This style of applying sparse but precise brushstrokes onto a developing but unfinished canvas evokes the diaphanously intangible pictures conjured by the mind in its ideational or dreamt gestures towards or, perhaps, away from 'the real' world. Edgeless sketches so typical of Ishiguro's chiaroscuro fictions – Etsuko's quasi-gothic dreamscape, Ryder's ongoing dissociative episode, Kathy's dislocated PTSD narrative, Ono's 'floating world' – mimic with remarkable fidelity the 'dreamy sense of unreality' which accompanies daydream, dream and fantasy (*U* 383). Although taking their cue from acquaintance with reality, both literary fiction and the imagination distort, transfigure, defamiliarize their raw, unrefined materials. For Sean Matthews and Sebastian Groes, 'Reality and Imagination' is one of several key 'grand, dialectical oppositions' around which Ishiguro's works are structured (2009: 7). Important as a theme, imagination is, self-evidently, vital for the creation of so many unique narratives that adhere just closely enough to the real to convince (sometimes too closely in Ishiguro's own assessment), with enough unreality to unsettle. Ishiguro, gifted, as Ryder thinks of the young aspiring pianist Stephan, with 'an imagination' of extraordinary 'originality and emotional subtlety', alludes often in interviews to the importance of imagination to his own creative process (*U* 150). We are reminded of his portraits of an 'imaginary' Japan vaguely recalled and playfully (re)constructed from partial fragmentary childhood memories; *The Remains of the Day*'s uncannily familiar England that is 'just an imaginary setting' (*Spiegel* 2005); the 'few lines [of Gawain] that described some imaginary ancient Britain that really caught my imagination' (*Geek's Guide to the Galaxy*, 2015); an 'imagination [which] came alive when I moved away from the immediate world around me' (Hunnewell 2008). Deceptively 'realistic', his fictional floating worlds are 'just another wilful quirk of his imagination', exploiting a deft skill to conceal the imaginary under a labile canvas sufficiently cognate with the real to encourage suspension of disbelief (*U* 41). Imagination might play a more fundamental role in Ishiguro's poetics than so far acknowledged, more so, or even being mistaken for memory.

Paradoxically, imagination is a necessary precondition for imaginatively distancing oneself from the world: for one's imagination to 'come alive' as it is dissevered from the 'immediate world' (what is writing but an act of mediating the world), that imagination must first perform the distancing. While allowing for the playful reinvention of the real, the imagination also presupposes both prior exposure and retroactive access to the phenomenal 'world of sense'. In David Hume's system, some form of sensory engagement with the material world is a prerequisite to subsequent neural processes, because 'neither the ideas of the memory nor imagination, neither the lively nor faint ideas can make their appearance in the mind, unless their correspondent impressions have gone before to prepare the way for them' (1874: 318). Ishiguro's imaginative worlds are predicated on 'impressions' of a real Japan, England and ancient Britain, or at least impressionistic sketches of them, although these are drawn from myriad sources both contemporaneous and subsequent, mediated and unmediated. If for Hume the world of sense precedes ideational constructs, for Rene Descartes the sensory apprehension of the real, or the sense data that arise from it, is a necessary (though not sufficient) condition of fantasy while also acting as a limiting factor: 'When painters try to create sirens and satyrs with the most extraordinary bodies, they cannot give them natures which are new in all respects; they simply jumble up the limbs of different animals' (Barthes's 'tissue of citations') (2017: 17). As Adorno writes, 'imagination in the production of a work of representational art is not pleasure in free invention, in creation *ex nihilo*' (1997b: 13). Indeed, many philosophers argue that pre-existing images are the medium of thought, imageless thought a logical absurdity: 'Thought simply can not go on without image' (Woodworth 1906: 702). Artists, as Ishiguro comments, need 'material to feed their imagination', and this material, the images on which thought depends, is mined from perceived reality in the form of impressions on the mind (inscribed neural traces) (Oe 1991: 121).

For both Descartes and Hume, memory and imagination are intricately co-related and complexly intertwined faculties that work by re-activating and re-engaging with the matter of the past (the 'details'). Meditating on the neurosensory transit of external objects to ideation, Descartes suggests that memory mediates between world and ideation, that it is 'with the assistance of memory' that these traces of the encountered world reach 'the imagination' (2017: 59). Scrupulously if unreliably introspective, Stevens mobilizes a metaphor most commonly associated with recall when desperately seeking a response to Mr Farraday's disconcerting American 'banter': 'I thus searched my imagination' (*RD* 130). In such an understanding, the process of thought involves sensory datum from the real world being atomized, internalized and subsequently reformed by the imagination via recall; in this paradigm, the recalled image is (always already) a secondary ekphrastic neural transfiguration of the primary ekphrastic sensory transfiguration of the real. We see in Stevens's confused rhetoric evidence of what Gaston Bachelard refers to as the 'solidarity of memory and imagination' in an acknowledgement of their interdependent cooperation in our experience of the world (1994: 6). Further questions arise about the kinds of access that our senses, and the mind, enable. Richard Rorty asks just such a question: 'How do we know whether what the Eye of the Mind sees is a mirror (even a distorted mirror – an enchanted glass) or a veil?' (2009: 46). Indeed, John Carey has commented on the 'inextricable fusion of memory, imagination, and dream' in Ishiguro's writing (2000). It is this fusion that produces narratives which seem to correlate with some form of objective reality while being repeatedly, if subtly, distorted, even veiled (by memory's murky lamp). The phenomenal world is not simply apprehended, eidetically mirrored in the mind for subsequent retrieval, but is rather wilfully and unwittingly reconfigured in transit in such a way that recall is, in essence, an act of the imagination. Whether recalled or constructed, sensory perception, or 'strange and extraordinary' creatures, all ideations undergo the same process of transfiguration before being rendered in the same (esem)plastic medium: pictures in the mind.

The imagination is an artist of sorts, reworking found materials to construct an approximate image both of self and of the world (in the same way that Hailsham's clones craft their art from discarded objects). In his attempt to analyse 'human nature', Hume discriminates between memory ('lively' ideas) and imagination ('faint' ideas), which he postulates to be discrete modes of the intellect. Relying on metaphors of painting, he suggests that

> [memory] paints its objects in more distinct colours, than any which are employ'd by the latter [imagination]. When we remember any past event, the idea of it flows in upon the mind in a forcible manner; whereas in the imagination the perception is faint and languid, and cannot without difficulty be preserv'd by the mind steddy and uniform for any considerable time. (1874: 318)

Hume's 'faint' and 'languid' recalls the vague echoes, the shadowy images and the 'dreamy sense of unreality' so characteristic of Ishiguro's narratives (*U* 383). Oddly, if we agree with Hume that memory, intriguingly personified as an artist (no recourse to photography as a simile in the eighteenth century), is distinguished by its distinct colours and forceful nature, Ishiguro seems more to exploit the faint, languid, diaphanous pastel sketches which emerge in the imagination. We might return here to Stevens's comparison of the evocative potential of photographs (memories) and sketches (imagination). Hume's proto-scientific taxonomy emerged in a period before the development of experimental psychology and neuroimaging technologies, and so cannot take account of the recently discovered fact that memories are 'labile and susceptible to interference' because 'neural plasticity is enhanced' during recall, enabling the 'integration of new information in the context of pre-existing memory representations' (Bridge and Paller 2012: 12149). Ishiguro's characters are deeply aware that impressions from the past must be repackaged and repurposed, or are so unwittingly, in the altered personal and political context of the present. As Etsuko admits, once more resorting to painterly metaphor: 'Memory, I realize, can be an unreliable thing; often it is heavily coloured by the circumstances in which one remembers' (*PVH* 156). This admission also acts, Yugin Teo remarks, as a 'warning of the continued unreliability of her memories', a warning the reader would be well advised to heed in each Ishiguro story (2014: 18).

In terms of the faculty of 'human understanding', Hume privileges the 'steddy and uniform' memory over the transient 'faint and languid' imagination. However, he does concede that imagination has the benefit of not being 'restrain'd to the same order and form with the original impressions; while the memory is in a manner ty'd down in that respect, without any power of variation' (1874: 318). Ishiguro's narrators would like to believe that memory is temporally and formally eidetic, its power of recall immune to the micro and macro, spatial and temporal deformations which, for Ishiguro, characterizes a faculty typified by willed and unwilled distortion. However, as Ishiguro's closest literary ancestor, Alain Robbe-Grillet, remarks:

> Memory belongs to the imagination. Human memory is not like a computer that records things; it is part of the imaginative process, on the same terms as invention. In other words, inventing a character or recalling a memory is part of the same process. (Guppy 1986)

It is the imagination which, for Coleridge, 'dissolves, diffuses, dissipates, in order to recreate: or where this process is rendered impossible, yet still at all events it struggles to idealize and to unify' (in Harvey 2013: 87). Coleridge's estimation of imagination's function shows a remarkable sensitivity to Ishiguro's defining preoccupation; in the absence of eidetic recall, it is the imagination which dissolves the elements of the lost past and reformulates them in the present, perhaps in order, as Kathy remarks, 'to get straight all the things that happened', but equally to construct a narrative of self more suited to the story told (*NLMG* 37).

Memory is equally susceptible to creative imperfections. Ryder, for example, recalling a trip to the cinema, collapses Stanley Kubrick's science fiction masterwork *2001: A Space Odyssey*, Clint Eastwood's spaghetti Westerns and *The Magnificent 7* (and by implication *The Seven Samurai*): he awaits 'the famous scene in which Yul Brynner comes into the room and tests Eastwood's speed on the draw by clapping his hands in front of him' (*U* 99). Ishiguro's first effort at fiction was a 'pulp Western', but Eastwood (*Unforgiven*/*Unconsoled*) and Brynner never appeared together, of course, and neither appeared in a Kubrick movie. Ryder's rare real-world referent provides quantitative evidence of the infidelity of his memory, as Richard Robinson comments, and the absurd slip gives the 'reader a foothold', 'breaks the author-reader contract' of the novel (2009: 74). However, the slip also illustrates imagination's capacity to connect and amalgamate disparate but categorically cognate experiences and to recall the composite product as a memory. Ryder's imagination produces a patchwork film seamlessly edited together from the elements abstracted by his imperfect memory from his favourite movies, bridging gaps with different but like materials. As Bachelard has remarked (in a language made more resonant by the recent introduction of virtual and augmented reality technologies), the 'imagination augments the values of reality' (1994: 3). The imagination, to borrow a term from Coleridge, is 'esemplastic', unifying, simply a variety of memory requiring the pre-existence of malleable raw materials which can be either wittingly or unwittingly manipulated and misaligned when retrieved. Problematically, over time and after repeated recalls, these imagined realities attain a degree of certainty for Ishiguro's ontologically insecure narrators, and one wonders how Ryder might reply if confronted with his error.

For Ishiguro, as for Coleridge, the imagination is transformative, esemplastic. In certain circumstances, it can produce the illusion that trauma can be overcome, forestalled or transfigured by and subsumed into narratives which sustain the possibility for a consolation unattainable in the real world. In this sense, like the arts for Vonnegut, imagination is another 'human way of making life more bearable' (2005: 24). Imagination is most developed in and associated with early childhood, often referred to as 'the age of imagination', characterized by 'long periods of day-dreaming, the tendency to invent "imaginary companions", to construct a world of fairyland into which temporarily to retreat from the world of sense' (Griffiths 2002: 6). Ishiguro's novels often explore childhood's shared idiosyncrasies: we might think of Ichiro, a Japanese boy pretending to be The Lone Ranger, whose father, to the consternation of his more 'traditional' grandfather, 'thinks the American heroes are the better models for children now', galloping on an imaginary Silver and muttering approximate sounds of American English; or Boris, a Westerner given to fantasies of karate battles, talking passionately about his favourite imaginary football character. Robinson has solved a naming code in the novel which connects the work to the real world, identifying the fact that 'a remarkable number of names in *The Unconsoled* derive from European (mainly West German) footballers' (2009: 68). These then the materials from which Ishiguro imaginatively constructs this recognizable yet slightly off-kilter alternate reality. Boris is passionate about his fantasy football squad, insisting that 'Number Nine's the best player so far in history', to an exasperated and aggressively unimaginative Geoffrey Saunders who complains to Ryder that 'if that's the sort of rubbish you fill your boy's brain with, God help him' (*U* 50). A sanction, here, from a Saunders 'overwhelmingly down-at-heel', against nurturing a possibly redemptive/consolatory but equally potentially misleading, even harmful imagination (*U* 44). Childhood imagination is expressed most clearly in the daydreaming, make-believe and the many drawings and sketches that feature so movingly in Ishiguro's novels. The faculty perseveres to greater or lesser extents into adulthood, and in certain circumstances, like Ryder, or Ono to the more 'adult' arts of painting and classical music (discussed in the next chapter). Part of Bachelard's topoanalytic project involves tracing the 'phenomenology of the daydream', which, he feels, 'can untangle the complex of memory and imagination' (1994: 26). Ishiguro, it seems, is on a similar quest.

In this chapter, I discuss the therapeutic use of solitary daydreaming, cooperative game playing and sketching in Ishiguro's works, in order to chart the development of the artistic and delusional tendencies of his narrators. Imagination, I will show, can be used in isolation or collaboration to evade and/or reconfigure the real world and memory of it in such a way that children can overcome or delay addressing traumatic moments, or even forestall the transition into adulthood (we might think here of C. S. Lewis's child evacuees in *The Chronicles of Narnia* (1950), or *Never Ending Story*'s (Warner Bros., 1984) Bastian escaping neighbourhood bullies in the local bookstore, or even Lewis Carol's Alice, bored to despair by her sister). Sketching, the material manifestation of the imagination, also plays an important role in coming to terms with the world while also making manifest Ishiguro's own compositional techniques. I argue that these two recurrent themes of Ishiguro's fictional canvases contribute to his evanescent gestural poetics, evidencing a recurring interest in ideational constructs which develops from his interrogations of realist and modernist poetics. Ideations, I argue, form virtually in the spaces limned by the absence of eidetic recall and the multiple failures of expression which besiege Ishiguro's fundamentally alone characters.

Part 1: Games

I

The belief that imagination might enable one to overcome trauma, or simply to 'forestall graver contemplation', as David James suggests of characters' digressions, appears throughout Ishiguro's writing (2009: 57). Arguably his most deeply and unconsolably traumatized character, internationally celebrated pianist Ryder, devotes his professional life (in so doing sacrificing his personal life with Boris and Sophie) to healing wounds, both personal and national. On his most recent visit to an anonymous but uncannily canny city, he recalls several childhood instances of retreating into the world of his own imagination in the face of his parents' escalating rows – ironically, and poignantly in a novel that is about repeating histories – just as Boris does as Ryder and Sophie's relationship violently deteriorates. One example occurs shortly after he arrives, alone, exhausted and disorientated, in an initially unwelcoming (spatially and temporally) labyrinthine hotel (which traces over, and is the trace of, his childhood room in England):

> I reached down a hand and let my fingers brush against the hotel rug, and as I did so a memory came back to me of one afternoon when I had been lost within my world of plastic soldiers and a furious row had broken out downstairs. The ferocity of the voices had been such that, even as a child of six or seven, I had realised this to be no ordinary row. But I had told myself it was nothing and, resting my cheek back down on the green mat, had continued with my battle plans. (*U* 16)

Here, we see perhaps the pivotal moment when Ryder develops an awareness that imagination can be used to obscure or overwrite the present, to become 'lost' in one's mind amidst the pragmatically inescapable chaos of domestic implosion. Language, in the form of self-talking, precipitates the first refiguration of reality; in this 'memory recaptured through daydreaming', Ryder notices the unusual intensity of the argument between his parents, yet is somehow able to reassure himself that it was 'nothing' (Bachelard 1994: 10). Equally remarkably, as Ryder in the immediacy of the recounted event switches his attention from the unsettling periphery to the managed centre, the atmosphere to the detail (his nascent myopia), he relives the initial retreat from the memory of the argument, and simultaneously from the unsure and disconcerting present of the hotel room, repeating as an adult his childhood introspection to a world of toy soldiers which this time exist only in his memory. This evidences a memory *of* imagination, keyed by and sensitive to the real, but only as an evasion of it. Touch, haptic, tactile memory rekindles, 'brings alive' and magically transports Ryder back to a previous moment as he brushes the rug. Imagination though invests impulsive childhood with the rational agency of the adulthood of recall, when it is more likely that, in the presence of his parents' furious argument, young Ryder was unaware of the purpose of his practiced inattention.

A similar scenario occurs in *When We Were Orphans*, when Banks recalls the details of the morning his father said his final farewell: 'All I remember of the rest of the morning is that I played with my toy soldiers on the rug in my bedroom' (*WWO* 101). Banks refers explicitly to 'the sanctuary of my playroom and my toy soldiers', a safe space ostensibly immune to and cloistered from conflictual 'adult' spaces (*WWO* 70). The feeling of safety is an illusion, however, one that maps the childhood space onto the 'relative safety of the International Settlement' in which Banks lives with his English family (*WWO* 54). Importantly, any memory of the day itself, the subsequent discovery of the 'kidnapping' is overwritten by the memory of playing soldiers (foreshadowing the later battle scenes). The short-term distractive strategy permanently replaces any possibly traumatic memory, or memory of trauma (the image of the palimpsest has been overused of recent). Returning to Ryder, imagination can do more than simply distract one from the present; it can also reconfigure its materials in such a way as to render them susceptible to remedy:

> Near the centre of that green mat had been a torn patch that had always been a source of much irritation to me. But that afternoon, as the voices raged on downstairs, it had occurred to me for the first time that this tear could be used as a sort of bush terrain for my soldiers to cross. This discovery – that the blemish that had always threatened to undermine my imaginary world could in fact be incorporated into it – had been one of some excitement for me, and that 'bush' was to become a key factor in many of the battles I subsequently orchestrated. (*U* 16)

The word 'orchestrated' is not accidental. Ryder is an amalgam of a diplomat and concert pianist (Lefebvre's 'Rythmnanalyst', as I'll suggest in the next chapter), using his knowledge of 'modern music' to orchestrate personal, social and political change, and to repair the various traumas of the cities he visits in search of his own harmony. Initially a source of irritation, confronted with the necessity of imaginative escape from the present, Ryder's imagination draws him further into the fabricated world of his toy soldiers and subsumes the real-world tear into a malleable fantasy terrain, something to be overcome, traversed, survived. Crucially, too, Ishiguro makes explicit a defining belief of each of his narrators; with the imagination, personal and national blemishes (the breakdown of family relationships, political disunity, organ harvesting, war crimes) can be reconstituted and incorporated into a redemptive narrative. Importantly, if the recalled 'furious row' itself was traumatic and precipitated the dissociative episode facilitated by imagination, the memory of his assumption of the redemptive possibilities of imagination sparked by that is itself repurposed as a positive memory. This crucial memory reveals a deeper motivation for the creative consolation that Ryder seeks to offer on his trips. This purposive inattention perseveres into adulthood for Ryder, fixated on the manageable details and matters of illusory import, he can at least create the illusion of 'control of dynamics' which are in reality careening chaotically out of control (*U* 136).

Boris, Ryder's possibly adoptive son, or the product of Sophie's infidelity (perhaps Beatrice too is guilty of this transgression), or her previous relationship, also takes recourse to imagination as a way to reconstruct family bonds, or to play through a series of extreme scenarios that would create that bond, in so doing healing wounds (he is figured as a ruptured and rupturing wound (a tear) shared by Ryder and Sophie). In one scene, he enacts in 'his imagination the latest version of a fantasy he had been playing through over and over during the past weeks' about an endless onslaught of 'thugs' threatening to invade the family's flat in a council development, rendering both Ryder and Sophie tremblingly ineffectual:

'No, I can't stand it!' Sophie would wail, then break down sobbing. I would hold her in my arms in an attempt to comfort her, but my own features would be crumpling. Faced with this pathetic spectacle, Boris and Gustav would not show a flicker of disparagement. Gustav would place a reassuring hand on my shoulder, saying: 'Don't worry. Boris and I will be here. And after this last attack, that will be the end of it'. (*U* 219–20)

As Ichiro, much to the dismay of Ono, has been exposed to US cowboy programmes, Boris has taken the influence of the Western media appropriation of the martial arts tradition in this cultural cross-seeding, developing with Gustav a 'blend of karate and other combat techniques' (*U* 221). The thugs represent for Boris the many social problems that besiege his family: poverty, implied alcoholism, infidelity and perpetual domestic conflict. Banks and Boris are each enmeshed in complexly motivated and seemingly irremediable matrices of emotional violence which they can neither 'orchestrate' or control: these seams, these rifts and ruptures in the adult world (torn rugs) are unamenable to real-world reconstitution. But, the world of toy soldiers and imagined karate fights fosters illusory agency. Boris wants nothing more than family harmony, the final scene in his fantasy a mundane domestic night: 'Boris, Sophie and I would settle in for the evening. Sophie would move in and out of the kitchen, preparing the meal, singing lightly to herself, while Boris and I lounged about on the floor of the living room, engrossed in the board game' (*U* 222). However, as Lewis remarks, such 'domestic bliss is unobtainable for Ryder, Sophie and Boris, except in the young boy's daydreams' (2000: 119). Movingly, both Boris and Banks retreat from a real world of chaotic conflict to a world of fantasy that is nonetheless saturated with and defined by conflict, simply of another order (they each also bring soldiers into their own sanctuary). If children have a capacity to reinvent, it is one delimited by real-world atmospherics, the inescapable context of a fabulation which is itself illusory in its assumption of radical freedom. In a way then they each imbibe the intangible and unfathomable emotional conflict and reconfigure that in a form that can be manipulated, resolved (defeated) before re-emerging into the unaltered (unconsoled) real world. Returning to *Narnia*, briefly, Peter, Susan, Lucy and Edmund are evacuated from blitzed London, only to find or place themselves at the centre of their very own war, only one in which *they* wield the power. Fantasy then, as Descartes, Hume and Coleridge remark, derives from and is delimited by reality, consolation's parameters curtailed by context.

Writing enigmatically about 'French Toys', Roland Barthes finds in them a manifestation of 'all the things the adult does not find unusual: war, bureaucracy, ugliness' (2000: 53). For Barthes, toys are not 'dynamic forms … which appeal to the spirit of do-it-yourself' but 'a microcosm of the adult world; they are all reduced copies of human objects, as if in the eyes of the public the child was, all told, nothing but a smaller man, a homunculus to whom must be supplied objects of his own size' (2000: 53). Yi-Fu Tuan agrees that children are overwhelmed by 'the world of adults', but he writes, they 'are giants in their own world of toys', 'they can command their fates' (2018: 27). In Barthes's less optimistic understanding, childhood is a myth; toys merely functional objects designed to 'condition' children for future socialized, gendered roles of fighting wars and child-rearing (2000: 45). Peculiarly sensitive to the power of the trivial, Ishiguro recalls that as a child, being taken from his childhood home in Nagasaki and away from his grandfather, his biggest regret is the loss of a much-prized toy:

> My grandfather and I had been to a department store in Nagasaki to buy this great toy: there was a picture of a hen, and you had a gun, and you fired at the hen. If you hit the right part, an egg would drop out. But I wasn't allowed to take the toy with me. That was the main thing I was disappointed about. (Hunnewell 2008)

Ishiguro is probably referring to the 'Mother Hen Target Game', an American toy produced variously by Eldon, Knickerbocker and Lakeside from the 1950s through to the mid-1970s (further evidence of the post-war Americanization so prevalent in his works). Of course, for an author who likes to narrativize his own life, this is a metaphor for the kind of ordinary but profound original loss that John Berryman approaches in 'The Ball Poem', asking 'What is the boy now, who has lost his ball / What, what is he to do?' (2014: 9). Banks too, fighting behind enemy lines as he closes in on his kidnapped parents, recalls that the eclectic detritus on the rubbish-strewn floor included 'children's toys, simple but much-loved items of family life, and I would find myself suddenly overcome with renewed anger towards those who had allowed such a fate to befall so many innocent people' (*WWO* 241). Ishiguro is a connoisseur of the trivial, the 'simple', and in this scene, as Banks moves through destroyed buildings and traumatized occupants, unsure as to whether they are European or Japanese, friend or foe, the domestic waste conveys war's indiscriminate nature. The lost, damaged, disregarded toy, for both Ishiguro and his characters, represents a childhood wound, a terribly misdirected brutality. Ishiguro does not so much mourn the loss of the toy as the toy's function as a material manifestation of his relationship with his grandfather, and the series of future adult losses presaged by this trivial bereavement. Banks has two culprits in mind for his anger: the social system that revels in war and, perhaps more, fighting parents and the implications for 'innocent' children. The battle ground through which Banks wades in his fantastically absurd journey is the playroom, no longer a sanctuary but simply another domestic warzone (hence the toy soldiers), exploded family life, comfort, security, the allegorical journey a reference to the internal mindscapes that resemble, constitute and nurture ongoing trauma of childhood through which Banks has and will continue to move.

As I suggest in Chapter 1, imagination often takes the form for many of Ishiguro's narrators of creative misremembering, recalling past events in such a way as to render them amenable to their conception of themselves in the present, and to some form of consolation: imagining the possibility of love when it has passed (Sophie, Ryder, Brodsky, Stevens, Kathy); reconciliation with children when they have died (Axl and Beatrice); family when it is irredeemably passed (Banks, despite his claim that the loss of his parents 'had by then long ceased to be of any great inconvenience to me'; Axl and Beatrice; Ryder who would pretend that his father's destructive moods were 'all a great game'); the triviality or importance of one's participation in personal and national history (Etsuko, Ono, Ogata, Stevens). In 'imagining' a version of Japan, Ishiguro himself therapeutically mitigates the abrupt loss of his grandparents. He speaks candidly of his move to Nagasaki: 'originally intended to be only a temporary stay, perhaps one year or maybe two years. And so as a small child, I was taken away from people I knew, like my grandparents and my friends. And I was led to expect that I would return to Japan' (Oe 1991: 110). Ishiguro reveals a deep wound, here, one conducive to some form of imaginative curative. In their explorations of the redemptive, consolatory potential of the imagination, his novels evidence his own need to work creatively through a traumatic rift, a torn rug. Unfortunately, as Melvin Rader observes:

> Even in grasping one's own past, one does not simply recover the experience of months or years before. The 'emotion remembered in tranquillity' is not the raw emotion initially felt; it is an ideated emotion, refined and contemplated … Whether it be an idea, a desire, or a feeling that is recalled, there is an abstracting and symbolizing and interpreting process that transforms the original experience. (Rader 1967: 160)

For Rader, the recalled emotion is purely ideational, a distillation, even purification of the original feeling. One's own recalled emotions, in this understanding, are nothing more than fictional fabrications which approximate past reality. Solitary imagination can be used to dissociate from a conflictual, traumatic present, and to create an illusory future point that will be the 'end of it', often one that involves the heroism of the dreaming child. Or, it can just heighten an already joyful experience, as in Tommy's goal celebrations, in which he 'always imagined I was splashing through water. Nothing deep, just up to the ankles at the most. That's what I used to imagine, every time. Splash, splash, splash' (*NLMG* 280). However, if we can make any generalizations about Ishiguro's narrators, it is that issues arising in childhood persist into adulthood and rarely have an end. One might also wonder, given this process of abstraction and ideation, how far or for how long imagination's consolations can last.

II

Sometimes, imagination is not a solitary act, performed alone. It can take the form of collaborative play that provides either an escape from the present or a way of safely engaging with its portentous implications (to face together a reimagined real-world scenario that cannot be approached alone). Banks, like Boris, has a tendency characteristic of childhood 'to dramatize in play remembered scenes', and also constructs a game that enables him to imagine a family reconciliation which is impossible in the real world (Griffiths 2002: 6). Shortly after the disappearance of Banks's father, his Japanese friend Akira proposes that they play a 'new game', 'about Christopher father. If you like … we play detective. We search for father. We rescue father' (*WWO* 107). Akira implicitly recognizes the usefulness of play and the potential therapeutic value of allowing Banks imaginatively to envisage his parents' circumstances and to find ways to (a) mitigate their suffering and (b) retreat from the powerlessness of the present to some imagined future point of power. It was, as Banks the adult thinks, his 'way of showing his concern and wish to help' (*WWO* 107). Despite the imagined nature of the play, Akira and Banks have an initial disagreement about the game's parameters. Banks refuses to cooperate when Akira proposes that his father is 'tied up', because such a scenario contradicts the ameliorating rationale for the fantasy. Subsequently, Akira 'took great care to ensure my father's comfort and dignity in all our dramas' (*WWO* 110). The game serves the function allotted to it only if both Banks and Akira agree to certain constraints on the discomfort of the kidnapped parent. His father is imagined, then, as a guest, the 'kidnappers always addressed him as though they were his servants, bringing him food, drink and newspaper' (*WWO* 110). The game had 'endless variations, but fairly quickly we established a basic recurring storyline. My father was held captive in a house somewhere beyond the Settlement boundaries. His captors were a gang intent on extorting a huge ransom' (*WWO* 109–10). By replaying and re-enacting the moment of a kidnapping (that it was a kidnapping is also an imaginative method to cope with abandonment after his 'father ran off one day with his mistress'), and by offering a scenario of rescue and redemption, Banks can at least have the illusion of agency, power, control, which is precisely what Boris searches for in his imagined karate battles. Once again, the raw materials for Banks's fantasy are mined from television, the world of imported mass media, film noir, detective shows, various pop culture appropriations. Indeed, the detective genre created something of a collective imaginary consolation, as Yugin Teo notes, although readers did not 'necessarily believe the simplistic depiction of life, crime and restoration in those novels', they did manage to help people 'imagine a better time and place' than their post-war reality (2014: 87).

The imagination as deployed in these scenarios offers both escape from perils of the present and the illusion of safety and familial reconciliation in the future. Perhaps most in need of this form of evasive consolation are the adolescent and poor-in-world residents of Hailsham, who could not possibly conceive of the depth of the body-horror that hovers menacingly off-page. Unlike Banks or Boris, they have no mothers or fathers, so cannot construct a sustaining fantasy of joyful family reunion (the category of orphans is inapplicable in this case). In one scene that shows the developing friendship between Ruth and Kathy, as if they were 'normal' children, they pretend to ride Ruth's imaginary horses:

I accepted the invisible rein she was holding out, and then we were off, riding up and down the fence, sometimes cantering, sometimes at a gallop. I'd been correct in my decision to tell Ruth I didn't have any horses of my own, because after a while with Bramble, she let me try her various other horses one by one, shouting all sorts of instructions about how to handle each animal's foibles. (*NLMG* 47)

Children have a heightened capacity to imagine; as Tuan observes, they 'will ride a stick as though it were a real horse' (2018: 33). Kathy had considered telling Ruth that she owned horses of her own, but now recognizes that her decision to say that she was horseless was correct, because she would otherwise have been limited by her own imagination. In riding Ruth's horses, she shares in Ruth's imaginative world, the horses and their natures constructed for her in such a way that the reality of the make-believe horses is gestured towards (they have characters, personalities, 'foibles'). Within the game's parameters, Kathy could have claimed to own an entire stable, so long as she had sufficient detailed knowledge of their personalities to facilitate shared play. Riding (Ryding) means adhering in play to the real-world constraints of both 'horse-riding' and the individual personalities of the horses. That is to say, constraints are required for effective freeplay. Banks and Akira often have 'disputes over how our game should proceed', which must be resolved before play can continue. The game then offers an important moment of bonding, complicity in an 'understanding', while relying on the acquiescence of both parties to unspoken rules which both constrain and make possible the fantasy. Rules give to fantasy a reality effect, the players consenting to adhere to the kinds of limitations that apply to the real-world objects of their play: Banks must resort to the detective mode if he is to succeed; Kathy must take the reins and respond to the quirks of Ruth's horses or she's liable to be dismounted. We might see this as another metaphor for reading: in order to participate in the 'imaginary' world of Ishiguro's novels, we must accept 'the invisible rein' proffered and participate in the mutual 'understanding' (Coleridge's 'willing suspension of disbelief'). Perhaps this accounts for some of the less positive reviews of his masterpiece, *The Unconsoled*, which refuses to play by the rules established in his own works: he goes 'too far'.

Sometimes, shared games, as with Banks's detective drama that will continue through and come to define his life as he perseveres in his ambition to be a 'celebrated detective', take on a very serious dimension, whether in imagination or reality. In *The Unconsoled*, Hoffman recalls a game played by himself and other children:

We'd rush around gathering up all the fallen leaves we could see, bring them up to the gardener's shed and pile them up against the side. There was a particular plank, about this high on the wall of the shed, it had a stain on it. What we told each other was that we had to collect enough leaves so that the pile reached up to that stain before the adults started to file into the building.

If we didn't, the whole city was going to explode into a million pieces, some such thing. (*U* 97)

Society itself is a game, requiring reciprocal acquiescence to a dynamic (national) mythos. It is the dynamism which causes such trouble for Stevens, Ono and Darlington, adhering strictly to the old rules as the game changes around them. Hoffman implies that the current adult community, the society into which Ryder has been thrown, is little more than a continuation of these childhood fancies. Absurd as this scenario seems, sincere belief in the possibilities of play is vital to Ryder, convinced as he is that an understanding of modern music might heal the city's political and personal wounds (and thereby further augment his reputation). He passionately, ludicrously shouts at Sophie that 'they don't understand the first thing about modern music and if you leave them to themselves, it's obvious, they'll just get deeper and deeper into trouble' (*U* 37). But fantasy *can* offer solutions, as Griffiths observes, 'problems, that will not yield their solution when attacked at the logical level, become clearer when the individual allows his thoughts to wander among adjacent topics' (2002: 9). It is demonstrably illogical that gathering leaves might prevent a city-wide cataclysm. However, it is not less absurd than Kathy, Ruth and Tommy thinking that they may get a 'deferral' for their naïve art, Banks thinking that solving a crime with a magnifying glass might allow him to 'root out single-handedly all the evil in the world', or that Ryder might find that 'very special one, the very important trip, the one that's very very important, not just for me but for everyone, everyone in the whole world', Stevens's and Darlington's belief that they can make a 'contribution to the creation of a better world' (*RD* 116).[1] As Sebastian Groes and Paul Daniel-Veyret comment, imagination 'can provide at once the potential for renewal and a dangerous dislocation from reality' (2009: 42). We might come back here to Saunders's sanction against Boris's football fantasy: for many of Ishiguro's characters, imagination enables a useful temporary escape from the traumatic present. However, as we see in a woefully deluded Banks (a kind of Walter Mitty), if the once-ameliorative game persists into adulthood, it prevents emotional development and the process of mourning. In this sense, the faculty does indeed forestall as opposed to facilitate healing. Uncle Philip asks Banks about his sleuthing, 'What good is [being a celebrated detective] to anyone? Stolen jewels, aristocrats murdered for their inheritance. Do you suppose that's all there is to contend with? Your mother, she wanted you to live in your enchanted world for ever. But it's impossible' (*WWO* 294). As another character tells an overprotective Ryder, 'Children always hear these things sooner or later', one has 'got to come to terms with the world, warts and all' (*U* 216).

If the cooperative imaginary can be employed to evade, displace or simply delay real-world fears, it can also be the site of 'older, less rational fears' (*WWO* 102). Bachelard identifies the duplicitous risks inherent in imagination, which can 'build "walls" of impalpable shadows, comfort itself with the illusion of protection – or, just the contrary, tremble behind thick walls, mistrust the staunchest ramparts' (1994: 5). Fantasy fears may be entirely irrational, but they may also manifest as yet unacknowledged subconscious anxieties about things 'told and not told' (*NLMG* 79). In *Never Let Me Go*, the 'drip-fed' students concoct 'all kinds of horrible stories about the woods ... beyond the Hailsham boundaries', but visible from their dorm window (*NLMG* 50). As Kathy recalls, they 'played on our imaginations the most after dark', especially the tale of a boy who ran into the woods, his 'body had been found two days later, up in those woods, tied to a tree with the hands and feet chopped off' (*NLMG* 50). At a point before they are let in on the secret that defines their lives, this seemingly unlikely terror comes startlingly close to the impending real-world horror of organ harvesting. For students 'habituated to the structure of knowing and not knowing', the woods represent a subconscious semiotic transfiguration of a future in which they will be systematically dismembered beyond the boundaries of Hailsham's temporary sanctuary (Eaglestone 2017: 22). As Kathy in her memoir adopts Hailsham's euphemisms and becomes complicit in its horror, the clone community becomes complicit in the horror of the woods. One night, to punish Marge K. for a minor transgression, they hold her 'face against the windowpane and ordering her to look up at the woods ... that was enough to ensure for her a sobbing night of terror' (*NLMG* 50). Again, this scenario is part of a necessary enrichment of the childhood imaginary, one that relies on a shared acquiescence to the rules of Hailsham's games. If Marge refuses to comply, she could simply look at the woods without fear. But, through such resistance, she would incur the more profound punishment of exclusion from the Hailsham imaginary and isolation from a community and shared mythos that sustains hope and home.

In *When We Were Orphans*, a bored Banks and Akira fantasize that Akira's servant, Ling Tien, is a sorcerer of the dark arts who

> had discovered a method by which he could turn severed hands into spiders ... Slowly the fingers would start to move by themselves – just little twitches at first, then coiling motions; finally, dark hairs would grow and Ling Tien would then take them out of the fluids and set them loose, as spiders, all around the neighbourhood. (*WWO* 91)

Ishiguro uses spiders to evoke fear in many of his works. In *A Pale View of Hills*, Mariko plays with a spider as Etsuko watches over her, she 'caught one of the spider's legs. The remaining legs crawled frantically around her hand as she brought it away from the wall' (*PVH* 81). In *Never Let Me Go*, Kathy and her friends discover that they themselves are a source of others' fear, that Madame 'was afraid of us in the same way someone might be afraid of spiders. We hadn't been ready for that. It had never occurred to us to wonder how we would feel, being seen like that, being the spiders' (*NLMG* 35). Banks and Akira play dangerously with Ling Tien's 'pale liquid with a vague smell of aniseed ... its nondescript appearance served our purpose well' (*WWO* 96). The shapelessness of the canvas, blank as it were, enables free rein, and the childhood friends become immersed in the dangerous alternate reality of their game: 'Akira warned that we should not let even a drop touch our hands lest we wake up the next day with spiders at the end of our arms' (*WWO* 96). It is unclear the degree to which Akira and Banks as children *believe* this, yet the residue of their playful fear lingers into the present. Banks recalls that, although he did not 'entirely believe these stories, they certainly upset me ... Indeed, as we grew older, we neither of us quite shook off our horror of Ling Tien' (*WWO* 92). Childhood superstitions and games persist, diffuse but free-floating, into an adulthood that is coloured by their memory. As Kathy recalls of the woods, 'you never really got away from them' (*NLMG* 50). In the case of Ling Tien, we also see a nascent racism, a fear of 'the other' derived from imagined exotic dangers. It is interesting, too, that this and other games cease when the real-world issue of Banks's father usurps the childhood imaginary, the students learn of their fates. It is as if the imagination is designed to facilitate distraction from trauma, that only in the absence of real threat does it exercise itself in creating fear.

Part 2: *Childhood arts*

I

Childhood imagination finds another outlet in art, as one character in *A Pale View of Hills* comments of her son: 'I think drawing is important too. A child should develop his imagination while he's young' (*PVH* 115). In one of the novel's more optimistic passages, Mariko, the *as if* orphan of Sachiko, 'psychologically damaged from the horrors she has witnessed during the war', enjoys a day trip with her mother and Etsuko, during which she sketches her surroundings with 'new crayons' (Lewis 2000: 21). Mariko remarks, possibly flippantly, or to convey a sense of mature artistic discernment, that 'it's harder to draw with new crayons', they 'weren't worn in enough' (*PVH* 114). Perhaps new crayons, sharp-edged, give too definite a line, too clean an image; 'worn' crayons, soft-edged, serve better the novel's impressionistic gestural aesthetics (how else to draw a pale view). One of Mariko's subjects is a butterfly, which attracts praise from Sachiko's friend, who remarks that 'it must have been very hard to draw it so well. It couldn't have stayed still for very long', to which Mariko replies that she 'remembered it', having seen 'one earlier on' (*PVH* 114). Seeing things 'earlier on' and responding to them in the present is a shared idiosyncrasy for Ishiguro's out-of-time narrators, as we have seen. Like the butterfly, very little in life stays still for long: all we have time for is a fleeting impression which can be subsequently embellished with recalled details in the subject's absence. Moreover, we have no way to determine what will turn out to be important, even 'turning points', in the fleeting immediacy of real-time encounters. Mariko's admiring viewer comments a little condescendingly to Mariko and Sachiko, that 'it's very commendable for a child to use her memory and imagination' (*PVH* 114). Mariko's butterfly relies not on imagination or memory alone; it is rather a composite image suggested by memory, creatively reimagined in the absence of the subject but with its trace (Hume's 'impressions') still in mind. Mariko's act of creative recall brings to mind Ishiguro's sketches of an 'imaginary' Japan from the shadowy details of always partial childhood memories. The butterfly is a curiously apt subject: transient, enigmatic, diaphanous and vivid while also highlighting the connection between the novel and Puccini's *Madame Butterfly*, and her own child aptly named Sorrow (Lewis discusses the relationship between these works in interesting ways). The subject of the sketch is not really the butterfly, but Mariko's memory and imagination, the butterfly a potent, labile, evanescent analogue of a fragility shared by the novel's narrator, Etsuko. Just like the shadowy reflections in the tiles of Ruth's recovery centre, Mariko's image is not of the real-world butterfly, but gestures towards its absence. It is also a moment of ekphrases, the reconfiguration of the material of the real into the two dimensions of paper (a butterfly is already almost two-dimensional), further removed in the prose of the novel.

Unfortunately for Mariko and her mother, they are accompanied on their excursion by a less sympathetic critic. The patronizing but kind woman has her son Akira (names recur often in Ishiguro's novels) with her. Unlike Mariko, Akira is fortunate enough to have a 'distinguished tutor for his drawing' (*PVH* 115). Spotting a picture of the harbour in Mariko's 'sketchbook', Akira remarks that 'those ships are too big ... if that's supposed to be a tree, then the ships would be much smaller' (*PVH* 115). Akira would take issue with Stevens's opinion that sketches are 'more evocative' than photographs. Mariko captures the flavour of her phenomenological presence in the moment, something which transcends geometry, spatial relations, rationality. The young critic though, as poor in imagination as Saunders, misses the point entirely, his judgment evidencing a category error; he assumes that art's function is mimetic, but Mariko's playful proportional distortions rework the material of the senses, imbuing them with personal significance. Also enacted in this churlish critique is a parody of the debate between realism and modernism, traditional figurative painting and the impressionistic, surrealistic, primitivist works of the anti-rational post-war period. Perhaps this too is an overreading, a critical error: Mariko renders her elusive subject with childhood's genuine naivete, not that which we might see in a Lowry, or indeed in the faux naivete of Ishiguro's sketches of sketches. This deformation of the labile material of the real world, the draping-over of the equally malleable canvas, reminds us of Ishiguro's own delicate experiments with proportion, attention, focus, when the mundane looms large, in the foreground, like Parmigianino's *Self Portrait in the Convex Mirror*, an everyday subject imbued with significance by the formal distortion which is nonetheless an accurate rendition of reality's experiential flavour.

Crayons, a medium associated with childhood, are the favoured tool of the apprentice. Masuji Ono, a once 'famous artist' with problematically imperialist leanings, tries to encourage his grandson Ichiro, obsessed with the Lone Ranger and US popular culture, to draw in his 'sketchbook' with, again, 'crayons'. As Valerie Purton has commented, the novel is about the 'relationship between the Japanese and Western traditions' (1993: 170). The subject of the work is a (recalled) poster for a monster movie, perhaps an early Gojira, to which Ono hopes to take Ichiro (if only he can get permission from the ladies of the house). Under Ono's guidance/scrutiny, 'Using a dark brown crayon, [Ichiro] drew on the lower part of the sheet a row of boxes – which soon became a skyline of city buildings. And then there emerged, looming above the city, a huge lizard-like creature up on its hind legs' (*AFW* 33). The process of creation is evocatively captured in these few words, Ichiro's drawn and Ishiguro's written lines coalescing to 'become' something more than themselves (more than boxes, more than text). Ono watches fascinated as the image emerges from the blank paper (as it does on the page of text in a simultaneous moment of creation, transfiguration, interpretation and ekphrasis), both because of his appreciation for the process and his desire to impress upon his grandson the pleasures of art. Ichiro acts as a potential proxy student to the now-disgraced sensei and, as Dominic Dean remarks, 'Ono's encouragement of the child's drawing is a vicarious way of retrieving some future for Ono himself, whose own paintings (aggressive imperialistic propaganda) are now hidden away' (2019: 4). Ichiro, however, quickly loses interest:

> He began to add more and more fleeing figures at the bottom of his sketch until the shapes merged and became meaningless. Eventually abandoning any sense of care, he started to scribble wildly all over the lower section of the sheet. (*AFW* 34)

Meaning is created and subsequently obliterated in Ichiro's beautiful portrait of art in action. Detail is overwritten, obscured by further detail which lacks the precision of that which it erases. Lines create, and lines obscure, but the matter which both produces and destroys is identical. Intriguingly, Ichiro first constructs and then eradicates the images of fleeing figures, capturing not the static moment of the poster or a still from a movie reel but re-creating the monster's imagined carnage in real time. Observed in process, the picture becomes a moving image, the absent film itself, as the crayon facsimile of the monster's fire ravages both the figures and the scene, reducing the clarity of distinct images to a singular point of dynamic chaos. In this scenario, art incorporates time as a vital dimension, suggesting that art is always processual and unfinished. Ichiro's joyful expunging of his own cityscape replicates the presumed primitive joy in wanton destruction of his marauding subject. For Ono, however, Ichiro goes too far and ruins the effect. Sketching though has no aetiology, no endpoint in a finished work; it is freeplay, unconstrained, active, dynamic and indifferent to critique.

A remarkably similar scenario occurs in *The Unconsoled*, during a scene in which Ryder, Sophie and Boris share a cosy evening in their small flat. The evening represents the almost perfect moment about which Boris fantasizes in his imagined karate battles. With studied inattention as he develops an 'understanding' of silence with his son (as is typical, hiding behind a newspaper as a barrier), Ryder observes a change in the room's always taut atmosphere:[2]

> Boris had managed to draw on his sheet a perfectly recognisable 'Superman'. He had been attempting to do just such a thing for weeks, but for all our encouragement had been unable to produce even a vague likeness. But now, perhaps owing to that mixture of fluke and genuine breakthrough so often experienced in childhood, he had suddenly succeeded. The sketch was not quite finished – the mouth and eyes needed completing – but for all that I had been able to see at once the huge triumph it represented for him. In fact I would have said something to him had I not noticed at that moment the way he was leaning forward in a state of great tension, his crayon held over the paper. He was, I had realised, hesitating whether to go on to refine his drawing at the risk of ruining it. I had been able to sense acutely his dilemma and had felt a temptation to say out loud: 'Boris, stop. That's enough. Stop there and show everyone what you've achieved. Show me, then show your mother, and then all those people talking now in the next room. What does it matter if it's not completely finished? Everyone will be astonished and so proud of you. Stop now before you lose it all.' But I had not said anything, continuing instead to watch him from around the edge of my newspaper. Finally Boris had made up his mind and begun to apply a few more touches with great care. Then, growing more confident, he had bent right forward and started to use the crayon with some recklessness. A moment later he had stopped abruptly, staring silently at his sheet. Then – and I could even now recall the anguish mounting within me – I had watched him attempting to salvage his picture, applying more and more crayon. Finally his face had fallen and, dropping the crayon onto the paper, he had risen and left the room without a word. (*U* 94–5)

Mariko's images are less politically loaded than those of Boris and Ichiro; she draws her environment, possibly because her mother is too poor to own a television and she is less exposed to the Americanization of post-war world culture that Ishiguro explores throughout his career. Ichiro sketches a radiation-mutated lizard which emerged during, and personifies ongoing fears in the Japanese psyche in the aftermath of, Hiroshima and Nagasaki; Boris sketches the crude popular symbol of US power and cultural domination, of 'truth, justice, and the American way', as he sits in a run-down estate in an anonymous Eastern European city. Imagination is in play here, of course, but so is memory. Boris, like Ichiro, is possibly recalling and re-creating a static image poster. They are though notably different in their approach – Boris, as we see, has struggled, rehearsed 'for weeks', and this, like Ryder and Stephan's concert performance, is the big night. Indeed, the novel has to do with 'performance anxiety' broadly construed, as Ishiguro told Charlie Rose, 'I feel that many of us are going through life with a sense that at some point, there is this very important performance that's coming up' (1995). We might imagine that Boris is disappointed artistically, but the novel shows us that the inhabitants of this city riven with artistic disunity view the arts as healing, curative. Attuned to the consolatory potential of imagination, Boris conceives of this moment as a vital opportunity to close the divide between his parents, narrow the distance between he and his sometime father, in the same way that Brodsky thinks music will reconcile him with Miss Collins, Hoffman with his wife, Stephan with his parents, and Ryder with the community. The pressure is high, and Boris cannot know because he is not told that the picture need not be complete, that its gestural qualities suffice to convey the idea of his subject. As with the tiles in the previous chapter, and Mariko's butterfly, Ishiguro uses this image to comment on his own art; incomplete, partial, at once formed and formless, his worlds emerge partially sketched but suggestively incomplete. Boris, though, like Ichiro, fails because, like Brodsky in his much-anticipated return to conducting, perhaps Ishiguro himself in this novel, had 'taken things too far', the audience 'exchanging worried looks, coughing uneasily, shaking their head' (*U* 494). Indeed, taking things too far is a recurring theme in the novel (*NLMG*'s Madame asks too 'do I go too far'), Ryder himself falls out of favour at the climax for the same reason, inadvertently posing with a politically incendiary building leading to the locals commenting anxiously that 'he'll take us too far. The Sattler monument, that's going too far' (*U* 370).

Boris's seemingly innocuous failure resonates with the novel's key theme of imaginative reconciliation promised by the arts. *The Unconsoled* is replete with examples of the outcome of perceived artistic failure and its lifelong repercussions. Previously a revered musician, Christoff suffers as a result of his own fall from grace on the art scene, the rift at the community's heart. Like Hoffman, he imagines that his wife's priority is artistic prowess: she had 'time for members of the artistic circle, and then only for the real elite. You couldn't get any respect from her otherwise' (*U* 105). As Christoff comments without bitterness, for 'Rosa, nothing else in life would be more important than to be married to someone in the position I was in' (*U* 189). Hotel manager Hoffman falls in love with his wife and she him on the pretence that he was a composer. Once she realizes her mistake, he is convinced that she 'would leave me. Sooner or later. It was just a matter of time'; he exists in the perpetual agony that she will leave him for 'someone like the man she thought I was before she realised', perhaps even someone like Ryder (*U* 353). Ironically, as Ryder points out, their marriage had lasted, and his wife seems blithely unaware of her own sense of failure. Nonetheless, convinced 'that his wife will leave him', as Lewis remarks, Hoffman 'invested all his ambitions in the possibility that his child might become the gifted musician he had never been' (2000: 112). Alas, Hoffman becomes deeply ashamed of his own son Stephan's piano-playing and assumes also that Stephan's mother is profoundly disappointed in both father and son:

> An embodiment, Mr Ryder! He's become an embodiment of the great mistake she made in her life ... Of course, as a mother, she loves Stephan utterly. But that's not to say she doesn't look at him and see in him her mistake. He's so like me, sir. (*U* 354)

As we have seen, Boris is figured and figures himself as a wound in the love between Ryder and Sophie, which is why his Superman failure assumes such devastating power. In the end, Ryder and Boris part ways, Sophie tells Ryder, 'You'll never feel towards him like a real father', and in the final scenes, she empowers Boris, deciding no longer to pursue a broken relationship, telling Ryder that 'he'll never love you like a real father' (*U* 532). Stephan is also regarded by his father as a manifestation both of his own artistic failure and the 'mistake', the 'misunderstanding' at the heart of his marriage. Stephan is a collaborative effort, unlike Boris who seems to be Sophie's biological son. An imperfect sketch, an inharmonious composition, Stephan manifests and memorializes all that Hoffman is ashamed of in himself. Hoffman originally believed that Stephan, if taught the piano, could make up for his own failure in his wife's eyes; Stephan comes to believe that if he can play proficiently, with passion, he can forge some deeper bond with and between his parents. He begs, 'Just come and listen, if only for a few minutes ... You'll both see then, I know you will', to which his father responds, perhaps with his own imagined failure in mind, displacing his wife's disappointment in him onto his son ('They fuck you up, your mum and dad'), 'I believe it would break your mother's heart to do so' (*U* 480). Again, as with Akira, the variety of criticism proposed here is in the wrong category: Stephan's work is an expression, a gesture towards his love for his parents, and so the aesthetic estimation that it would in fact perform the opposite role is inappropriate. We return here to Henri Lefebvre's argument, 'If you take it for what it is (a paint-daubed or coloured scrap of paper [recital]), it falls short of its goal. If you take it for what it seeks to evoke, it accomplishes it' (2019: 32).

II

The stakes of childhood games and sketches are sometimes high, either factually or in the imagination, or simply because of a misunderstanding of the nature of art's redemptive possibilities. Nowhere is this illustrated more powerfully than in *Never Let Me Go*, where the capacity to imagine and to render externally the products of imagination is a criterion to determine whether or not the clones 'have souls at all', whether they might deserve a stay of execution, a 'deferral' of 'donations'. Drawing and painting play a vital (in a literal sense) role in the impressionable imaginations of Hailsham's young clones, believing, at least later, that 'the soul is a captive, treated humanely, kept / In suspension' in the convex mirror of the canvas, and that essence can be adduced as evidence of something like a spirit (Ashbery 1974: 248). An outsider in Hailsham, prone to bouts of extreme anger, Tommy identifies a turning point in his alienation from his peers in a painting he had somewhat casually composed in art class. Kathy recalls it was a 'particular watercolour – of an elephant standing in some tall grass – and that was what started it all off. He'd done it, he claimed, as a kind of joke' (*NLMG* 19). Evidently, Tommy is embarrassed by his own efforts and pretends that the painting was in jest. But the damage is done. 'For a while,' Kathy relates, 'he'd only had to suffer during art lessons ... But then it grew bigger. He got left out of games, boys refused to sit next to him at dinner, or pretended not to hear if he said anything in his dorm after lights-out' (*NLMG* 19–20). As with the Peace Park statue, Tommy's own artwork inspires a shared silence, though for slightly different reasons. Hailsham is a society, of sorts, and Tommy's failure to adhere to the spoken and unspoken rules of the game results in his ostracization from a community united by necessary belief in the value of art and the imagination.

Tommy recovers from these various exclusions, partially because Miss Lucy reassures him that 'if I didn't want to be creative, if I really didn't feel like it, that was perfectly all right. Nothing wrong with it, she said' (*NLMG*). Prone to spite when slighted, Kathy finds it hard to believe that Miss Lucy could have made such a claim, or worse that she could have shared so intimately with Tommy and not her: 'That's just rubbish, Tommy. If you're going to play stupid games, I can't be bothered'; she was, she confides in us, 'genuinely angry, because I thought he was lying to me, just when I deserved to be taken into his confidence' (*NLMG* 23). Kathy's rhetoric operates from the novel's themes of being 'rubbish', 'trash' and also of game-playing. Kathy is very willing to play games, but she is unwilling to play this 'stupid' game because it challenges the rules of the more meaningful game in which she is participating. Indeed, the novel and its many disagreements reflect the idea that society, 'history', is little more than a series of overlapping and often conflictual games. We know that being taken into confidences is vital to the integrity of Kathy's fragile self-image; immured in a world of profound deceit, things 'told and not told', she takes consolation in intimate understandings (which is why her horse-riding escapades with Ruth are so important). This might also explain her anger with Ruth over the pencil case incident: Ruth had not taken Kathy into her confidence in the trust that she would either (a) not announce that it was a gift or (b) not announce that it was not a gift (the fact is irrelevant, the gesture of confidence central). Crucially, Hailsham masquerades a liberal arts school, and the students' lives depend upon the assumed radically redemptive possibilities of creative practice. Although unaware that they are the tokens in a high-stakes game, the function of Hailsham is to determine whether the clone's art can convince a public reliant on organ donation that the clones have souls and are worthy of more humane treatment. Not human rights, though. Tommy's claim that creativity is optional constitutes a threat to the core of Kathy's necessary self-sustaining beliefs, one which poses a genuine challenge to her hopes for a deferral of donations, for love, extended life. Miss Lucy later recants, perhaps because she has been let in on the secret of Hailsham's post-humanist project. A further possible rationale for the importance that Kathy accords to art, to creativity, is that 'none of us could have babies ... we could have sex without worrying about all of that' (*NLMG* 72). Coleridge famously sees a parallel between the original creative act and artistic creation, as 'a repetition in the finite mind of the eternal act of creation in the infinite I AM'. Creativity for the clones serves a double function: Art is a demonstration that they are human (or that they have fundamentally human qualities), that they 'have souls at all' while also being their only medium for procreation (Tommy later produces microsketches of his own imagined progeny).

Art in Hailsham also creates a niche culture and economy of exchange:

> Four times a year – Spring, Summer, Autumn, Winter – we had a kind of big exhibition-cum-sale of all the things we'd been creating in the three months since the last exchange. Paintings, drawing, pottery; all sorts of sculptures made from whatever was the craze of the day – bashed-up cans, maybe, or bottle tops stuck into cardboard. (*NLMG* 15–16)

The exchanges are entirely appropriate; the art exchanged is produced by posthumans for posthumans, although it is, necessarily, modelled on and aspiring to the human arts. Poignantly, the students' art is modelled from trash, things discarded by the public they exist to service. Part of the sadness in the novel is that each of the clones believes they have a 'possible', someone in the real world from whom they are modelled. In ways despairingly limited by their own profoundly curtailed freedoms, they dream that they may be modelled on ordinary people, most often office workers. Ruth, though, towards the end, after a failed search for her possible, suggests that, once again, there is a truth about their origins and, therefore, their natures that has lingered just in the periphery, unspoken, 'told and not told': 'We all know it. We're modelled from *trash*. Junkies, prostitutes, winos, tramps. Convicts, maybe, just so long as they aren't psychos. That's what we come from. We all know it, so why don't we say it' (*NLMG* 164). As they drive around, Ruth suggests that they have been looking in the wrong places, that to find their models 'you look in rubbish bins. Look down the toilet, that's where you'll find where we all came from' (*NLMG* 164). We might return here to Saunders's comment that imagination is a 'sort of rubbish' with which children's heads should not be filled. Ruth, who 'always wanted to believe in things', is deeply affected by the failure of their hopeful trip and makes a direct correlation between the materials of their art and the materials from which they are constructed: They too are composed from 'trash'. Later, she implies that the clones themselves are in fact creative products, asking whether someone had ever been a 'clone model' (*NLMG* 164). Of course, the work of art is emergent, supervening upon the totality rather than deriving any direct value from the quality of its materials (Marcel Duchamp's 1917 'Fountain' is evidence that the artwork is more than its matter). That is to say, the materials may be trash, the details 'dull', 'mundane', but the esemplastic, unified form undergoes a refiguration into a dynamic whole whose meaning transcends its elements. The failure to find a possible model undermines the shared game in which they have participated; as a community, the clones culture a consolatory imaginary predicated on the faint hope that somewhere, albeit in a parallel reality, they live long and meaningful lives. Necessarily, this consoling hope relies on an acknowledgement that the clones are merely mechanically reproduced copies (Kathy A, Kathy B...) of an original not itself a clone, and, in this sense, they lack Walter Benjamin's 'aura', the unique work's intangible soul, paradoxically negating any possibility of the sustaining legend of deferrals. This moment sees Ruth, and Tommy, Chrissie, Kathy and Rodney, letting go of the 'invisible reins' of a game that had, until this very moment, enabled them to countenance their terrible fates.

Galleries play an important role in the novel. A myth develops, no one is quite sure the origin, that 'Madame', a mysterious figure who visits Hailsham periodically, has a gallery of the children's work, and that the best work is selected for inclusion in the gallery. Kathy is peculiarly concerned with the gallery, and it may indeed be her that inadvertently gives rise to the legend of deferrals, asking, 'But what *is* her gallery? She keeps coming here and taking away our best work. She must have stacks of it by now ... What *is* this gallery? Why should she have a gallery of things done by us?' (*NLMG* 30). The myth deepens when Tommy has another conversation with a fraught Miss Lucy, who retracts her previous advice about Tommy not having to be creative, telling him now that 'your art, it *is* important. And not just because it's evidence. But for your own sake. You'll get a lot from it, just for yourself' (*NLMG* 106). Kathy, intrigued, asks 'what did she mean, "evidence"'? (*NLMG* 106). Tommy recalls a later moment that Miss Emily 'let drop' that art 'revealed what you were like inside. She said *they revealed your soul*' (*NLMG* 173). In a world of therapeutic clones, whose insides are valuable in a material sense because they offer continued life for the 'normal' population at the cost of the clone, the implication that some fundamental non-material essence might exist 'inside' and be revealed through art is deeply attractive. This and other scenes lead to a legend developing that if two people were in love, and that they could prove that love, they could apply to Madame for a deferral of donations. Crucially, the only way that love could be judged true is through art, they think, 'there has to be a way to judge if they're really telling the truth', '*they need something to go on*' (*NLMG* 173). Not only does art 'reveal our souls' but it can also demonstrate, if read correctly, that two people 'fit'. Again, we might suggest that this is a misunderstanding both of aesthetics and of the being of art – here it is conceived as functional, a record of something that can be read like a text, or at least a guide to the feelings of the author. Another implication is that art does more than simply gesture towards world's noumenal ground, that it can indeed eff the ineffable. Sadly, after Ruth dies during complications in her third donation, Kathy and Tommy (himself in the final stages of the process) track down Madame, who relieves them of the myth of deferral. In the meantime, Tommy has continued secretly composing 'fantastic creatures', 'imaginary animals' in his sketchbook, which he intends to submit as 'evidence'. Madame is herself in a wheelchair, with ailing health. She tells them that Hailsham was a kind of experiment, but a failed one, that that deferrals could never happen because 'such a thing would always have been beyond us to grant' (*NLMG* 256). Madame reveals that they had taken the artworks as part of a campaign for the rights of clones, but that the works were not to prove love or to reveal individual souls, but to '*prove you had souls at all*' (*NLMG* 255). An ambition as naïve and ill-conceived as the students' own delusions.

Deferrals are an imaginative coping strategy for lives brutally sacrificed. However, 'completion' is also, potentially, simply another strategy to manage the inescapable hopelessness of their condition. Clones are expected to complete at the fourth donation, but this consolatory death is itself possibly fantasy, as Tommy speculates:

> You know why it is, Kath, why everyone worries so much about the fourth? It's because they're not sure they'll really complete. If you knew for certain you'd complete, it would be easier. But they never tell us for sure … You'll have heard the same talk. How maybe, after the fourth donation, even if you've technically completed, you're still conscious in some sort of way; how then you find there are more donations, plenty of them, on the other side of that line; how there are no more recovery centres, no carers, no friends; how there's nothing to do except watch your remaining donations until they switch you off. It's horror movie stuff, and most of the time people don't want to think about it. (*NLMG* 274)

Portrayed as Hailsham's buffoon, Tommy often has the most perceptive insights into the plight of the clones. His frequent bouts of rage seem, in hindsight, to have been very appropriate responses to the knowledge that has somehow installed itself deep in his preconscious mind. Here, he imagines a horror that escapes Ruth and Kathy, and possibly the reader. In this scenario, death becomes the sole consolation, the only evasion of a progressive and total dismemberment.

The relationship between real world and thought is bidirectional. Just as thought offers material to the imagination, 'Phantasy supplies the subject matter of thought' (Griffiths 2002: 6). Memories themselves are episodic, autobiographically constructed personal narratives, 'emotionally-laden contributions to the structure of the self image' (Baddeley 1992: 14). For Ishiguro, we all begin as artists, of sorts (Picasso agrees that 'every child is an artist'), with the heightened capacity for transformative imagination typical of childhood, reconfiguring an often-mundane, sometimes traumatic reality, obscuring the present and subsequently overwriting the past. Imagination then provides a therapeutic means to cope with trauma, and to refigure the daunting worries of the real world into a form which is amenable to action, whether in the present or the (deferred) future. Perhaps the most poignant example is the final scene of *Never Let Me Go*, when Kathy, alone, bereft of friends and Hailsham, shortly after the death of Tommy, stands in a field

> thinking about the rubbish, the flapping plastic in the branches, the shoreline of odd stuff caught along the fencing, and I half-closed my eyes and imagined this was the spot where everything I'd ever lost since my childhood had washed up, and I was now standing here in front of it, and if I waited long enough, a tiny figure would appear on the horizon across the field, and gradually get larger until I'd see it was Tommy, and he'd wave, maybe even call. The fantasy never got beyond that – I didn't let it. (*NLMG* 281–2)

Once more we return to the image of scattered rubbish in a visual that brings to mind the lyrics to Suede's 1996 'Trash', Brett Anderson crooning 'But we're trash you and me / We're the litter on the breeze'. No longer innocent, certainly less naïve, Kathy recognizes the dangers of unreined imagination and allows the reverie to go only so far. As Yugin Teo remarks of this moment, 'Kathy's memory comes alive through her imagination, but she never allows this moment of fantasy to carry her away' (2014: 37). An interesting turn of phrase as she prepares to be carried away by the brutal realities of her condition that have forced her to let go her friends. Kathy's imagination paints a picture here, not simply of the return of a loved companion but the possible end of a terrible nightmare.

III

Ishiguro's deployment of imagination, and sketching, works from the gestural poetics that defines his writing. Both are partial, again in both senses, unfinished, but suggestive of a whole that is not or cannot be rendered mimetically. In part, this exploits his fascination with 'the texture of memory', as he commented in an interview, any 'scene pulled from the narrator's memory is blurred at the edges' (*The Punch Magazine*, 2017). Profound things are subtly implied, lines limned, some detail dotted on the page, but the surrounding space hazy with ambiguity and aporia. This is apt; sketches are abstracted details, focused points in a larger canvas that may or may not come to fruition. Their contexts then are also gestural, nascent, entirely speculative. To sketch is to prepare, imaginatively, for an *as if* context that may remain imaginary. Once more then we have a sense, an impression of detail, but hazily rendered, abstracted from context. Perhaps this is because the worlds in which Stevens, Banks, Ryder,

Etsuko et al. live are indeed imaginary in both senses; they are the fictional space of their author and of the characters. However, each of the scenarios here, of imagination, daydreaming, shared fantasy and artwork, demonstrates the unwitting political engagement of the childhood arts, their works somehow responding to environmental prompts. Perhaps this is because, as Bachelard poeticizes, 'thought and experience are not the only things that sanction human values. The values that belong to daydreaming mark humanity in its depths' (1994: 6). Daydreaming however, as we have seen, is delimited by a real world which it futilely attempts to refigure to release some consolatory potential.

Notes

1 The Sherlock Holmes films of the 1940s are a likely inspiration here – in *The Voice of Terror* (1942), Basil Rathbone does indeed thwart a Nazi invasion with the aid of his intuition and his trusty magnifying glass. The film is a work of propaganda; one character is told of her murdered husband in London that 'the Nazis killed him'.
2 Quoted at length partially because it is not amenable to abridgment but also for its beauty.

Chapter 3

AESTHETICS

Unspoken understandings, daydreams, childhood games and crayon sketches are not the only gestures towards giving form to the 'innumerable atoms' that make up everyday life (Woolf 1986: 160). Such often purposively partial (in both senses) ideational renderings cannot capture 'all the details', as it were, or tell us 'how everything was'. Neither are these the only method of imaginatively reworking life's complexly subtle traumas. Just as Ishiguro is interested in the communicative possibilities and limitations of written and spoken language, his works are sensitive to the political potential and the affective limitations of the arts more broadly. Sebastian Groes and Paul-Daniel Veyret insist on the importance of considering Ishiguro's 'lifelong engagement with other modes of representation' in any critical appreciation of his work (2009: 32). Drawn to many possible creative outlets, pragmatism persuaded Ishiguro to devote his own 'limited' time to the art of fiction:

> I used to want to be a musician, I wanted to be a filmmaker and a writer, but I'm now kind of sticking to writing, because I realize that there's only a limited amount of time left. Me and writing, it was never my great passion, but it's what I've been allowed to do. It's a little like an arranged marriage. I wanted to be a rock and roll star first. (Rose 1995)

Although ('kind of') settling with the arrangement and putting aside his musical and filmic aspirations,[1] he has since co-written song lyrics and authored several screenplays for television and film.[2] His passion for the arts finds expression in his impressionistic prose and narrative structure, as well as the way he describes his own work. Through writing, he recalls, he could 'compose almost in the way an abstract painter might choose to place shapes and colours around a canvas' (*The Guardian*, 2016). Music too features prominently as a metaphor for his compositions, like *Nocturnes*, which he describes as being 'divided into these five movements' (Aitkenhead 2009). Drawing an analogy between music and literature, Roland Barthes discerns 'the same constraint in the gradual order of melody and in the equally gradual order of the narrative sequence' (1990: 30). Ishiguro's works, particularly his novels (the short form does not allow him the same luxury), are powerful precisely because their individual melodies unfold gradually and because each novel is a movement in an ongoing symphony, a sketch in an unfinished painting.[3]

Whether reluctantly or not, Ishiguro's poetics evidences a joy in literature's polysemic potentialities. In part this is because he can incorporate various painterly techniques into his writing. His narratives are composed in impasto, layers of detail producing a rich textural depth that seems to be calm single surface but which reveals the artist's brush strokes (Ishiguro allowing alternative perspectives to challenge Ono, Stevens, Banks and Kathy's memories, for example). As I suggested in Chapter 1, his characters have a tendency to isolate and examine areas of their lives in clinical detail while leaving the periphery in darkness, mimicking the chiaroscuro effect that we might see on a Caravaggio or Joseph Wright canvas. Alternatively, Yugin Teo sees this as a nod towards the 'world of light and shade' characteristic of film noir (2014: 32). Literary art also offers a dynamically responsive canvas that can incorporate – or, at the very least, be overlaid onto thus accommodating the shape of – other representational modes, albeit with varying degrees of fidelity. Writing *about* art, though, is another challenge altogether; however analogous, writing, painting and music are very different media. Stephen Cheeke warns of the risks inherent in the transfiguration of the plastic arts into the literary, 'the impossibility of ekphrasis – the doom of an ultimate and inevitable failure', asking, 'How can literary language find a parallel or an analogy with art?' (2008: 1). Deleuze and Guattari pose a similar question, rhetorically pondering whether it can 'be that literature sometimes catches up with painting, and even music?' (2005: 304). In writing art, one simply engages more directly with the defining paradox in all creative endeavour: the 'real' world and memory of it are always (already) imagistic, and so representation, whether in sculpture, music, painting or text, is always an ekphrastic reworking of the 'real' in a malleable medium.

For Barthes, this is a characteristic of literature, of writing:

> Every literary description is *a view* ... in order to speak about it, the writer ... transforms the 'real' into a depicted (framed) object; having done this, he can take down this object, remove it from his picture: in short: de-depict it (to depict is to unroll the carpet of the codes, to refer not from a language to a referent but from one code to another). (1990: 54–5)

We might also think back, here, to the literal rug/carpet (of codes) of Ryder's childhood, unrolled and reformulated into the recuperative imaginary, slipping once more along the order of simulacra through the act of imaginative recall. Or, Melvin Rader's remarkably similar description of the process of memory: 'Whether it be an idea, a desire, or a feeling that is recalled, there is an abstracting and symbolizing and interpreting process that transforms the original experience' (1967: 160). Literature, like memory, relies on a process of abstraction, transformation and depiction of a decontextualized real to achieve its effect.

Although the depicted object is abstracted from its surroundings before being symbolically transfigured, Arthur Schopenhauer argues that 'æsthetic pleasure is one and the same whether it is called forth by a work of art or directly by the contemplation of nature and life' (1909: 259). Schopenhauer goes a little further to suggest that the ekphrastic depiction of the real retrieves from its subject a purer Idea extricated from the arbitrary contingencies of worldly context:

> That the Idea comes to us more easily from the work of art than directly from nature and the real world, arises from the fact that the artist, who knew only the Idea, no longer the actual, has reproduced in his work the pure Idea, has abstracted it from the actual, omitting all disturbing accidents. (1909: 259)

Returning to the concerns of Chapter 1, perhaps Ishiguro's 'imaginary' Japan is so convincing precisely because the artist 'knew only the Idea', and not the actual. In this understanding the artist, through abstraction and distillation, might approach more closely the ineffable noumenal ground beneath the phenomenal subject. However, as our narrators come to realize, detail without context is wrought with ambiguity (is even meaningless if we take a structuralist approach). Ekphrastic transfiguration from one medium to another is a semiotic translation (a moving across) from one signifying system to another, neither of which is overly concerned with fidelity to the real-world referent (the object of Hume's 'impression'). If 'to write' is to frame, to depict, to abstract and to render in a different medium, then writing art is simply rewriting a 'real' already rewritten by perception. Yet, because of the inherent difficulties of such translation, the process is never truly mimetic. According to Deleuze and Guattari (intriguingly borrowing Schopenhauer's rhetoric of purity), 'No art is imitative, no art can be imitative or figurative' because, in the moment of composition, the depicted object 'itself is in the process of becoming something else, a pure line and pure color' (2005: 304). Figurative painting becomes a radical impossibility in this paradigm which involves the dynamic transfiguration of the apprehended subject. If the world as subject is essentially undisclosable, the project of mimesis is undermined by artistic attention's inevitable transformative abstraction. Further, like Mariko's butterfly, much of the work of the artist takes place in the absence of the subject but intangible quasi-presence of its memory.

The manipulability of memory ('memory is always an art' according to Harold Bloom) has proven to be the most hauntingly recurrent spectre of Ishiguro's writing and, reciprocally, the ever-expanding body of scholarly responses to his works (a canvas draped over a canvas draped over…).[4] His texts (re)trace the pale lines of personal/autobiographic-public/historical recall, actuating and exploiting memory's resonantly suggestive failures. Ishiguro and his narrators are perversely susceptible to 'retrieval induced distortion', a neural phenomenon in which 'memories are updated with information produced during retrieval', leading to the 'distortion, or even mostly false recollection' that has come to be so typical of his works (Paller and Bridge 2012: 12144). This tendency is revealed in Etsuko's honest assessment that memory, her own in this reflective meditation on the paradox of lingering past loss's simultaneous irretrievability and inescapability, 'can be an unreliable thing; often it is heavily coloured by the circumstances in which one remembers' (*PVH* 156). Etsuko recurs with a minor lexical modification as Setsuko to haunt Ishiguro's following novel, the spectral trace of the earlier incarnation (a preparatory sketch) remaining (snagged like the sinisterly polysemic rope of the first work). Ishiguro's reluctantly ambiguous narratives emerge, partially, from the torsional forces generated at the juncture between the private/subjective and public/objective; predominantly first-person, individual memory is foregrounded, however, and the background social memory, the wider 'context of recall', mistily limned (with a 'worn' crayon), but never quite coalescing (the constitutive sketches remain speculative, abstracted from a projected but perpetually unrealized and unrealizable whole). Hinting at the generative seed of *The Buried Giant*, Ishiguro notes his own interest in memory and a desire to move beyond the personal: 'I remain fascinated by memory. What I would like to tackle next is how a whole society or nation remembers or forgets. When is it healthy to remember, and when is it healthy to forget?' (Spiegel 2005). Very self-evidently the extended conceit of *The Buried Giant*, but also the question that pervades each work on many levels: How and why do we capture and 'order' memories, and how and why, once memorialized, might we forget them? As he commented in his Spiegel interview, 'Some people say, bury that, move on' (Spiegel 2005). Ishiguro shows us, most explicitly in *The Buried Giant*, that things buried take deep root, germinating when environmental conditions become conducive, producing 'a heap of broken images' in need of retrospective ordering (Eliot 2004: 69).

The arts, as well as their curation, contribute to the institutionalization of historical memory, with music, painting, architecture (the subject of the following chapter) acting as a narrativized repository (what is culture but shared memories). For Georges Bataille, the 'museum is the colossal mirror in which man [sic] finally contemplates himself [sic] in every aspect' (1997: 23). Indeed, architectural and ideological spaces such as galleries, museums and libraries are considered to be 'memory institutions'. Yi-Fu Tuan agrees, asking rhetorically 'what better aid to memory than the tangible evidences of the past – old furniture, old buildings, and museum collections' (2018: 194). David Carrier views these hollow yet replete public sculptures as 'memory theatres', interactive archives, suggesting that a 'walk in an art museum is a narrative under another name, for you need but describe what you see as you walk to write a history' (2003: 61). Describing what one sees is a fraught process, as Ishiguro goes to great lengths to demonstrate. Clive Bell feels that art history, more than history, captures the 'spirit' of a culture and an age: 'If I am right in thinking that art is a manifestation – a manifestation, mark, and not an expression – of man's [sic] spiritual state, then in the history of art we shall read the spiritual history of the race' (1914: 96). Bell's conception of history as singular is a bit reductive; as Gianni Vattimo reminds us, 'history presupposes literary rhetorical schemata, different ways of telling stories', and 'therefore, is not history, but histories' (1997: 149). As true of individual as it is national and global history, as Ishiguro illustrates. The arts, in both gesture and gestures towards gesture, reify moments from the past and imaginative reinterpretations of those moments, working from and providing materials for variants of history. But, if for Bell to understand the 'history of an age must we know and understand the history of its art', the converse does not hold: 'to understand art we need know nothing whatever about history' (1914: 98). If we agree with Bell that art serves so vital a function as archiving the 'historical spirit of a whole culture', presumably the artist does, as Masuji Ono thinks, necessarily and correctly occupy a 'position of large influence' in society as a custodian of cultural memory (*AFW* 139).

Just as the imagination can be used to forge communities from individuals, so too the arts, emerging from one mind to unite many in a mutual 'understanding' of a shared 'historical spirit'. Bell poses a poignant question about the salvation of childhood's innate, primal imagination, asking whether it is possible to 'save the artist that is in almost every child?' (1914: 286). Maybe, as Bachelard argues, 'it is on the plane of the daydream' alone that 'childhood remains alive and poetically useful' (1994: 16). As an innocently naïve child caught up in plots both domestic and political, *When We Were Orphans*'s Christopher Banks daydreams with his friend Akira that he might enact meaningful change in the world, until he comes to recognize the limitations of childhood play. However, reunited, or at least believing he is reunited with Akira as an adult in the search for his kidnapped parents, he consoles his lost friend by reminding him about 'how we used to pretend we were detectives searching for my father?', optimistically assuring a dying 'Akira' (misrecognized, simply a Japanese soldier), 'now we're grown, we can at last put things right' (*WWO* 263). Ironically, and somewhat pitifully, Banks has not 'grown' up, and his fantasy of being a celebrated detective and healing his own familial wound continues into the war-torn present. Indeed, proxy-Akira is mortally wounded, yet Banks seamlessly incorporates this brutal reality into his ongoing delusion.

Ishiguro asks how the arts might be actuated productively and palliatively in personal, familial, local and global communities. This is the question he addressed when asked about the significance of winning the Nobel Prize:

> I think the Nobel Prize is a truly international prize, and it emphasizes what human beings do together to try and push civilisation and knowledge onwards. I think it symbolizes, for most people, the idea of people striving together to do something good, rather than dividing into factions, and

bitterly fighting each other, and arguing with each other, for resources. (Ishiguro 2017)

Ishiguro remarks on the ethos of the prize which, so he argues, celebrates those areas of human endeavour devoted to doing 'something good' while binding people together with some sense of shared identity, shared struggle. Ishiguro shares Banks's ultimately misplaced optimism, in the belief that fiction can achieve so admirable yet ambitious a goal of galvanizing disparate communities and enabling them to overlook their own needs. Leo Tolstoy believed in art's capacity to do just this, because art 'begins when one person, with the object of joining another or others to himself in one and the same feeling, expresses that feeling by certain external indications' (Tolstoy 1996: 50). Somewhat ironically, even perversely, the Nobel committee praised Ishiguro for uncovering 'the abyss beneath our illusory sense of connection with the world' (remarkably similar to Harold Pinter: 'who in his plays uncovers the precipice under everyday prattle and forces entry into oppression's closed rooms', The Nobel Prize in Literature 2017). Once more, Ishiguro recognizes that the global community is the product of a shared imaginary, an acceptance of the proffered 'invisible reins'. 'Whatever it is in reality', he goes on, 'what's important is what it symbolizes for people', because, foremost, the laurel is 'an idea that people have all around the world' (2017). Community is an idea, a concept, as Uncle Philip (channelling Georges Sorel's theory of 'social myth') tells Banks, 'people need to feel they belong. To a nation, to a race' (*WWO* 76–7). Like imagination, then, cultural production has the capacity to create affinities between both individuals and communities through generative synthetic sympathies.

Ishiguro's use of the arts in his own art is an attempt to grapple directly with a problem encountered by both he and his characters: How might an individual (artist) see 'clearly above the dogmatic fervours of one's day' (*The Guardian*, 2016). Consistently exploiting the symbolic potency of the arts and imagination within his own literary creations, Ishiguro participates in wider cultural discussions to do with the limitations and failures of representation, and the cultural, political, personal function of artistic expression. Perhaps Sebastian Groes and Paul Daniel-Veyret's comment in relation to *The Saddest Music in the World* (2003), that 'we are all bound together by forms of art and the imagination', could be applied to his works in toto (2009: 40). We might here misremember and reformulate Ishiguro's earlier question: When is it healthy to be bound together? And when is it healthy to be unbound? As Shameem Black remarks of *Never Let Me Go*: because 'the students become more and more emotionally bound to each other through the exchange of art, they gradually lose their ability to imagine themselves outside the system that governs their collective lives' (2009: 795). Banks's Uncle Philip (offering a comment on the causes of war as does Mr Cardinal in Darlington's gardens) argues: it might be wiser to be a 'mongrel', 'be less of these wars for one thing … because people have changed. They'll be like you, Puffin. More a mixture. So why not become a mongrel? It's healthy' (*WWO* 76). If people were less bound to concepts of nationhood, he suggests, or even race, wars would end. Indeed, without such allegiances, often inspired by shared arts and the memories they evoke (Ono's wartime propaganda, for example), 'dogmatic fervour' might very well be unthinkable.

In this chapter, I discuss several examples of painting and music in Ishiguro's novels and short stories. In the previous chapter, I argued that his child artists and daydreamers were unwittingly politically and socially attuned to their wider worlds, using imagination to overcome trauma or to form alliances in challenging times while still illustrating the degree of their immersion in those worlds and their conflicts. Through his literary deployment of painting and music, Ishiguro engages with a range of salient and pressing questions about the relationship between aural and visual aesthetics and ethics. As Sean Matthews and Sebastian Groes note, 'the interrelations of art and life, of aesthetics and ethics' is 'central to Ishiguro's vision' (2009: 2). Recalling Hoffman's childhood game of leaf-piling to prevent a city-wide cataclysm (a comment on the failure of the global political community to prevent world war, the Holocaust, Hiroshima and Nagasaki, and the sense that the burden shifts intergenerationally from prevention to palliative amelioration), we might again suggest that, in Ishiguro's worlds, children become adults and assume adult roles, but that they remain embedded within imaginative communities which are sustained by shared arts (the 'invisible reins'). That is to say, the adult arts, though perhaps more practised, refined, aware, nonetheless have the same unifying functional currency as childhood imagination and sketches. In the same way that childhood imagination resolves personal wounds, the adult arts often serve personal prestige, the desire to occupy a 'position of large influence' (*AFW* 139). As Carlos Garrido Castellano comments of Ryder, despite ostensibly offering a kind of music therapy, he is foremost determined to keep his 'prestigious image intact' (2020: 245). Masquerading as artists using their talents to 'fill the cracks in the social bond', they exploit the personal palliative dimension of art as therapy (Bourriaud 2002: 36). Ostensibly cultivating affinity, they unwittingly foster disaffinity precisely because they co-opt public performance for personal healing. As we'll see later, failed art is that which memorializes wounds, personal and national, which it may in fact be 'healthier' to bury. If art is relationally operative, failed art dissolves rather than strengthens familial, community, national and international bonds, deepening divides in performances of radical aesthetic alterity.

I

The relationship between art and politics is a complex one, more so in periods such as modernism that arise during or preceding conflict, when the political world is more fractious, divisive. Rachel Potter reminds us that the 'politics of modernism' has come to be associated with a 'number of prominent writers with fascist ideas', foremost perhaps Ezra Pound (2012: 178). Mark Antliff makes the same connection, arguing that, in order to appraise modernism, an 'understanding of the profound interrelation' of '*fascism* and *modern art*' is essential (2002: 148). This is one reason that in the period of late modernism, according to John Barth, the 'democratic West seems eager to have done with ... the "omniscient" author of older fiction', while the 'very idea of the controlling artist, has been condemned as politically reactionary, authoritarian, even fascist' (1984: 65). Modernism in this understanding is highly politically charged. On the other hand, in his eulogy *In Memory of W.B. Yeats*, W. H. Auden polemically suggests that 'poetry makes nothing happen' (1995: 78). 'Nothing' is a complex term (perhaps, as Wittgenstein might say, nothing itself 'is not a something, but not a nothing either'), more so after Eliot despairingly connects 'nothing with nothing' on Margate sands (Eliot 2004: 70). As John Lyon has remarked, at least 'since Shakespeare the word has been something of a riddle' (2009: 280). The 'nothing' that Auden and Eliot manipulate might be the appropriate artistic response to the perceived failure of pre- and interwar politics, when

> artists saw themselves as engaged in their own legitimate, modern vocation, one that challenged rival vocations and practices – politics now especially, in large part because politics was seen as leading to catastrophes like the Great War. (Levenson 2011: 222)

A political turning away, then, one which José Ortega y Gasset sees as central to the modernist 'dehumanization of art': modernism, he argues, is 'not an art for men in general but for a special class of men' (1972: 8). Some have argued that to expect poetry or the arts to achieve, or even aspire to, anything beyond the purely aesthetic is to misunderstand art's purpose. According to Arthur Salmon, 'Politics have no place in' art; for Bell to 'associate art with politics is always a mistake' (Bell 1914: 20; Salmon 1925: 21). '*L'art pour l'art*', as Théophile Gautier famously has it. Bertolt Brecht, the most prominent modernist playwright, would disagree, arguing that 'art is never without consequences', a dictum which formed the basis of his development of the deeply politically revolutionary techniques of 'epic theatre' (1978: 150–1). Adorno goes as far as to suggest that autonomous apolitical art is a logical impossibility, posing the paradox that 'art becomes social by its opposition to society, and it occupies this position only as autonomous art' (quoted in Kania and Gracyk 2011: 398). These various and often antagonistic perspectives evidence the ongoing uncertainty about the relationship between ethics and aesthetics and what Ishiguro calls the '"role of the artist" in a time of political change' (*The Guardian*, 2016). War is certainly such a time. And the world is always at war.

Although painting, drawing and sketching, as well as questions of aesthetics and ethics, play prominent roles throughout Ishiguro's novels and short stories, it is in *An Artist of the Floating World* that he tackles the conundrum most directly. Ishiguro stages a dialogue between two diametrically opposed modes of art. On the one hand, 'decorative' paintings commissioned for export to a West offering a 'quaint' view of Japan; on the other, 'political' art which serves a function of provoking nationalist fervour in the build-up to the Second World War. The former works towards aesthetic beauty, its responsibility simply to capture the fleeting and transient delights of the peculiarly Japanese 'floating world' (decadent); the latter views art as politically and ideologically active in binding people together in a cause (propagandistic). These questions were raised in the philosophy of aestheticism, which came to define and inform much art in the period of the *fin de siècle*. Oscar Wilde's *The Picture of Dorian Gray* (1890) is possibly the most famous example, a creative philosophical treatise on the hypothetical attraction (Lord Henry Wotton) and the pragmatic dangers (Dorian) of aestheticism which revolves ideologically around J. K. Huysmann's Decadent masterpiece *À rebours* (1884). The novel is suffused with references to Eastern art, 'producing a kind of momentary Japanese effect' (Wilde 2005: 5). Aestheticism was itself influenced by Japanese art to which the West was exposed after Japan was forced to open its borders to trade in 1853. As Pamela Genova notes, in 1872, Philippe Burty coined the term 'japonisme' to describe a trend in 'writers from such varied ideological schools as Naturalism, Symbolism, and Decadence [who] actively sought to integrate fundamental Japanese aesthetic theories into their poetics' (1997: 268–9). Modernism too, developing from and inheriting the theoretical heritage of aestheticism, asks the same questions of the arts – What can and what should art try to recover from the stony rubbish of post-war civilization.

Ono's double bind is that, for his pride, he needs to believe that he had 'great influence' before the war as a propagandist while also recognizing that this poses problems both personal and political in the present. However, he finds himself having to, or believing that he has to justify some of the decisions that he made in his career, primarily because he assumes that his now dubious past is preventing his daughter from finding a husband (a continuation of his need to feel 'influential' rather than concern for her). Like that of his successor Stevens, his story is interested in being guided or misguided, particularly in relation to tutorship: Ono is taught by Seiji Moriyama until Ono changes his technique and is called a traitor and banished from the villa; Ono decides to change his aesthetic philosophy when he meets the confused Marxist Chishi Matsuda. Ultimately, as Lewis writes, Ono sets up 'an agitprop school' before 'reaching [his] lowest ebb' after he 'betrays his most talented pupil', Karuda (2000: 59). This betrayal represents a turning point in Ono's professional life. Tutorship plays a prominent role in Ishiguro's fictions more widely (most explicitly perhaps in *NLMG*), a theme played out in *A Pale View of Hills* through Ogata, an influential teacher in Japan before the war, like Ono, who 'cared deeply for the country [and] worked hard to ensure the correct values were preserved and handed on' (*PVH* 147). But, young Shigeo, who like Matsuda is something of a communist, tells Ogata that his 'energies were spent in a misguided direction, an evil direction. You weren't to know this ... you shouldn't be blamed for not realizing the true consequences of your actions' (*PVH* 147–8). Shigeo's at once accusatory, forgiving, even patronizing suggestion that Ogata was 'misguided', a term that recurs throughout his works, is important in a work and oeuvre which teases out the economies of intergenerational responsibility in post-war Europe and Japan.

In *An Artist of the Floating World*, under the guidance of Mori-san at his bohemian villa, there are, informally, two schools. There are 'the engineers' (Ono's faction), named for 'the intense and frantic way we worked once an idea had struck [like] an engine driver shovelling on coal for fear the steam would at any moment run out' (the opposite of Marinetti's Futurist poet who works with the 'cool detachment of an engineer') (*AFW* 196). Alongside these are the 'slow faction', nicknamed the 'backwarders'. A 'backwarder' is 'someone who, in a room crowded with people working at easels, insisted on stepping backwards every few minutes to view his canvas – with the result that he continually collided with colleagues working behind him' (*AFW* 160). The engineers are 'full of passionate intensity' as Yeats might have it, the backwarders, though not essentially bad, 'lack all conviction'. If the engineers respond to the 'dogmatic fervours of one's day', the backwarders are complacently immured in the past. Perhaps, though, this is appropriate; as Søren Kierkegaard noted in his diary, 'It occurs to me that artists go forward by going backward' (1967: 51). History provides a lesson, and art can reflect on the present only by carefully and patiently drawing on the material of the past, unless we agree with Bell that 'to understand art we need know nothing whatever about history'. In bumping into others in her community, the backwarder is made repeatedly aware that art is not produced in isolation. Art in Ono's taxonomy can be either forward-facing (progressive) or backward-facing (regressive), the latter, he implies, less socially aware in the literal sense of the villa and metaphorically Japan.

Ono is intellectually seduced by Matsuda, member of the Okada-Shingen (New Life) Society, and 'a government stooge who recruits artists for the nationalist cause' (Lewis 2000: 57). Matsuda is a gesture towards a poorly interpreted Marxism, at one point asking Ono what he understands of communism. Oddly, Marxism was well established in Japan since around 1890, according to Yukiko Koshiro, who also remarks that 'throughout the war, Japan's Marxists, both political and intellectual, remained the most eminent antiwar and anti government' force (2001: 427). One memorable day, a 'turning point' for Ono, Matsuda takes him on a tour of the Nishizuru district, 'some derelict site half-way to demolition', bringing to mind the 'reservations' from Aldous Huxley's *Brave New World* (1932). Attempting to encourage Ono to be politically aware, Matsuda tells him that as 'a breed, you artists are desperately naïve'; like children they use their art to 'hide away from the real world', that his 'knowledge of the world is like a child's' (*AFW* 171). Matsuda invokes a crude

Marxism, though his hope is not for 'revolution' but simply to wrest power back from businessmen to the emperor, returning to an earlier historical moment. Marx himself might consider Matsuda a petite bourgeoise 'reactionary', very literally trying 'to roll back the wheel of history' (Marx 2008: 24). In Nishizuru, Ono and Matsuda encounter 'three small boys bowed over something on the ground, prodding at it with sticks. As we approached, they spun around with scowls on their faces' (*AFW* 167). Unwittingly exchanging one master for another, yet adamant that he has an ability to 'think and judge' for himself (*AFW* 69), Ono takes inspiration from this squalid scene and his educative trip with Matsuda for his first political composition, 'Complacency':

> Although they stood in front of a squalid shanty hut, and their clothes were the same rags the original boys wore, the scowls on their faces would not have been guilty, defensive scowls of the little criminals caught in the act; rather, they would have been the manly scowls of samurai warriors ready to fight. (*AFW* 168)

Returning to a concern central to Stevens, the image carries the motto 'but the young are ready to fight for their dignity' (*AFW* 168). Ono misreads the scowls on the boy's faces, the description of them as 'guilty' implying that the children are somehow responsible for their own poverty: They are, he surmises, 'criminals'. Despite the failure of his shared enterprise, Ono clearly retains pride in this work, his present description as impassioned as the moment of composition. For his own purpose, he reworks the suffering of the impoverished Japanese (we might think here of Niki's young English friend writing a poem for Etsuko's experiences of post-atomic Nagasaki) while also espousing a philosophy that very likely led to the death of the study's scowling subjects. Ono's artistic development is one from a pure aesthetics to propaganda, spurred by the fervent belief that the latter is somehow more truthful, less decadent than the former. Rebecca Walkowitz has commented on the use of 'truth' in propaganda, arguing, 'The propagandist style acts as if it is true, whereas the impressionist style never makes this claim: in this sense, Ishiguro suggests, the style that claims openness and truth is most deceptive' (2001: 1058). As Walkowitz notes, propaganda gestures towards style-less representation, but its subject is political, conceptual, and the figurative rendition of that ideation performs a kind of distortion (denegation) of both reality and the truth which is ostensibly the meta-subject. However, if impressionism (decadent art) makes no claims to truth, it does so only because of its refusal to engage with political reality, a negation no less political (to return to Adorno's paradox).

During a discussion in a bar following their visit to the Nishizuru district, Matsuda returns to his intentionally provocative refrain that artists are an 'astonishingly decadent crowd. Often with no more than a child's knowledge of the affairs of this world' (*AFW* 170). In response, Ono proposes an 'exhibition-cum-art' (to borrow Kathy's words) sale of beautiful images, to raise money for the poor of the city and open 'the eyes of us decadent artists' (*AFW* 172). Matsuda replies that 'Japan is headed for crisis' and that Ono is misguided if he believes 'a little good-hearted charity can help the poor of our country' (*AFW* 172). Rather, Matsuda views art as one wave of a cumulative political tsunami. Ono counters that Matsuda himself is naïve in his estimation of the kinds of things that artists and the arts can accomplish:

> [An] artist's concern is to capture beauty wherever he finds it. But however skilfully he may come to do this, he will have little influence on the sort of matters you talk of [which] seems to be founded on a naïve mistake about what art can and cannot do. (*AFW* 172)

Ono raises explicitly the defining question about the efficacy of art: What it 'can and cannot do'. Understanding the political potential of the arts, Matsuda envisages a generational change, 'in politics, in the military', to which the arts can contribute as part of a developing 'new spirit'. Matsuda passionately tells Ono that 'it is simply not enough for an artist to hide away somewhere, perfecting pictures of courtesans', that 'Japan is no longer a backward country of peasant farmers. We are now a mighty nation, capable of matching any of the Western nations. In the Asian hemisphere, Japan stands like a giant amidst cripples and dwarfs' (*AFW* 173). As H. Byron Earhart notes, the 'putative rationale for the Japanese war machine was to relieve Asians of the colonial yoke of the European powers' (2011: 170). In an age of eugenics, radical social planning, ethnic cleansing and fascistic fascination with genetic purity, Matsuda's language is deeply troubling. The word 'backward' too returns us to the non-reactionary painters of Mori-san's stable, those complacent recorders of the floating world. Matsuda believes in the supremacy of Japan and the imperialist ideal, encouraging Ono to devote his art to support the effort. This is a pivotal period in Ono's radicalization, capturing the precise moment that he moves from aestheticism to propaganda, necessitating the very narrative amelioration the reader holds, in which Ono is compelled to simultaneously celebrate and renounce the part he played in a game whose rules have now changed.

Mori-san, Ono's master until he comes under the (mis)guidance of Matsuda, has a different philosophy about the purpose of art and the artist's responsibility. For Mori-san, an aestheticist who banishes from his commune any artist with political motivations, 'the finest, most fragile beauty an artist can hope to capture drifts within those pleasure houses after dark' (*AFW* 150). Mori's contention that the floating world is the single most beautiful subject of art is irrelevant if one disagrees with the premise that art's subject is beauty (it begs the question under debate). Ono implies that, in producing artworks for the international market, Mori unwittingly participates in the cultural reduction of Japan to a few stock images, recalling that the essential point about the sort of things we were commissioned to paint – geishas, cherry trees, swimming carps, temples – was that they look 'Japanese' to the foreigners to whom they were shipped out, and all finer points of style were quite likely to go unnoticed. (*AFW* 69)

Ironically, Ishiguro's tatami-strewn 'Japanese' novels have suffered just this fate. In the villa, Mori and his eager acolytes do indeed hide from the world. This is not to say that art understood as pure aesthetics serves no deeper purpose for Mori, who also speaks of responsibilities: 'As the new generation of Japanese artists, you have a great responsibility towards the culture of this nation' (*AFW* 151). Mori-san is an aestheticist, living by the principle of art for art's sake. But, he makes clear, art participates in the preservation of a traditional national culture which is transcendently ahistorical. In abrogating responsibility for reacting to the politically transient present moment, the artist, as Mori sees it, dedicates her life to capturing something that is at once fleeting yet permanent, an 'autonomous work of art that transcends its context' as Claire Bishop has it (2004: 53–4).

After his sketch for 'Complacency' is discovered, Ono remarks to his former master that

> I have learnt much in contemplating the world of pleasure, and recognizing its fragile beauty … it is my belief that in such troubled times as these, artists must learn to value something more tangible than those pleasurable things that disappear with the morning light. It is not necessary that artists always occupy a decadent and enclosed world. (*AFW* 179–80)

This passage brings us back to the tension between the tangible and intangible of which Heidegger speaks in *The Origin of the Work of Art* (see intro). Ono makes a direct allusion to Walter Pater's famous lines of *The Renaissance* (1873), seen by many as the ur text of aestheticism: 'art comes to you professing frankly to give nothing but the highest quality to your moments as they pass, and simply for those moments' sake' (1994: 29). Ono's rejection of ephemeral aestheticism in favour of a more politically engaged practice is not his 'belief' but Matsuda's. After sharing his work with his colleagues, he is called a 'traitor' by his one-time friend and admirer Nakahara. To be a traitor in this context is merely to favour one guide over another, to hold contrary theoretical positions. No objective, absolute judgement can be made as to which is the 'correct' path; rather, it is simply the shared criteria by which the community includes or excludes members. In this sense, Ono is simultaneously a traitor and not a traitor, occupying an ambiguous state of interpretative uncertainty. How might we reconcile these two approaches to art? Walkowitz argues that while 'Ono tells us that the political message of his later art was starkly opposed to the aesthetic project of his earlier, Ishiguro makes it clear that Mori-san's aestheticism has its own commitments, and the realism of the political work is not without deceit' (2001: 1057). Perhaps in a time of war, or the build-up to war and the radical changes likely to follow in its wake, each enterprise is necessary. It is not that one or the other of these modes is the 'correct path' or expresses 'correct values'; rather, the issue that Ishiguro explores is being guided and misguided, both by one's own ego and by the ego of others. That is to say, neither Mori nor Matsuda are 'right', as such, but both are wrong in their unreflective inflexible commitment to their own or others' unexamined ideals. However, if art has the potential for symbolically uniting diverse communities via a relational aesthetics, then each of these modes fosters artistic divisions which develop from and exaggerate political factions.

II

Ishiguro, who wanted to be a 'rock and roll star' until he settled on writing, has over the past decade or so co-written lyrics for several of American jazz musician Stacey Kent's albums, some of which develop scenes from his novels (a transfiguration of the literary to the aural). 'Breakfast on the Morning Tram', inspired by the final scene of *The Unconsoled*, somewhat optimistically reads that as a moment of (deferred) consolation: 'Very soon you'll forget your heartache / When you have breakfast on the morning tram' (Tomlinson/Ishiguro 2007). Soothing though the sentiment is, it is rather at odds with the novel, which poignantly shows that time compounds heartache, which becomes pervasively diffuse rather than forgotten, and that even were Ryder to be in a position to forget, he's unlikely to do so. Like all of Ishiguro's characters, Ryder likes to nurture and so keep open his psychical and emotional wounds. As Etsuko thinks, 'as with a wound on one's own body, it is possible to develop an intimacy with the most disturbing of things' (*PVH* 54). So important is popular music to Ishiguro that the end of *Remains of the Day* was fundamentally redrafted after he heard Tom Waits singing 'Ruby's Arms', leading him to reverse

> a decision I'd made, that Stevens would remain emotionally buttoned up right to the bitter end. I decided that at just one point – which I'd have to choose very carefully – his rigid defence would crack, and a hitherto concealed tragic romanticism would be glimpsed. (*The Guardian*, 2014)

Certainly, the final scene between Miss Kenton/Mrs Benn and Stevens, when he declares that his 'heart was breaking', derives effective force because it is in such (jarring) contrast to the restrained, 'buttoned up' butler preoccupied with personal and professional dignity.[5] One might argue that the novel would have been more powerful had Stevens, in fact, not emerged so radically changed at this single point, his heartache modestly implied: his romantic side is already 'glimpsed' through his interrupted evening reading and his motoring trip. Or, one might argue that it is at only this singular instant that Stevens truly recognizes that Miss Kenton has become another person, has let him go and that he must reciprocally (he addresses Mrs Benn here, uniquely).

The title of *Never Let Me Go* is taken from a track on the fictional album *Songs after Dark* (*Nocturnes*, perhaps) by Judy Bridgewater. Kathy's favourite song, she listens clutching a pillow as she dances imagining herself as a 'woman who'd been told she couldn't have babies, who'd really, really wanted them all her life. Then there's a sort of miracle and she has a baby' (*NLMG* 66–7). Kathy, of course, cannot have babies, something she has been 'told and not told'; the proxy offspring in this ameliorative imaginary scenario (some immaculate conception) is as proximate as she'll come to parenthood in her brutally attenuated gesture life. The use of the song as an empathetic prompt is ambiguous, Madame herself misreading its significance, or reading into the song another kind of meaning which resonates with her own role in Hailsham's sham.[6] Polysemic through simplicity, the song is trite, naïve, American, popular and unimaginative. The startling unoriginality of the lyrics ('Never let me go … Oh baby, baby … Never let me go') caress Kathy with sentiments themselves clones of a sort, vacuous phrases, as Orwell might say, 'tacked together like the sections of a prefabricated hen-house', to appeal to the innocent romantic naivete of adolescence (another kind of ignorance of the reality of adult life in this extended allegory). Indeed, the phrase so potentially potent in the context of the novel is used as the title of at least seven generic pop songs between 1954's version by Johnny Ace, Stacey Kent's own 2007 arrangement of Ray Evans and Jay Livingstone's version, and Jess Glynne's in 2018. Theodor Adorno has suggested that popular music serves a more dubious function: 'music that permits its listeners the confession of their unhappiness reconciles them, by means of this "release", to their social dependence' (Adorno 1991: 313–14). If the exchanges of art invest the students' lives with deceptive meaning in Ishiguro's metaphor, popular culture performs the same function for the reader.

It is in *Nocturnes* (a reference perhaps to the story cycle *Night Pieces* by E. T. A. Hoffman, given the use of that name also in *The Unconsoled*) that Ishiguro most directly explores the cultural role of popular music, and more specifically popular American music (if in the estranged context of Venice). Appropriately, the collection contains his most informal, colloquial writing, in contrast to his other works which led Philip Hensher to comment that he 'hardly ever uses a phrasal verb. He is a writer who always prefers to say "depart" rather than "set off", "discover" rather than "find out"' (2000). As Christopher Tayler observed in a contemporary review, *Nocturnes* is 'more discursive and less formal than that of his earlier books' (2009). Christopher Hitchens was unimpressed by the collection and its language, frustrated that 'Ishiguro almost never chose a formulation or phrase that could be called his own when a stock expression would do' (2009). As David James has argued of Stevens's modesty, however, the lexicon and grammar of each work is determined by the characters: to attribute these traits to the author is to profoundly misunderstand the books (did Burgess speak in Nadsat?). The collection is replete with names – Tony

Gardner and Marcus Lightfoot – that would be at home on the sleeve of a long play record from the late 1950s. A shared appreciation of this period of music is the subject of 'Come Rain or Come Shine', when Ray thinks back to his university friendship with Emily, who loved 'the Great American Songbook. She favoured Sarah Vaughan and Chet Baker. I preferred Julie London and Peggy Lee' (*N* 38). Their reconciliation at story's end is facilitated by 'Vaughan's 1954 version of "April in Paris"' (*N* 86).

Often the stories are about degrees of artistic disaffinity. As Tom Fleming observed in his review on the collection's release, they explore 'the conflict between what music promises and what life delivers' (2009). *Nocturnes* is also about musical affinities, some unexpected. In 'Malvern Hills', an aspiring singer-songwriter, disillusioned with the 'inauthentic' London music scene, travels to spend time in the country (perhaps Worcestershire which features in *The Unconsoled*) with his sister and brother-in-law. One day, as he plays his own composition on a guitar, two Swiss tourists looking to find Elgar's inspiration in the hills stop by to listen: 'They seemed on the verge of getting carried away, like they'd just come across another Elgar in the hills' (*N* 106). Tilo and Sonja are also musicians, 'professionals', 'but first and foremost [they] play because we believe in the music. I can see it is the same for you' (*N* 108). It transpires the couple have fallen out in a marital disharmony prompted by aesthetic disharmony: They play 'In hotels, restaurants. At weddings, at parties' rather than the more 'radical' music of Sonja's taste. Tilo, the more accommodating, pragmatic, 'realist' of the two, is unperturbed by this, but for a grudging Sonja, 'in this real world, much of the time, we must play what our audience is most likely to appreciate. So we perform many hits. Beatles, the Carpenters. Some more recent songs' (*N* 110). Audiences dictate taste; Tilo, Sonja and the narrator must adapt their art to the world, to mimic rather than create. We might ask questions to do with authenticity and function, here: Is art a personal exploration of creative possibility or simply a mode of communication through entertainment (lobby/elevator music)? This depends on whether, as Sonja poses it, an artist is prepared to 'take inspiration from great composers who took a similar path' (*N* 109–10). Taking another's path is a mistake made by many of Ishiguro's characters.

In 'Cellists', Tibor, a young classically trained musician on the wrong 'path', is spotted playing by and comes under the tutelage of Eloise McCormack, a young American connoisseur of the cello. Unlike many of his circle of itinerant café musicians, Tibor 'studied at the Royal Academy of Music in London, then spent two years in Vienna under Oleg Petrovic', until demand for classical concerts waned and he had found himself auditioning in hotels and cafes (*N* 192). Like Tilo and Sonja, Tibor plays simple melodies, arrangements of pop songs and renditions of film scores such as the perennial favourite 'The Godfather' in cafés and hotel lobbies. Posing as a 'distinguished musician', using politically loaded language that would be equally suited to *The Remains of the Day* and *An Artist of the Floating World*, Eloise offers Tibor personal lessons in her hotel room.

She remarks to Tibor that he is 'not quite on the *correct path* just now. And when I heard you, I so wanted to help you find it. Sooner rather than later' (*N* 197, 198, my italics). A concern that recurs in Ishiguro's writing, and his interest in education, echoing Ogata's rhetoric: 'We devoted ourselves to ensuring that proper qualities were handed down, that children grew up with the *correct attitude* to their country, to their fellows. There was a spirit in Japan once, it bound us all together' (my italics). For Eloise, correcting the paths of musicians with 'potential' is a 'mission': 'I don't know what else to call it. I want all cellists to play well. To play beautifully. So often, they play in a misguided way' (*N* 197). This linguistic trace of the political in the musical makes a connection with the same conflation in *The Unconsoled*. Misguided occurs frequently in conjunction with notions of responsibility, as we saw with Shigeo, once more evidencing Ishiguro's interest in the idea of influence and authority.

Eloise imagines herself as a saviour, of sorts, working in the interests of a music, and instrument to which she feels deeply personally connected. Interestingly, Nicolas Bourriaud (more of whom later) feels that 'through a series of gestures art is like an angelic programme' (2002: 36). However, it transpires that Eloise is not in fact a 'distinguished musician' or even an amateur cellist. She confesses to Tibor that

> the fact that I've not yet learned to play the cello doesn't really change anything. You have to understand, I am a virtuoso. But I'm one who's yet to be *unwrapped*. You too, you're still not entirely unwrapped, and that's what I've been doing these past few weeks. I've been trying to help you shed those layers. (*N* 212)

In this rhetoric, there is something inside Tibor, underneath the exterior, which needs to be disclosed (the ineffable essence). Eloise is a teacher without practical expertise. The question then is whether it is necessary to be an artist to appreciate and guide the creation of art, and whether to study is either a necessary or sufficient condition. If, as Schopenhauer argues, 'no one ever became an artist by the study of æsthetics; that a noble character was never formed by the study of ethics', then Eloise may be perfectly capable, even peculiarly sensitive to the possibilities of the cello (1909: 77). Tibor disagrees, although his insistence on the necessity to play has to do not with musical expertise rather with conviction: artists 'have to take our courage in our hands and we unwrap ourselves, as you put it, all the time unsure what we will find underneath. Yet you, you do not care for this unwrapping. You do nothing. But you are so sure you are this virtuoso' (*N* 213). Like Stevens, Ono and Ogata, Eloise is happier on the side-lines. Hers then is a somewhat safer path, one that might, in years to come, allow her to both claim credit and deny absolute responsibility for the path that Tibor takes.

Ironically, Eloise is not a fan of music teachers herself, precisely because they misguide one into believing that here is 'someone to help me, he's one of us.

Then you realize he's nothing of the kind. And that's when you have to be tough and shut yourself off'. Etsuko too dislikes music teachers, thinking back to her daughters' tutor, 'a very limited pianist and her attitude to music in general had often irritated me; for instance, she would refer to works by Chopin and Tchaikovsky alike as "charming melodies"' (*PVH* 50). To be charming is to be quaint, innocuous. Above, Ono suggested that it was a decadent abrogation of responsibility to compose in an 'enclosed world', 'to hide away from the world', producing art that is not connected to or lacks affinity with the cultural and political present. Eloise's hiding is of a deeper, more intimate variety; she wants to remain unwrapped, cloistered, virginal in order to not be misguided. There is in this personal sacrifice a misguided conviction: 'to protect my gift against people who, however well intentioned they were, could completely destroy it. So I shut them out' (*N* 213). Perhaps she, like Sonja, Ono and Etsuko, would worry that, under the wrong influence, art, like Tibor's, can be reduced to a series of 'charming' melodies, stripped of political, aesthetic or emotional value.

III

Symbolically dynamic, open to recontextualization, misreading and appropriation, the arts have an ambiguous relationship with politics precisely because of their inherent polysemy (we might think of Bruce Springsteen or Neil Young demanding, respectively, that George W. Bush and Donald Trump refrain from using their music during rallies). As Segal remarks, 'Even when the artist has well-defined ideas about the political meaning of his or her work, critics can interpret it in a radically different way [because the] arts cannot easily be reduced to unambiguous statements or clear-cut arguments' (2016: 8). One person's political responsibility is another's cultural irresponsibility. If art is to be used to build bridges between diverse communities, as Ishiguro proposes, it needs to operate relationally. The theory of 'relational aesthetics' emerged in Paris in the 1990s, the term itself coined by Bourriaud, art critic and curator, in 1996. Community-minded Jeff Warren notes that the theory 'makes claims that "art is the state of encounter" and aims to transform the practice of art making to transforming social relations' (2017: 32).[7] Working from Bourriaud's 1997 collection of essays titled *Esthetique Relationelle*, Bishop summarizes:

> Relational art works seek to establish intersubjective encounters (be these literal or potential) in which meaning is elaborated collectively (RA, p. 18) rather than in the privatized space of individual consumption ... Rather than a discrete, portable, autonomous work of art that transcends its context, relational art is entirely beholden to the contingencies of its environment and audience. Moreover, this audience is envisaged as a community: rather than a one-to-one relationship between work of art and viewer, relational art sets up situations in which viewers are not just addressed as a collective, social

entity, but are actually given the wherewithal to create a community, however temporary or utopian this may be. (2004: 53–4)

Relational aesthetics, 'consisting in judging artworks on the basis of the interhuman relations which they represent, produce, or prompt', reconfigures the personal aesthetic encounter as a communal social encounter (Bourriaud 2002: 112). In this understanding, meaning is not the product of a singular consumerist or aesthetic act but an aggregate of interpretative acts which strives towards shared meanings, the striving itself, paradoxically, constitutes that very meaning. Art produced with the intention of performing this social function is a variety of gesture: regardless of the aesthetic merit of the work, 'what's important is what it symbolizes for people', as Ishiguro would say, as they participate in the 'collective elaboration of meaning' (Bourriaud 2002: 15). Communities (of readers, viewers, listeners, persons) form around the aesthetic encounter which itself is little more than a prompt to a more meaningful communion. Art's value manifests virtually in the space vacated by singular semiosis. If, as Schopenhauer proposes, the aesthetic encounter facilitates the 'forgetting of self as an individual', then it may create conditions ontologically conducive to egoless community formation (1909: 264). However, as Bishop notes, these communities are transient, evaporating on dispersal. They are also highly contingent, 'micro-utopian' social transformations reliant on the arbitrary vagaries of environment and audience (Castellano 2020: 239).

It is unlikely (or I have found no evidence) that Ishiguro was aware of relational aesthetics as a philosophy. Nonetheless, his works are deeply invested in the community-building possibilities of the arts, in relation to his own practice (as his comments about the Nobel illustrate) but also his fictional worlds. Hailsham's 'students' develop close quasi-familial bonds around the 'exchanges' of art that they themselves produce (although they do not work together, but produce individual works for bartering). As Anne Whitehead remarks, the education at Hailsham is 'firmly rooted in the arts' (2011: 56). The novel's great tragedy is that the artworks have limited cultural currency; the value accorded to their crafts by the students themselves is restricted to the 'environment and audience' of Hailsham and does not extend into the community beyond the bordering woods and barbed wire fence. Disillusioned by her own once-prized collection, Ruth asks Keffers to donate them to a charity shop: 'Keffers rummaged in the bag a bit, he didn't know what any of it was – why should he? – and he did this laugh and said no shop he knew would want stuff like that' (*NLMG* 129). Although of central importance to the poor-in-world clones, the works resemble little more than trash to those in the 'real world'. The sadness of the novel is partly attributable to the fact that the clones' work does not, as Madame and Miss Emily hope, enable the clones to enter into to become part of human community. Theirs is an ephemeral micro-utopia, founded hopelessly on a misguided belief in the value of their esoteric and radically limited art, and by implication their lives.

Although relational aesthetics is an important aspect of *Never Let Me Go*, it is in *The Unconsoled* that the potential affinities and disaffinities created by the arts are explored most directly. In fact, in *The Unconsoled* (and *Nocturnes*, see later), we have relational aesthetics' aural equivalent: 'relational musicology'. As Georgina Born argues, like its forerunner, it 'responds to the problematic assumption that the social is outside of the music itself' (quoted in Warren 2017: 32). The context of Ryder's diplomatic visit is the sociocultural disintegration of the non-descript city following the deaths of 'Mr Bernd, the painter, and Mr Vollmoller, a very fine composer', both of whom 'had for so long been at the helm of [the] cultural life' of the community but who had 'died within months of each other [leaving] a certain feeling … well, a kind of *unsettled* feeling' (*U* 98–9).[8] *Unsettled, Unconsoled*. The novel ostensibly moves towards an evening of personal, familial and national consolations in the form of three headline musical performances at which the entire town will attend to witness its own reconciliation enacted through the personal consolatory performances of Brodsky (attempting to rehabilitate himself, his love for Miss Collins and the town); Stephan (hoping to bring together his parents and to inspire their validation); and Ryder (waiting in vain for his parents' return, hoping also to perform his designated diplomatic role of healing communal rifts). Boris also unconsciously envisages his crayon rendition of Superman as a conduit through which to re-establish his relationship with his estranged father, to rekindle his parent's love and, ultimately, to act as the foundation for some dreamed-of but entirely fantastic domestic harmony. However, the failure of these efforts conveys Ishiguro's uncertainty about art's community-building potential. Indeed, as with the failures of language, art's failures enact yet deeper regrets, often enforcing, performing radical disaffinities between persons and groups. James argues that Ishiguro's narratives gesture towards a kind 'consolation [that] may endure against backdrops of dread'; in the examples here, we see the oft-illusory solace offered by creativity, but also the compromised comfort (James's discrepant solace) (2019: 180).

Nocturnes is equally preoccupied with the possibilities of music, both personal and interpersonal. In the title story, Steven (once more the trace of earlier incarnations), a saxophonist with ambitions to be not 'just big-league session player, but big-league headliner' (a great bugler, as it were), is encouraged by his agent to undergo cosmetic surgery because he's the 'wrong type of ugly' to move from studio to spotlight. Negotiating the space between music as commodity (charming) and music as art (aesthetic/radical), he dreams of producing music for its own sake, in isolation:

Why should I have to join in this game? Why couldn't I just play my music the best way I knew, and keep getting better, if only in my cubicle, and maybe some day, just maybe, genuine music lovers would hear me and appreciate what I was doing. (*N* 131)

We might ask what a 'genuine music lover' is: not a critic, not an agent, but a casual listener, a fan of the art for its own sake. Again, this raises the questions posed by the rest of the collection about musical integrity and authenticity, ones which re-activate the aestheticist/propagandist debate begun with Mori and Ono. Mori would perhaps agree, in his villa, that the artist has a duty only to the form itself; or, as Matsuda informs Ono, one might argue that 'it is simply not enough for an artist to hide away somewhere'. Helen, Steven's ex-wife, jokingly remarks that 'it was like [Steven] was going to the toilet' when he practised alone in his room. Steven, though, is happy with this analogy, admitting that that's 'how it felt. That's to say, it was like I was sitting in that dim, airless cubicle taking care of personal business no one else would ever care to come across' (*N* 131). Steven imagines an ideal space of artistic intimacy, viewing art not as a medium for community building (the average listener is not a 'genuine fan' of music) but for self-gratification that also privileges the art itself. Like Eloise, there is a desire to retain art's pure essence, safely isolated from society. Bell might agree with such recourse, because, he thinks, the 'one good thing Society can do for the artist is to leave him [*sic*] alone' (1914: 252). To listen, to (step back and unwittingly) bump into music, involves altering the course of that art in an aesthetic reapplication of Heisenberg's uncertainty principle. But there is also a radical political dimension to Steven's isolation; as Bourriaud remarks, the 'enemy' that artists 'have to fight' is the 'spread of supplier/client relations to every level of human life' (2002: 83). It is this 'spread' that has affected Tilo and Sonja, and it is against this that Eloise and Steven protect themselves.

Steven is not the only musician to find himself practising in a 'cubicle'. Despairing in the realization that he had not 'had a chance to touch a piano now for many days' as the big performance approaches, an increasingly agitated Ryder is led by Hoffman to a private room in the hotel that seems uncannily like a men's room:

> I entered a long narrow room with a grey stone floor. The walls were covered to the ceiling with white tiles. I had the impression there was a row of sinks to my left ... The doors to the two outer cubicles were closed, but the central cubicle – which looked to have slightly broader dimensions – had its door ajar and I could see inside it a piano, the lid left open to display the keys. (*U* 341)

In order to take this time to practise for his solo performance, Ryder cancels an important meeting with the 'Citizens' Mutual Support Group', in a direct rejection of the relational aesthetics he ostensibly advocates. As Castellano remarks, he also 'maintains an aura of artistic genius', which creates a distance between he and his audience even 'while embarking on situations of social engagement' (2020: 241). Ryder experiences the kind of performance anxiety one might associate with the public lavatory: 'I was unable to ... It's been the same since I was a child. I've never been able to practise unless I had complete, utter privacy' (*U* 341). We might read this as a fear of intimacy, a concern for showing something, revealing oneself (in both senses) when unprepared: the work/artist must be polished before being 'unwrapped', 'shedding layers' publicly. Ishiguro himself wrote 'during self-imposed "lock-in" sessions when he literally would not leave his study morning to night for weeks' (Ennis 2016). Being cloistered poses two related risks to communication. The outside world neither penetrates nor is penetrated, as one character remarks to Steven, 'that sound-proofing in that cupboard of yours … It works both ways' (*N* 131). To shut oneself off from the world is also to shut off the world from oneself. However, the world – as Coleridge, Hume, Descartes, Schopenhauer, Barthes et al. argue – is the fertile ground from which artists take the 'material to feed their imagination' (Oe 1991: 121). Art performed alone for self-gratification brings to mind the thoughts of David Foster Wallace on 1960s metafiction, which he views as 'the act of a lonely solipsist's self-love … It's lovers not being lovers. Kissing their own spine. Fucking themselves' (2009: 332). Wallace's concern here is that writing that is inbent, self-directed and isolated cannot serve a bridging function of offering 'imaginative access to other selves' (McCaffery 2011: 22).

IV

Ryder has been called upon by Pederson and the city council to harmonize a community divided by fundamental and seemingly irresolvable disagreements about modern art. As Ryder tells Sophie, the citizens 'don't understand the first thing about modern music and if you leave them to themselves, it's obvious, they'll just get deeper and deeper into trouble' (*U* 37). Artistic differences arise, which create and sustain deep wounds between factions. For Lefebvre, all societies are subject to these states of eurythmia (accord, alliance) and arrythmia (discord, disharmony). *The Unconsoled* dramatizes Lefebvre's hypothesis that 'alliance supposes harmony between different rhythms; conflict supposes arrythmia', and his contention that 'intervention through rhythm' can 'strengthen or re-establish eurhythmia' (2019: 78). Unfortunately for Ryder, the failure of his mission to establish such harmony is somewhat inevitable, given the city's predilection for 'modern' art. As Ortega y Gasset writes, modernism is wilfully unconducive to community building because it is not simply unpopular but deliberately 'anti-popular'; he goes on to argue that it even has 'the masses against it', precisely because, as Ryder correctly suggests, 'the mass of the people, does not *understand it*' (1972: 6). For Ortega y Gasset, this is not an unwanted side-effect; rather, modern art is conceived with the specific intention of creating such a divide in society, between those who understand and those who do not, what he terms the class of 'the illustrious and the vulgar' (1972: 7). According to John Carey, Ortega y Gasset 'welcomes this process' for its ability to create rifts in a population bifurcated into the 'intellectuals and the masses'

(1992: 17). If we agree with Ortega y Gasset that modern art is definitionally divisive, then the failure of Ryder's project, predicated on using modern art in the service of a reconciliatory relational aesthetics, is utterly inexorable. As Castellano remarks, although Ryder may be perceived (and perceive himself) as 'investing in "social interrelations" at the expense of his "modernist appeal" as a virtuoso pianist', he also illustrates the 'limitations of the "micro-utopian" social transformations predicated by Bourriaud' (2020: 239). Problematically, Ryder is not fully able to forego his own creative ambition, or his ego, and so is prevented from realizing his aims. For Wong, he merely 'symbolizes the possibility of resolution' but 'remains unaware' of how such a role might be met (2005: 77). This failure is neither surprising nor unexpected: the novel works only if we and the city accord acclaim to Ryder as a solitary virtuoso. His art is modernist, individual, even in performance, and his investment in his art as a solo practice disables any possibility for socially recuperative performance. Indeed, one might suggest that the virtuoso is inherently isolated, symbolically separated from the orchestra which acts as little more than a background for the main subject. Ryder, then, is always privileged, and that is the premise upon which his visit is paradoxically grounded, a further fact alongside the divisive method, which from the outset renders artistic consolation a radical impossibility.

We might think of Ryder as what Lefebvre has called a 'Rhythmanalyst', someone (at least in principle) sensitively attuned to the polyrhythmic vibrations of space, the city, the emotions, society. Perhaps Ryder believes he has the ability to '"listen" to a house, a street, a town, as an audience listens to a symphony' and, in so doing, to re-establish a lost harmony (Lefebvre 2019: 32). Ryder is an accomplished listener, overhearing not simply conversations behind walls and in distant rooms, but even the thoughts of the conversers. Lefebvre suggests that 'once one discerns relations of force in social relations and relations of alliance, one perceives their link with rhythm' (2019: 78). *The Unconsoled* construes this literally. Christoff is the perceived cause of the city's disharmony. Originally 'celebrated', 'flattered' by the town which 'made it clear we looked to him for enlightenment and initiative'; they concede to Ryder that at 'least some of the responsibility for what happened lies with us' (*U* 98). It was after a rather 'cold', 'functional' rendition of 'Kazan's *Grotesqueries for Cello and Three Flutes*' that it became time for the cultural elite, persons in 'positions of influence', much like *An Artist of the Floating World*'s Ono, to 'own up to our error, however far-reaching the implication' (*U* 101–2). In many ways the novel is a modern retelling of the absurd conflicts that beset the Lilliputians in Jonathan Swift's satirical masterpiece *Gulliver's Travels* (1726). The two factions, the 'Tramecksan and Slamecksan', disagree violently over 'the high and low heels of their shoes, by which they distinguish themselves' (2004: 53). Worse, they have been involved in a protracted war with their neighbour Blefescu over whether or not one should break a boiled egg at the large or small end. The current political crisis faced by the community in *The Unconsoled* is entirely attributable to an aesthetic assessment (certainly justification for Plato's expulsion of poets and musicians from the ideal Republic). However, this discord merely reflects fashion, intergenerational transition; as Lefebvre comments, the 'relationship between music and society changes with *eras* and societies themselves' (2019: 74). If generations play games by different rules, they play also from different scores.

Typically for many of Ishiguro's anachronistic characters, Christoff finds himself violently separated from the aesthetic, political, social context in which he was formed. To a degree, his tragic flaw is the artistic integrity which at first drew the attention of the city's leaders. However, he shares with *Nocturne*'s Steven a belief that the problem lies not with the music or musician, but rather the uneducated audience:

> To be perfectly fair, it's not their fault. The modern forms, they're so complex now. Kazan, Mullery, Yoshimoto. Even for a trained musician such as myself, it's hard now, very hard … They're out of their depth, they'll never understand how modern music works. Once it was simply Mozart, Bach, Tchaikovsky. Even the man in the street could make a reasoned guess about that sort of music. But the modern forms! How can people like this, untrained, provincial people, how can they ever understand such things, however great a sense of duty they feel towards the community? … They can't distinguish a crushed cadence from a struck motif. Or a fractured time signature from a sequence of vented rests. (*U* 185–6)

Once more we find support for Ortega y Gasset and Ryder's contention that modern art is definitionally, deliberately beyond the limited understanding of the culturally uninitiated masses. Presumably, Ishiguro has in mind John Cage, Philip Glass (one piece in the novel is called *Glass Passions*), Terry Reilly, Julius Eastman, the archetypal minimalist composers who appeared in the 1950s, instigating a revolution in music. Christoff may be perfectly correct: Ligeti, Reilly, Cage are notoriously complex, rejecting melody, formal constraints, often even recognizable instruments (or sound at all in Cage's infamous 4'33). For Ortega y Gasset, difficulty is the essence of modern art and its endeavour to challenge the 'profound injustice of the assumption that men [*sic*] are actually equal' (1972: 7). Ortega y Gasset and Christoff's troubling elitism, prejudice against 'untrained, provincial people', consolidates the already present 'profound interrelation' of '*fascism* and *modern art*' that Potter and Antliff have written of (Antliff 2002: 148). Congressman Lewis in *The Remains of the Day* also thinks that the modern moment is too sophisticated for amateurs, informing Darlington's conference guests that they are 'a bunch of naive dreamers. And if you didn't insist on meddling in large affairs that affect the globe, you would actually be charming' (*RD* 102). The reoccurrence of the key terms of Ishiguro's aesthetico-political debate, 'naïve' and 'charming', is not coincidental. Christoff too has come to believe that modern music, as modern politics, is too nuanced for amateur audiences, and that professionals are required now to mediate between art and its reception; 'It's not their fault music has become so difficult and complicated. It's unreasonable to expect anyone in a place like this to comprehend it' (*U* 186). We are reminded here of Shigeo, yet another character-in-trace, telling Ogata that he 'shouldn't be blamed for not realizing the true consequences of your actions'. At once conciliatory, consolatory and condescending.

Ryder has a tendency to forget his own purpose in the town or to conflate various purposes. After being invited to speak with Christoff and his colleagues (his own agitprop community), he takes the opportunity to critique Christoff's use of modern music, implying that Christoff lacks the courage of his experimental convictions:

> These failures of nerve are, in my experience, very often associated with certain other unattractive traits. A hostility towards the introspective tone, most often characterised by an over-use of the crushed cadence. A fondness for pointlessly matching fragmented passages with each other. And at the more personal level, a megalomania masquerading behind a modest and kindly manner. (*U* 202)

Ryder comes back precisely to those devices which Christoff mentions as being beyond the understanding of his 'provincial' audience. Here, though, his acolytes form an alternative community around Ryder's more radical vision, appearing to think, remarkably similarly to Eloise's repeated disillusionment with teachers ('someone to help me, he's one of us'), that 'yes, yes, here at last is someone who really knows', in response to an excited Ryder's suggestion, in conflict with Christoff, that a 'pigmented triad has no intrinsic emotional properties. In fact, its emotional colour can change significantly not only according to context, but according to volume. This is my personal opinion' (*U* 198). 'No one spoke,' he recalls, 'but the impact of my statement was discernible. One by one, hard gazes turned towards Christoff' (*U* 198). His listeners are impressionable, eager to be guided, even if that means misguided. Ironically, Ryder goes on to implicate himself – he is indeed a megalomaniac masquerading as a modest and self-deprecating diplomat. Despite being in town to 'fill the cracks in the social bond', his ego encourages him to misuse relational aesthetics to form a faction which, rather than healing rifts, creates further or compounds existing rifts (tearing the rug, as it were).

Ryder's is one of three main attractions at the planned prestigious concert. Once prominent conductor but now disgraced alcoholic, Brodsky has been rehabilitated by Hoffman for a performance which he hopes will reunite him with his love Miss Collins while also settling the 'unsettled' community. Brodsky's daring, possibly foolhardy choice for a re-entry onto the cultural scene is *Verticality*, a notoriously complex modern composition. In the beginning, he impresses with his sensitivity, his ability to tease out from the music the 'peculiar life-forms hiding just under the shell' (*U* 492). Brodsky exploits the 'looser form', perhaps in the manner that Ishiguro does in this, his most experimental fiction. Indeed, this description of the 'peculiar life-forms' might be applied equally well to *The Unconsoled*. Brodsky is carried away by the 'sordid' perversity of his own performance and loses touch with the audience who begin to leave, and the orchestra who begin to rebel. Taking things 'too far', Ryder notices that 'a disaffinity between a conductor and his musicians had entered the orchestra's sound' (*U* 491). Relentless in his pursuit (like Melville's Ahab in his search for his own peculiar nemesis beneath the ocean's surface), Brodsky's conducting 'took on a manic quality and the music veered dangerously towards the realms of perversity', ultimately ending in a catastrophic disaffinity (*U* 491–2).[9] Brodsky confirms Miss Collins's suspicions that he will 'never be able to serve the people of this city, even if they wanted you to. Because you care nothing for their lives. That's the truth of it. Your music will only ever be about that silly little wound' (*U* 499). She shouts that 'you were never a real musician', only 'a charlatan. A cowardly, irresponsible fraud' (*U* 499). Collins returns us to the central concern of the novel and Ishiguro's ongoing preoccupation with the arts, one that we see in *Nocturnes* with Steven, Sonja and Tilo, Eloise and Tibor, and in *An Artist of the Floating World*: Is art a personal exploration of form, a purely aesthetic endeavour, a political tool, or simply a mode of entertainment? However, modern music is not suited to such a task. Yugin Teo notes that the city's 'inhabitants long for art to mean something positive regarding their collective hopes for the future'; unfortunately, they look in the wrong place for an aesthetic experience that can 'traverse cultures rather than being associated with any one culture' (2014: 102). One might equally suggest that Brodsky sacrifices his romantic life for his art, which is here in its purest form, personal, expressive, radical and, ultimately, fatal. If, as Ortega y Gasset comments, 'concern with the human element of the work is strictly incompatible with aesthetic gratification', or 'true artistic enjoyment', Brodsky's audience are incapable of directing 'their attention to the work of art itself', seeking instead the absent 'human sensibility' (Ortega y Gasset 1972: 68; 11).

Somewhat naïve, Hoffman nonetheless offers the most idealistic conception of the joys of music. Talking with Ryder, he declares:

> How beautiful it must be inside your head, Mr Ryder! How I would love to be able to accompany you on the journey you will embark on the moment your fingers touch the keys. But of course, you will go where I can't possibly follow. How I envy you, sir! (*U* 344–55)

Music, as understood by Hoffman, is delight, sublime, a truly glorious gift. However, the public have access only to those moments selected by the artist, and so Hoffman, forever outside, must await the product. Of course, we have been immersed inside Ryder's head for the duration of the novel and have witnessed his chaos, distraction, narcissism, self-interest and anger. Perversely, *The Unconsoled* is a comment on the failure of the experimental that takes place in Ishiguro's most complex, challenging, unapproachable novel, 'a blot on the landscape' which 'many reviewers loathed' as Rachel Cooke comments (2011). Nicholas Wroe recalls that the novel 'left readers and reviewers baffled and occasionally angry. Critic James Wood went so far as to claim the book had "invented its own category of badness"' (2005). Amit Chaudhuri, taking aim at Ishiguro's (perceived) imprecise imitation of Kafka, concludes a survey of the work with the simple claim that 'the novel is a failure' (1995). An argument could very easily be made, elsewhere, that Kafka does not have a monopoly on the kind of defamiliarization with which his name has become associated, that only a reading lacking nuance could find Ishiguro's work an imitation (Bernhard, Robbe-Grillet, Abe, Lewis Carroll are much more useful points of comparison). Salmon argued at the height of the modernist period 'that our consciousness is' becoming 'more complex' in modern life, that our 'imaginative elements crave a different measure of utterance. The old set forms suited their more simple and definite purpose' (1925: 21). But, often those most enigmatic and unfathomable works affect us most, haunting us like recurring dreams permeating the porous boundary between the imaginary and the real: As Ishiguro has written of Franz Kafka's *The Trial* (in an appropriately watery metaphor of uncharted depths, things beneath the surface), 'This book is so deep and mysterious, it is almost unfathomable. the [*sic*] metaphors are so unspecified, and yet at the same time, seem so pertinent, that one coul [*sic*] drive oneself mad thinking of applications, or interpretations' (Tisdale 2015). Perhaps the saddest music in the world, the saddest writing, is that which no one hears or understands. Whether purely aesthetic or deeply political, if we ask with Bell 'What might Art do for Society?' we might also conclude that it can 'leaven it; perhaps even redeem it: for Society needs redemption' (1914: 276). For Lefebvre, music 'brings compensation for the miseries of everydayness, for its deficiencies and failures' (2019: 75). The arts can inspire community, forge bonds between disparate groups, but only if that art is relational, committed to others often at the cost of the art itself and the artist's own needs. However, Ishiguro warns in *An Artist of the Floating World*; *Never Let Me Go*; and *The Unconsoled* about overburdening art, expecting from it too much. As Miss Lucy wisely tells Tommy, 'You'll get a lot from it, just for yourself' (*NLMG* 106).

Notes

1 He does sneak 'Axl rose' into *The Buried Giant* (173).
2 Guy Maddin's dizzying reworking of *The Saddest Music in the World* (2003) beautifully transfigures the ethereal edgelessness of Ishiguro's 'dim torch narrative mode' and, although departing in significant ways from the screenplay, remains sensitive to the atmospherics. I comment on this in more detail in 'Screenplays and Film Scripts', in *The Cambridge Companion to Kazuo Ishiguro*, ed. Andrew Bennett (Cambridge: Cambridge University Press, forthcoming).

3   The fact that Ishiguro relies on gradual impasto might account for the less positive reception of his shorter works.
4   In some ways, Stevens in his search for greatness is a parody of Bloom who tries from his own ethnocentric position 'to confront greatness directly' in his efforts to define the 'great' writer (Bloom 1994: 3).
5   What is most noteworthy in this response is Ishiguro's use of idiomatic phrases (buttoned up, bitter end, etc.), which are so glaringly absent in his fictions.
6   I develop this idea in 'Empathy and the Ethics of Posthuman Reading', in *Kazuo Ishiguro*, ed. Peter Sloane and Kristian Shaw (Manchester: Manchester University Press, forthcoming).
7   At the time of writing, no use of Bourriaud had been made in relation to this work, but in the intervening period, Carlos Garrido Castellano published an article making the connection while also drawing out the failures of the movement which he attributes, interestingly, to neoliberalism's appropriation of the arts.
8   Oddly, and possibly purely by coincidence with *AFW*, Ryder is the name of an American journalist (David Warren Ryder, 1892–1975) who was imprisoned for funding Japanese propaganda in 1942.
9   This entire sequence is reminiscent of the dancehall scene in *Back to the Future*, as Marty McFly takes the guitar playing too far, and the other musicians and the audience look on with the 'incredulity, distress, even disgust' that Ryder sees in Brodksy's performance (*U* 494).

Chapter 4

ARCHITEXT

Ishiguro's painterly, musical narratives are negative phenomena, emerging from the interstitial spaces between a series of overlapping sketches and movements which do little more than gesture towards a perpetually potential canvas, an unfinished symphony. Ishiguro is also a builder, of sorts, exploiting an architectonic poetics to construct intricately designed textual spaces from which 'tangled knots of emotion [rise] languidly to the surface', as Ryder might say (*U* 357). Analogies between architecture and music are not new. Indeed, as Theodor Adorno laments in the preamble to a lecture on the two forms, the 'common elements between music and architecture have been discussed repeatedly, almost to the point of ennui' (1997b: 5). It is not just music, however, but also the literary work. Enamoured with the 'armature' of 'reinforced concrete' which made it possible for 'the architectural ensemble to free itself from arborescent models', Gilles Deleuze and Felix Guattari suggest that in this paradigm of 'different sections and variable intervals', 'the literary or musical work has an architecture' which, like a contemporary building, 'holds heterogeneities together without their ceasing to be heterogeneous' (2005: 329). Like modernist poetics, modern materials' peculiar qualities enable the construction of discrete structures while resisting homogeneity, in the same way that Ishiguro's (modernist) novels are composed of 'innumerable atoms', multiple often-conflicting viewpoints which never fully coalesce into a (realist) singularity, 'as if their true resolution took place in some as yet invisible dimension', as J. G. Ballard might say (2014: 2).

In Yi-Fu Tuan's more affective reading, while structurally analogous, language and architecture are also uniquely attuned to human emotion: 'The built environment, like language, has the power to define and refine sensibility' (2018: 107). David Spurr also identifies a deep interconnectedness between the two art forms and their sensitivity to 'human existence':

> Architecture, as the art of building, gives concrete form to the external world according to the structures of imagination; whereas literature, as the art of written language, gives symbolic form to the same world. In their respective manners architecture and literature are potentially the most unlimited of all

art forms in their comprehension of human existence itself, and this fact alone justifies the task of putting them into relation with one another. (2012: 3)

Although manipulating different materials, both give rise to a 'tangible world that articulates experiences … individual as well as collective', aiding our 'comprehension' of the human condition (Tuan 2018: 100). In this sense, architecture, like literature, is a phenomenal gesture towards its own ineffable noumenal ground. Intriguingly, reading itself relies on a process that developmental psychologists refer to as 'ideational scaffolding', which is 'a high-level schema' in the mind with cognitive 'slots into which some of the specific information described' in a text will fit, helping 'the reader determine which are the important text elements' (Anderson et al. 1978: 438, 434). We might return here to Martin Heidegger's suggestion that we encounter and make sense of the world through an 'imagined framework added by our representation' (2011: 108). Ishiguro's novels play explicitly with ideational scaffolding; we are 'drip-fed little pieces of information' in Ishiguro's words, or 'told and not told' as Tommy has it, before a schema for the revealed information's significance emerges during, and often after, reading the books (*The Guardian*, 2006). *Never Let Me Go*, *The Unconsoled* and *The Buried Giant* foreground the profound absence of frameworks of meaning and their gradual, devastating emergence from the texts' intricate structures (the revelation of donations, Axl and Beatrice's visit to their son, Ryder and we come to realize gradually the nature of his past in the apparently foreign city). The dilemma faced by each of his characters in the present is that, within sociopolitically and personally reconstructed frameworks, they must review their pasts and retroactively slot details into a schema which was at the time unavailable. It is for this reason that turning points arise only in retrospect; they present themselves as insignificant because the schema within which they accrue meaning has yet to evolve.

Ishiguro comments often during interviews on his compositional process, insisting that each of his works begins with a concept, before the appropriate structure is designed and subsequently carefully erected. We might think of *Never Let Me Go*, a work for which he 'was looking for a situation to talk about the whole aging process, but in such an odd way that we'd have to look at it all in a new way' (Wong and Crummett 2008: 213). Cloning and bioharvesting provided Ishiguro with a suitable metaphorical structure to defamiliarize the terrifyingly mundane (Wood's 'bland') horrors of ageing and death, in what Rosemarie Garland-Thomson has called 'a subtle and complicated exploration of our psycho-emotional response to mortality' (2017). Reminiscing about *An Artist of the Floating World*, Ishiguro recalls that 'I knew I'd need a much larger, more complex architecture to build the idea into the novel I could already see, tantalisingly, in my imagination' (*The Guardian*, 2016). For Ishiguro, a novel's shape, its 'concrete' form, is determined by a generative idea that acts as the armature (which is, perversely, hidden from view behind the trivial façade, emerging for the reader during reading, as the ideational scaffolding).

Understood as such, he is something of a functionalist, pragmatically structuring textual space around the emotional and conceptual requirements of the inhabitant. In order to house the evasive ambiguity that has come to be so typical of his gestural poetics, his fictional architectures mirror the meandering, digressive, labyrinthine narratives. Critics have continued the metaphor: Writing of *When We Were Orphans*, Philip Hensher remarks that Ishiguro's 'virtues are all architectural ones'; for Tim Adams, Ishiguro is 'an architect of singular, self-enclosed worlds' (Hensher 2000; Adams 2005). Ishiguro's novels are edifices with misleading corridors, hastily constructed semi-opaque partitions, areas of light and darkness (the chiaroscuro), suffused with memory reactivated through daydream, resulting in a beguilingly distinctive architexture.

It is not simply on the level of form, however, that Ishiguro exploits the symbolic potency of architecture and its acute sensitivity to human emotion. Each of Ishiguro's narratives and narrators is attached (almost umbilically) to iconic structures which are at once material (they represent buildings) and symbolic (those buildings manifest expressionistically the novel's central concerns).[1] Each, whether Darlington Hall, Hailsham or The Warren, sustains tenuous dreams of home, belonging, community while also memorializing the emergent loss or absence of feelings of domesticity as the characters come to realize that these were never homes at all. Home, in this sense, was always a forlorn dream. As Gaston Bachelard has written, the 'house we were born in is more than an embodiment of home, it is also an embodiment of dreams' (1994: 15). Ishiguro's gestural poetics actuates daydreams, the imagination, misty memory and so seems peculiarly apposite for his metaphorical use of buildings, more particularly the concept of home. Ishiguro has spoken of the importance of Proust's *À la Recherche du Temps Perdu* to his early writing (although he was not taken with the work as a whole). Confined to bed with a cold, he 'went over' the Combray sections 'again and again' in a 'key turning point in [his] writing life' (*The Guardian*, 2016). These passages are fruitful, here too:

> But in my dreams of Combray ... I leave not a stone of the modern edifice standing, I pierce through it and 'restore' the Rue des Perchamps. And for such reconstruction memory furnishes me with more detailed guidance than is generally at the disposal of restorers; the pictures which it has preserved – perhaps the last surviving in the world to-day, and soon to follow the rest into oblivion – of what Combray looked like in my childhood's days; pictures which ... traced their outlines upon my mind before it vanished. (1943: 228)

Dreamed reapprehension is figured as an ideational deconstruction of the 'modern edifice' to uncover, 'restore' the overwritten original. Like Combray, Darlington Hall and Hailsham have 'traced their outlines' imagistically in Kathy and Stevens's impressionable psychic infrastructure at the precise moment of their spiritual, if not structural, collapse. Unlike blueprints or precise architectural drawings (objective, photographs), mental images (subjective, sketches) incorporate dream-memory into the material edifice, which comes to be haunted by the lost past and imagined futures which, certainly for Kathy and Stevens, never materialize. During the disintegration of her proxy family, Kathy remarks with touching naivete that 'I'll have Hailsham with me, safely in my head, and that'll be something no one can take away' (*NLMG* 281). However, even if, as Tuan suggests, home evokes 'enchanted images of the past', these images of domesticity housed safely in our minds, Ishiguro illustrates, are likely to be entirely fictitious (2018: 144). Kathy's Hailsham is not a clone-conditioning experiment but a fabulated family home nourished by fertile childhood imagination. Stevens and Kathy witness the end of their respective eras, the still-frame collapse of various deeply held illusions, documented through a series of sketches of the buildings which sustain memories of hopes past. These spaces, like Axl and Beatrice's warren, Ono's prestigious house, Ryder's hotel, are as enigmatic and symbolically laden as the narrative structures which they inhabit while also being equally partial, unreliable.

Ishiguro's architectural spaces problematize the idea of 'home', of domestic 'dwelling'. Although often inextricably tethered by intricate memory skeins and complex emotional networks to what might be described as proxy-homes, his characters are nevertheless 'homeless' (Herr Bremann in *RD* is literally 'homeless for some time').[2] They are, as Ching-Chih Wang titles her study of 'strangers' in Ishiguro's novels, 'floating characters in a floating world'. This both explains and is explained by the fact that Ishiguro rarely writes about recognizable urban spaces, communities; his characters live as outsiders in hotels, in institutions, as servants in others' homes. As Barry Lewis identifies in his important monograph, 'the main characters in Ishiguro's novels live in houses that are not quite homes' (2000: 7). This is eminently suitable for, and perhaps a knowing comment on, the novel form, which itself is 'like no other, an expression of ... transcendental homelessness' (Lukacs 1971: 41). Hailsham is not a home, of course (unless in the euphemistic institutional sense of a care home, children's home, etc.), the naïve clones merely find temporary refuge before transferring to transitional cottages that prepare the way for completion; Darlington is both home and work, Stevens (a house in motion) adapting his personal and professional persona (are they the same thing?) to the needs of the Master; living in hotels (his vagrant state's causal correlate), Ryder searches with Boris and Sophie for home future and past, Sophie's hopeless hope that 'once I find a proper home for us ... then everything will go better'; Axl and Beatrice are pushed to 'the outer fringes' of the warren in their senescence, no longer productive, they are literally expelled like pathogens from the organistic hive (*BG* 89). If, for Bachelard, 'a house constitutes a body of images that give mankind proofs or illusions of stability', necessarily the absence of home experienced by these characters must profoundly undermine this imagined stability (1994: 17). Visitors proliferate in Ishiguro's novels, which feature relatives in spare rooms, childhood friends, party guests, hotel clients, each redolent of transience and the loss of 'dwelling', manifesting a kind of existential betweenness.

The most influential contribution to the poetics of home is Bachelard's *The Poetics of Space* (1957), a seminal study of the symbolic and ontological import of what he refers to as the 'oneiric house'. In this 'phenomenology of the imagination', Bachelard introduces the term 'topoanalyis', which he defines as 'the systematic psychological study of the site of our intimate lives' (1994: 80). Bachelard argues that houses support Being on the most profound ontological level. Although we might leave our homes, he suggests, those psycho-architectures with their uniquely calibrated dream-memories never quite leave us (they may remain, as Kathy hopes, 'safely in [our] head'). Jeff Malpas summarizes that, for Bachelard, the 'life of the mind is given form in the places and spaces in which human beings dwell, and those places are taken themselves to influence human memories, feelings, and thoughts' (2018: 6). Bachelard is concerned with the idiosyncratic qualities which he attributes to the house of birth. In Ishiguro's writing, these qualities are amenable to transference from one structure to another (they can, paradoxically, be transient, mobile). In this reading, not tied to a single material structure, 'home' is an epiphenomenal substance, an emotional conceptual admixture which adheres to, inheres within the absent dweller. Kathy, Stevens, Axl and Beatrice neither leave nor are left by Hailsham, Darlington or the warren:

> The house we were born in becomes imbued with dream values which remain after the house is gone. Centers of boredom, centers of solitude, centers of daydream group together to constitute the oneiric house which is more lasting than the scattered memories of the birthplace. (1994: 17)

Even in the advent of the demolition (and scattering) of the material place of birth, it persists ideationally in the oneiric house which 'holds childhood motionless' (Bachelard 1994: 5). This imaginary structure that 'exists for each of us' is a 'house of dream-memory, that is lost in the shadows of a beyond of the real past' (Bachelard 1994: 15). Not only is it *for* each of us, but *in* each; the home that previously encapsulates one's dreams becomes encapsulated in one's dreams. Each of Ishiguro's central characters occupies and is (pre) occupied by an 'oneiric house', one that is lost or in the process of being lost, yet recorded in and inspiring later dream-memory (a peculiarly apt description of Ishiguro's stories). It is often the felt loss of the oneiric house and its symbolic value which textures the narratives with diffuse, inescapable mourning. If, as Bachelard suggests, 'memories are motionless, and the more securely they are fixed in space, the sounder they are', then the absence of home might account for the wayward recall so distinctive of Ishiguro's writing (1994: 9). Yugin Teo makes a similar suggestion that 'home provides the elements that allow for the chronicling of an individual's life history, and it is where an individual's memories always return to' (2014: 73). Memory is not so much unreliable as unanchored, vagrant.

Many of Ishiguro's characters have been described as homeless. As Timothy Wright has suggested, his characters 'embody a more modernist sense of being-at-home nowhere' (2014: 84). Wright enigmatically implies a peculiar comfort in this domestic 'nowhere' (oneiric homelessness, perhaps). This concern with homelessness is unsurprising, given Ishiguro's background as a social worker:

> At formative points in my growing up, I did social work. I worked in community development in Scotland for a short while and I worked with homeless people in London for two or three years. Those periods of experience did go into my first novels, but not in a direct way. I was never tempted to write about the homelessness scene in a realistic way. I felt a bit guilty about this, but I used to work in a homeless hostel in west London ... It certainly helped in the way I look at characters and to some extent the way I create the worlds in my novels. (Doran 2016)

Expressing the condition of homelessness is crucial to Ishiguro's novels, indirectly in most cases, but in others more direct, in turn necessitating his vagrant architexture. During interview with Oe, he remarked that he considers himself 'a kind of homeless writer' (Oe 1991: 115). What is so disconcerting for his narrators is that they *feel* a sense of homeliness, one which is itself ungrounded, homeless. In this chapter, I draw out the symbolism of Ishiguro's most iconic architecture: through readings of Darlington Hall, Hailsham, Masuji Ono's house, the warren, Ryder's hotel and the ruined or dilapidated buildings that linger in decay on his landscape's hazy peripheries, I argue that these structures play fundamental roles both in their specific narrative occurrence and in Ishiguro's gestural poetics. They sustain characters, offering 'enjoyment of the condition of being bounded in a spatial environment while at the same time being free or mobile within those bounds' (Louis Hammer 1981: 385). This sense of being bound (tethered) yet mobile is important; many of Ishiguro's novels are road trips (Kathy drives as she reminisces, as does Stevens), but as Kathy, Stevens, Axl and Beatrice break off from Hailsham, Darlington and the warren in search of past and future, they carry with them these spaces in imagistic and emotional trace, in the case of the first two becoming ambassadors for their idealized (mis)conceptions. Structures both grand and humble, which are the core symbolic centre of every Ishiguro narrative, are both material and ideational, generated by and generating dream-memories which simultaneously occupy and are occupied by their transient inhabitants. Many narratives are motivated by fantasies of returning to a home that was always imaginarily felt to be present in buildings not designed for the domestic. From this confusion arises what Lewis refers to as the 'tug-of-war between a sense of homelessness and being "at home"' (2000: 3). Perhaps this is another of Ishiguro's engagements with the politics of modernism, as

David Spurr argues, 'for modern architects and writers alike, the traditionally idealized concept of dwelling is a false promise, one that modern art forms reject in order to strive for a more authentic definition of human existence in its spatial dimension' (2012: 53). Drawing on the salient relationship between architecture and textuality, he suggests that 'literature and architecture share a profoundly ambiguous and yet productive response to' modernity (Spurr 2012: 51). Both are homes, of sorts, each reluctantly housing and being housed by characters adrift in unhomely modernity.

I

The importance of architectural anchors to Ishiguro's work emerges in his debut novel, a spatiotemporally itinerant narrative loosely tethered between three domestic spaces: Sachiko's hut, Etsuko's Japanese apartment and Etsuko's home in the English countryside of the narration's present. Etsuko's two homes act as fixed spatiotemporal coordinates for her recollected narrative and that of her present. The cottage, on the other hand, functions as a malleable ideational mediator between these other two, a multidimensional portal encapsulating Etsuko's (and Japan's) past, present and future in a projected space of pure (possibly therapeutic) potential. Etsuko is comparatively fortunate, living in a newly constructed building on the symbolic and literal edge of a bulldozed wasteland in post-war Nagasaki:

> The occupants of the apartment blocks were much like ourselves – young married couples, the husbands having found good employment with expanding firms ... Each apartment was identical; the floors were tatami, the bathrooms and kitchens of a Western design. They were small and rather difficult to keep cool during the warmer months, but on the whole the feeling amongst the occupants seemed one of satisfaction. And yet I remember an unmistakable air of transience there, as if we were all of us waiting for the day we could move to something better. (*PVH* 11–12)

Once again, we see evidence of the growing influence of Western design on post-war Japan that Ono mistakenly interprets as yet another symptom of Japanese 'weakness of will'. This trend began much earlier; as Peter McNeil has argued, the 'adoption of western-style architecture ... commenced in the Meiji period (1868–1911)' (1992: 282).[3] Etsuko's small apartment creates a sense of 'satisfaction', not quite happiness or homeliness but a more utilitarian feeling of temporary sufficiency. However, the space, though new and newly occupied, is suffuse with the 'transience' so typical of Ishiguro's dwellings. Like a waiting room, the space encourages thoughts of leaving, its identical newness deflecting attempts to settle. It is not simply a case of an otherwise settled person feeling unsettled in waiting; Etsuko is existentially unsettled by a space which is not, for her, conducive to permanence, futurity, dwelling. Etsuko's desire to 'move to something better' seems, at first, to do with accommodation, but in fact crystalizes the novel's key theme of geographical relocation (Sachiko, Etsuko, Keiko, Niki, all move and desire to move). Sachiko wants to emigrate to America because she feels 'it's a better place for a child to grow up … life's much better for a woman in America', but we know, of course, that she wants to follow her American lover, to pursue her dreams at the expense of her daughter (*PVH* 46). Etsuko too reflects on her Japanese past from the felt security of her detached, idyllic English house. The apartment then becomes a metaphorical expression of a desire to settle elsewhere in a permanence obviated by the precarious transience of post-war Japan. Troublingly, these relocations often end in tragedy.

Etsuko's pristine new build is in stark architectural contrast with her neighbour's dilapidated peripheral dwelling, yet each is felt to be temporary. Sachiko lives both out of time and out of space, enigmatically, hauntingly liminal in a cottage which belongs to an era irrecoverably passed (and here in no danger of being romanticized as some idealistic remnant from a better time):

> One wooden cottage had survived both the devastation of the war and the government bulldozers. I could see it from our window, standing alone at the end of that expanse of wasteground, practically on the edge of the river. It was the kind of cottage often seen in the countryside, with a tiled roof sloping almost to the ground. Often, during my empty moments, I would stand at my window gazing at it. (*PVH* 11–12)[4]

These diametrically opposed structures necessarily house (or at least temporarily contain) what appear, initially, to be different (distinct and dissimilar) characters. Sachiko is worryingly preoccupied with her own clearly ill-fated ambitions of moving to America and is abusively neglectful of her daughter Mariko; Etsuko, pregnant with her own daughter, shows more concern (or recalls showing more concern now, in the aftermath of her daughter's suicide) for Mariko (although both children have similar fates). Sachiko wants to leave the cottage, the city, the country and even appears reluctant to dwell in Etsuko's narrative, always absent or in haste to leave the page she is homeless by virtue of this fact, as opposed simply to her domestic vagrancy. Sachiko's cottage and its inhabitants become memory houses for Etsuko, material manifestations, imaginative explorations of a lingering guilt in the present for her own felt responsibility for the subsequent suicide of the child she carries in this scene (in another transient but formative space). Indeed, the tone of the passages which house the cottage scenes is gothic, revealing a past paradoxically haunted by the retroactive despair of Etsuko's present. What is remarkable in Ishiguro's play with the gothic is that the remembered past is haunted by the narrated present. Etsuko repeatedly projects herself onto Sachiko, Keiko onto Mariko, the cottage standing as an architectural externalization of her internal emotional penumbra. Etsuko displaces, evicts Sachiko, appropriates the lived space of the cottage and its inhabitants for her ideational purposes.

The degradation, the 'stark shabbiness', the 'old and insecure' structure', the 'faint odour of dampness [that] lingered everywhere' are indications both of the material decay of the single surviving pre-war cottage but also of Etsuko's regret-infused memories. Etsuko ports the cottage's atmospheric matrix of loss, regret and hopelessness and re-creates this space in her contemporary home, more specifically in Keiko's bedroom:

> It had been Keiko's fanatically guarded domain for so long, a strange spell seemed to linger there even now, six years after she had left it – a spell that had grown all the stronger now that Keiko was dead … For the two or three years before she finally left us, Keiko had retreated into the bedroom, shutting us out of her life … the rest of us were forbidden entry into her room. At mealtimes I would leave her plate in the kitchen and she would come down to get it, then shut herself in again. The room, I realized, was in a terrible condition. An odour of stale perfume and dirty linen came from within. (*PVH* 53–4)

Reminiscent of a hermit's cell, or even a hotel suite, Keiko's sanctuary absorbs something of the essence both of its occupant and the taut tonal atmospherics created by that presence. Not only are the family shut out of the room, but, according to Etsuko developing a metaphor of exclusions, they are in this way excluded from Keiko's life. Lewis argues that the novel 'plays with the recipe of the paradigmatic European ghost tale'; haunting in this scenario has something to do with traces left behind, spectral, yes, but also sensual, energetic (2000: 31).[5] Keiko's room once more manifests mood, its foreboding spatiality transforming the 'most pleasant' room in the house back into Sachiko's dank foreboding cottage, a connection maintained by the word 'linger'. That word itself is telling; 'To stay behind, tarry, loiter on one's way; to stay on or hang about in a place beyond the proper or usual time, esp. from reluctance to leave it' (*OED*). Lingering involves staying unwanted in places intended for temporary occupancy. Memories of trauma linger in the mind's dark recesses.

Her 'spell' lingering, Keiko leaves 'home' to take up residence in Manchester; alone and far from family, she apparently retreats into yet deeper isolation. Early in the narrative, we discover that she 'had hung herself in her room', one which most likely replicated the one she left at Etsuko's, but which the latter never sees:

> I never saw Keiko's room in Manchester, the room in which she died …
> I have found myself continually bringing to mind that picture – of my daughter hanging in her room for days on end. The horror of that image has never diminished, but it has long ceased to be a morbid matter; as with a

wound on one's own body, it is possible to develop an intimacy with the most disturbing of things. (*PVH* 54)

As we have seen with Ryder and Brodsky, wounds can be nurtured, kept open, sustained and sustaining. There is also a lingering denial in the choice of the passive description of 'in which she died'; Keiko's role was more participatory, and Etsuko ponders the extent of her own responsibility for past action and inaction. Keiko's earlier retreat into self-imposed isolation suggests a chronic depressive episode, and it is little surprise that left alone with no one to replenish the dinner tray that she fatally succumbs to an ennui beyond endurance. Perhaps, like both Sachiko and Etsuko, Keiko saw life as 'just a few empty rooms' and, with Sachiko, would agree that 'I could sit there in and grow old. Other than that there'll be nothing. Just empty rooms, that's all' (*PVH* 171). Etsuko often dwells on the 'emptiness of those long afternoons I spent in that apartment' (*PVH* 99). It is hard, here, to not see this as a comment on female experience, the lingering at home passively waiting for improvement in an era and culture that prevented women's self-actuation (Sachiko is entirely reliant on her American boyfriend). Etsuko's second daughter, Niki, is more 'modern', resistant to marriage and to traditional conceptions of womanhood, with no desire to have 'kids screaming around me' (as they might have during the war (*PVH* 48)).

II

A closed door is a partition that provides both intimacy and seclusion, one that Ishiguro works into many of the most crucial moments in his characters' memories. We might think of Beatrice, on 'the outer fringes of the warren', and the 'barrier' of the 'large wooden frame criss-crossed with branches' that had 'become an object of considerable pride' to her as she and her husband are expelled from the warm centre, possibly after they caused a candle fire (*BG* 6). Pride comes from accepting the enforced exclusion and erecting a barrier between the couple and their persecutors. Doors also act as bidirectional spatial and interpersonal barriers (like the sound-proofed 'cubicle' in 'Nocturnes'), effecting what Bachelard refers to as a 'dialectics of outside and inside', segregating space to create rooms with the quantum uncertainty of a Schrodinger experiment. As Georg Simmel argues, the door forms a 'linkage between the space of human beings and everything that remains outside it' (1997: 67). For Keiko, 'It was the landlady who had opened the door' to find the ghastly decoration, a moment of revelation to which Etsuko returns on sleepless nights, thinking 'how [the landlady] had finally opened the door of that room in Manchester' (*PVH* 54). The definition of lingering takes on a peculiar resonance here: to '*hang* about in a place beyond the proper or usual time'. Multiple potential realities lingered behind the closed door; doors enable the imagination to construct innumerable possible scenarios about the space beyond, each one of which being very real until the moment of observation when the gaze reifies one possible state.

Many momentous events in the lives of Ishiguro's narrators centre around closed doors. Stevens recalls a turning point in his relationship with Miss Kenton, standing in the service corridor outside her room, meditating somewhat incredulously that 'it was not impossible that Miss Kenton, at that very moment, and only a few feet from me, was actually crying' (*RD* 212). Stevens remains, not wanting to 'intrude upon her private grief' (*RD* 176). States of possibility, moments of regret. Stephan, in *The Unconsoled*, attempting to ameliorate Miss Collins's lingering dislike of Brodsky, reminds her of an incident from Brodsky's past, in which his 'father went to listen at the door and heard him sobbing' (*U* 59). In the same novel, Gustav recalls the precise moment at which his 'understanding' with Sophie developed; after she had found her pet hamster dead, he 'became aware that in the living room Sophie was sobbing uncontrollably' (*U* 83). 'Well', he confides in Ryder, 'the door between the bedroom and the living room was closed, and as I say, the radio was up loud, so it would have been perfectly conceivable [possibility] I might not have heard her. So I remained in the bedroom, my ear close to the door, the concert playing behind me' (*U* 83-4). In a pivotal moment in *Never Let Me Go*, Kathy recalls dancing to the eponymous song as Madame was 'standing out there, sobbing and sobbing, staring at me through the doorway' (*NLMG* 71). Banks conflates the literal and figurative, thinking back to his rise to fame when 'many new doors suddenly opened to me; invitations poured in from entirely new sources; those who previously had been no more than pleasant to me exclaimed with great enthusiasm when I entered a room' (*WWO* 19). The opening of figurative doors inflects the opening of literal doors. In another reference to the Americanization of the orient, Banks thinks back to Akira's house, with a pair of 'replica' (skilful, but mock, as Mrs Wakefield might say) Japanese rooms, and 'the doors to these rooms being especially curious; on the outer, "Western" side, they were oak-panelled with shining brass knobs; on the inner, "Japanese" side, delicate paper with lacquer inlays' (*WWO* 72). Confusingly, the western door leads to an eastern room, and vice versa. Banks reminisces about a defining moment in his childhood, as he and Akira encourage one another to enter the frightening domain of Ling Tien: 'For some time yet, though, it was to remain beyond either of us to walk right up to the door, let alone to go through it. By the time we finally entered Ling Tien's room, we were both ten, and it was – although of course I did not know it then – my last year in Shanghai' (*WWO* 93). For Simmel, doors enact a series of hopeful metaphysical possibilities, 'life flows forth out of the door from the limitation of isolated separate existence into the limitlessness of all possible directions' (1997: 68). Banks certainly has such expectations of the world.

These moments behind doors are turning points (hinges are mechanical turning points upon which pivot innumerable possibilities) of central importance, literal and figurative instances of doorways of possibility being closed. Stevens and Gustav miss unrepeated opportunities for reconciliation or deeper union. Kathy's extended deferral results from a single careless moment with the door ajar as she dances; Banks recognizes this event, days before his father's disappearance, as the end of his childhood, the moment at which he crosses a boundary into more adult game playing. Doors are literal and also portals of opportunity that might be missed, as they are by Ryder ushered through a door he 'had not noticed', or Banks's identical door that 'I had not noticed' (*U* 337; *WWO* 221). We might wonder with Bachelard whether 'he who opens a door and he who closes it are the same being' (1994: 224). Perhaps this explains the ambiguity of Robert Frost's meditation on roads not taken: 'Yet knowing how way leads on to way, / I doubted if I should ever come back' (2002: 219). Frost is interested in the consoling illusion that one might be able to revisit roads not taken while also hinting that the decision to choose one path is to irretrievably become another person; the same person cannot pass through the same door twice, neither can she return to the previous moment. Doors are Heraclitan, playing on flux, 'an entire cosmos of the Half-open', offering 'the temptation to open up the ultimate depths of being, and the desire to conquer all reticent beings' so tantalizing yet threatening to Ishiguro's risk-averse narrators, whose stories always involve doors passed but sought frantically thereafter (Bachelard 1994: 222). Bachelard proposes that if 'one were to give an account of all the doors one has closed and opened, of all the doors one would like to re-open, one would have to tell the story of one's entire life' (1994: 224). In passing through doors, and declining others, a multitude of possible selves come into being and vanish from being in the plenum of potentials (1994: 224). As Eliot famously expresses it, 'What might have been and what has been / Point to one end, which is always present. / Footfalls echo in the memory / Down the passage which we did not take / Towards the door we never opened' (2004: 171). For Eliot, Ryder, Frost, Stevens and Gustav, steps are retraced in memory to doors unopened and forever unopenable.

III

Darlington Hall is perhaps the most typical and iconic building in Ishiguro's oeuvre, home once to the now-disgraced Lord Darlington and in the present of narration to the American businessman Mr Farraday (Congressman Lewis in the film), intent on capturing, or at least purchasing, a lingering remnant of the quaint British past. As John J. Su remarks, the 'decline of the estate in *The Remains of the Day* mirrors the decay of the British Empire – at a time when ever larger sections of Darlington Hall are being closed off and dust-sheeted, Great Britain finds itself shedding its colonies' (2002: 563). At one point, Farraday asks Stevens for reassurance that 'this is a genuine grand old English house, isn't it? That's what I paid for' (*RD* 124). Stevens thinks of

Darlington as England, telling Farraday that 'it has been my privilege to see the best of England over the years, sir, within these very walls' (*RD* 4). For Farraday, and more so Stevens, Darlington Hall is associated with a prestige that can be passed on to the building's inhabitant, a belief made more poignant if, as Stevens insists, 'association with a truly distinguished household is a prerequisite of "greatness"' (*RD* 32). Prestige is also important for Ono, who desires 'a house in keeping with our status' and is rewarded by winning what he recalls as 'an auction of prestige' based on 'moral conduct and achievement' to purchase the house of a deceased local dignitary (*AFW* 9). Ono necessarily thinks that such prestige can be imbued by the building and its history, as does Stevens. Each thinks that their association with great houses might act as some form of guarantee of their morality. History spectrally inheres within the spatial, the essence distilled then suffusing the occupant. It is not simply that 'history could well be made under this roof', history saturates space, infiltrating bricks and mortar in a kind of fossilization (*RD* 77). As Spurr writes, the mode of being of literature, like that of architecture, is historical: 'It brings the past down to us in the space of the present' (2012: 3). Like all buildings, Darlington has entered the 'age of electricity and modern heating systems', brought about by Farraday's almost-namesake Michael Faraday. The house is also now too large, with many unused 'dust-sheeted areas' (*RD* 8). Ono's house too, built by famed Akira Sugimura, suffers from the war, this time more directly; areas have been bombed, notably the 'garden corridor' overtaken with 'cobwebs and mould' (much like Sachiko's cottage). Dust-sheeting and war damage are literal, of course, but these figurative closures are also symbolically valent in novels that have to do with covering things up, shutting things off and, in the act of narration and recalling, removing the dust sheets, walking 'the passage which we did not take'.

Darlington Hall might be considered more a spatiotemporal composite of potential spaces overlaid onto the built structure that is 'Darlington Hall', rather than simply a single-material edifice. The stately home, also a domestic home, also a professional lodging, is a virtual space, quantum even, a series of parallel experiential, historical and material domains flickering between possible states while remaining multiply co-present. Darlington Hall's quantum state is peculiarly damaging to Stevens, who is perpetually at work in a professional space which is also simultaneously his only gesture towards a domestic space (like many of Ishiguro's characters, he welcomes as guest his aged father, who is then also employed). As Lewis comments, Stevens attempts valiantly, but ultimately misguidedly, to maintain a 'self-space in which all traces of a personal life have been extinguished' (2000: 94). Tuan discerns a socializing but also existential function of buildings, in that they clarify 'social roles and relations. People know who they are and how they ought to behave when the arena is humanly designed' (2018: 102). For Stevens, however, who lives and labours in the same building, the space is fraught with uncertainties. Such uncertainty accounts for his confusion over whether he is professionally required to respond in kind to Farraday's disconcerting banter: Farraday is at home, Stevens at work *and* quasi-home, Farraday's wordplay an ambiguous invitation to transgress irreconcilably distinct ontological domains in a way that imperils Stevens's fragile personal/professional equilibrium. Erving Goffman discusses such difficulties in *The Presentation of Self in Everyday Life*: 'We find that the performer can be fully taken in by his [sic] own act; he can be sincerely convinced that the impression of reality which he [sic] stages is the real reality' (1956: 10). A further implication of this radical uncertainty of being is that it is categorically impossible for Stevens to form a romantic relationship with Kenton if Darlington is always work. Stevens's private personhood is negated by the space, partially resulting from a constitutional inability to be both person and butler, to shut off one element of his identity from another. Rushdie remarks that 'the butler as liminal figure, standing on the border between the worlds of "upstairs" and "downstairs"' (*The Guardian*, 2012). Certainly, this is true, but Stevens's professional/personal vacillations are more ontological than simply liminal: rather than a singular coherent subject caught between realms, Stevens is multiple immanent subjects oscillating between states (he frequently cries while denying that fact). Stevens never leaves Darlington, and it is the house as both architecture and imaginary that determines his observations over the course of the novel. It is both eternally in his mind in the memories he recounts but is also the point against which he measures the world outside (his ideational scaffolding).

As is the river for Etsuko (more in Chapter 5), the 'butler's pantry' is the vibrating multidimensional portal of Steven's radical uncertainty, which enacts the move from the 'limitation of isolated separate existence into the limitlessness of all possible directions' that Simmel mentions. Stevens thinks of the pantry as 'the heart of the house's operations; not unlike a general's headquarters during a battle [it] must be the one place in the house where privacy and solitude are guaranteed' (*RD* 165). A biological metaphor that runs through the book (as does the military), the 'back corridor' 'serves as a sort of backbone' (*RD* 78). Unknowingly referring back to Keiko's room, Miss Kenton quips that Stevens's pantry is a 'prison cell'; she frequently brings flowers (as one might to a sick relative). But on one such evening when Miss Kenton intrudes, Stevens 'was not in fact engaged in professional matters. That is to say, it was towards the end of the day during a quiet week and I had been enjoying a rare hour or so off duty' (*RD* 165). Stevens cannot take recourse to personal dignity to enforce his right to free time and prevent Kenton crossing a threshold that is not simply a door but an imaginary boundary between work and leisure, because he has no person as such, he is always and only a butler. As Lewis suggests, Stevens's 'commitment to being a butler has almost an existential fervour' (2000: 85). Therefore, he can claim a right to solitude only if the room is professionally vital. He offers the defence that he is reading to improve his language proficiency, asking Kenton repeatedly to not 'invade', continuing the military metaphor, his 'private moments'. As Lewis writes with a suitably martial metaphor, she alone is 'able to pierce the butler's shield of dignity' (2000: 95). The pantry is a battle ground, Stevens's only haven, rudely broken by the playful aggression of Kenton who not only insists on entering but takes the book from Stevens's grasp. In this moment, Stevens recognizes the room's susceptibility to dimensional shift, to quantum plurality: 'Suddenly the atmosphere underwent a peculiar change almost as though the two of us had been suddenly thrust on to some other plane of being altogether' (*RD* 166–7). Christine Berberich, with other critics, sees this as a romantic provocation in which Stevens, although 'pulling away from the intimacy', nonetheless 'reveals the truth' of his feelings but fear about such intimacy (2007: 26). However, it is a far more complex scene: Stevens feels the space's oscillation between private/public, personal/professional in such a way that he and Kenton in this moment are very literally conveyed into 'another dimension altogether', a midway space that is located within but also existing virtually beside the coordinates of the pantry (*RD* 16). This forced intimacy reconfigures the professional space as the transgressed private and so constitutes the single moment in the novel that Stevens, for the briefest second, finds a model of domesticity. His powerfully felt yet inarticulable emotion is simply that of being home; 'it is not easy' for him 'to describe clearly what I mean here' because it invests the pantry with a fleetingly felt homeliness which Stevens has never experienced, and because in this moment he very literally becomes, for a flash outside of time and space, another person, one who lacks the informal vocabulary to express a feeling so deeply uncanny (*RD* 166–7).

This quantum potential of rooms rearises in *The Unconsoled*, a novel in which, as Daniel Bedggood observes, 'the oneiric domain is foregrounded more often' than in any other of Ishiguro's works (2017: 111). On what appears to be his first night in his new hotel, Ryder recognizes the space, but not simply because he has visited before and forgotten:

> I was just starting to doze off when something suddenly made me open my eyes again and stare up at the ceiling ... the sense of recognition growing stronger by the second. The room I was now in, I realised, was the very room that had served as my bedroom during the two years my parents and I had lived at my aunt's house on the borders of England and Wales. (*U* 16)

Even remaining 'highly conscious of how all around the room features had been altered or removed', that 'its dimensions had been enlarged, the cornices had been removed, the decorations around the light fitting had been entirely altered', he is utterly convinced that 'it was unmistakably the same ceiling I had so often stared up at from my narrow creaking bed of those days' (*U* 16). This is typical of the novel, in which, as Lewis notes, 'buildings and landscape keep melting into something else, in a Daliesque way' (2000: 109). It is no coincidence that the realization occurs in the hypnogogic state between waking and sleeping, a kind of dream within a dream (or nightmare) which typifies Ryder's Dissociative Fugue. The feeling is one of home, 'the realisation that after all this time I was once more back in my old childhood sanctuary [the same word that Banks uses of his playroom] caused a profound feeling of peace to come over me' (*U* 17). Ryder takes consolatory recourse to the 'body of images that give mankind proofs or illusions of stability' so seductive in his psycho-geographical drift. If we take this literally, viewing space as materially situated, it is abundantly clear that the room *cannot* be the same room. However, if this is the oneiric house, housed *by* Ryder (safely in his head, as it were), then it is indeed the case that he projects his dream-memory of his childhood room onto the bricks and plaster of the strange room thereby transforming it. The hotel supports such ideational refiguration, which in turn enables retreat to a domain, a sanctuary of peace that may or may not have a real-world correlate. Ryder's memory of a home that never was (he was a guest of his auntie, presumably after his mother left his father and the imploded family home) constitutes an oneiric home, one itself not restricted to or a function of architectural space. A similar event occurs elsewhere (indeed, the word 'recognition' in various forms appears with remarkable frequency in the novel), when Ryder and Boris search for their old dwelling and find themselves in an apartment: 'The room was by now growing steadily more familiar to me', because it resembles his childhood home in Manchester (the trace of Keiko lingers here) which offered hope to 'a nine-year-old ... that a fresh, happier chapter was unfolding for us all' (*U* 214). New space, new family. Of course, we know that this is not to be, and that his parents' fights would continue catastrophically.[6]

Remarkably, Banks has exactly the same (mis)recognition as he is shown around a house by his St Dunstan's school friend Morgan. He recalls early in the narrative his family's 'big white house', making a connection with the oneiric house of birth: 'I am able to bring back that picture very vividly ... a huge white edifice with numerous wings and trellised balconies. I suspect this memory of the house is very much a child's' (*WWO* 51). With Morgan, he apparently rediscovers this house:

> Then finally I stepped through a door and felt something tugging at my memory. It took a few seconds more, but I then recognised with a wave of emotion our old 'library'. It had been greatly altered: the ceiling was much higher, a wall had been knocked through to make the space L-shaped; and where there had once been double doors through into our dining room, there was now a partition against which were stacked more crates of rice wine. But it was unmistakably the same room where as a child I had done much of my homework. (*WWO* 190)

The new owner apologizes to Banks (why would he not, given Banks's global fame) for the changes made, just as the imagined occupant of Boris's old family home does: 'You'll notice straight away how much the place has changed since you were there, and the husband will see this and at first he'll be a little apologetic' (*U* 208). Ryder's 'unmistakably the same ceiling' becomes Banks's 'unmistakably the same room'. It is certainly conceivable that walls are removed, but raising a ceiling is an altogether different task. Banks acknowledges that 'a house undergoes alteration whenever its occupants change', spaces expanding and contracting to suit the needs of the new inhabitants (as they do in Alex Proyas's *Dark City*, 1998). In precisely the same manner as Ryder, Banks 'recognizes' the space despite the absolute lack of any indication that this is the same space at all, the dimensions themselves altered: Memory and emotion are either prompted by a genuine recognition of a profoundly altered space, or evidence Banks's (clearly operating very similarly to Ryder) own dissociative delusional state. He even comments that he could not 'work out at all how the areas through which Morgan and I had just entered related to our old hall' (*WWO* 186). Once again, recognition returns to consciousness the oneiric house at precisely that point which stability is most desired, Banks recalling his childhood, a moment before the collapse of family and the inception of a trauma that induces the homeless state which remains into adulthood. Rooms here are purely ideational, portable and virtual. Just as the architext is suffused with moments of recognition, refiguration, so the architecture within that space becomes imbued with comparable immanence. At stake always, however, is the feeling of homeliness.

IV

Home is a powerfully felt absence throughout *Never Let Me Go*, texturing the already bleak narrative with a loss made more resonant because of the childlike qualities of the story's subjects. Hailsham is *a* home, of sorts, but not home in any meaningful domestic or familial sense (it is, after all, a 'sham'). Hailsham seems, on first reading, to both reader and student to be an elite boarding school, perhaps like St Dunstan's which Banks attends. But, as Rachel Carroll remarks, a 'residential school setting can signify either economic privilege or social marginalisation; belonging to the latter category, Hailsham's legacy in terms of childhood memory is comparable to that of other casualties of reproductive and familial norms: the abandoned, the illegitimate and the disabled child' (2012: 140). Institutions – (care, children's) 'homes' as they often euphemistically called – speak of either great privilege or great deprivation. For Ishiguro, the setting is vital to the novel's themes and the workings of the narrative:

> The boarding school setting, I might add, appealed to me because it struck me as a physical manifestation of the way all children are separated off from the adult world, and are drip-fed little pieces of information about the world that awaits them, often with generous doses of deception – kindly meant or

otherwise. In other words, it serves as a decent metaphor for childhood in general. (*The Guardian*, 2006)

This drip feeding in 'the bubble of innocence', what Tommy refers to as being 'told and not told', is crucial to both veiling and unveiling the novel's sinister armature (Adams 2015). Ironically, Kathy drip-feeds the reader, as she imbibes and replicates the ethos of the building, her carceral home, while also exploiting the text's refusal to provide a schema within which to situate information. Of course, Hailsham is not the home in which she was born because she was not born at all, but rather mechanically produced and decanted in a laboratory (is she an Alpha or a Delta?). Tellingly, the word 'born' is as absent in the text as the nurturing family and traditional home the word connotes. This is troubling too if we agree with Marc Augé that one's 'place of birth is a constituent of individual identity' (2008: 43). Nonetheless, Hailsham is Kathy's only home (although she thinks in the presence of narration that others may be resentful 'about my bedsit'), and it carries much weight with the community of clones less fortunate that she comes to meet in the cottages and recovery centres. Regardless of its new significance, Hailsham maintains the prestige of Darlington and Ono's house; being a 'Hailsham student', in Kathy's ongoing euphemism, 'is enough by itself sometimes to get people's backs up. Kathy H., they say, she gets to pick and choose, and she always chooses her own kind: people from Hailsham, or one of the other privileged estates' (*NLMG* 3–4). What privilege, one may ask.

As is the case for anyone attending a boarding school or residential institution, there comes a time when Kathy must leave the imagined sanctuary of Hailsham. But the memories she has of those comparatively 'normal' childhood times stay with her as she becomes a carer and, after reuniting her proxy family, eventually oversees her friends'/children's/siblings' deaths. Kathy is in a difficult position at the time of narration; 'dominated by memories of an institutionalised childhood', she recognizes the harms perpetrated by Hailsham, but also that it is the closest thing she'll have to a home, its community her only family (Carroll 2012: 134). It is the absence of 'real' family that makes it so hard for her to abandon her fond memories of her proxy siblings and the times they spent at Hailsham. She confides in us that 'there have been times over the years when I've tried to leave Hailsham behind', meditating late in the novel that

> I suppose I lost Hailsham too. You still hear stories about some ex-Hailsham student trying to find it, or rather the place where it used to be. And the odd rumour will go round sometimes about what Hailsham's become these days – a hotel, a school, a ruin. Myself, for all the driving I do, I've never tried to find it. I'm not really interested in seeing it, whatever way it is now. (*NLMG* 4–5, 280)

Like Stevens on his motoring journey, Kathy in her car is all that remains of a unique time in Hailsham's troubled history, a period in which the house gestured towards the ultimately unrealized possibility of a more humanistic treatment of clones. Despite her claim that she has 'lost' Hailsham, Kathy's memoir is firmly anchored to the building, which sits at the heart of her self-narrative (and personal identity) as it does the novel's. It is Kathy who constructs, traces the edifice for us, describing the gardens and grounds, boundaries and fences, rooms and the guardians, the students and their foibles. As the original Combray becomes ideational, so the original Hailsham thrives only in Kathy's dream-memory. Perhaps if people have oneiric houses, as Bachelard suggests, houses also have oneiric occupants which sustain their dreams. Returning again to their intertwining, symbiotic ideational co-extension, Hailsham is Kathy's armature, she its; each is finely integrated into the material and symbolic fabric of the other (she is, after all, one of the organs of the house). Regardless of the biomedical horrors of the reality that gave rise to Hailsham, ex-students seek it out precisely because it was their only home, the single space that offered a sense of homeliness, however tragically misconstrued. Kathy may not attempt to find her Hailsham, yet she does re-create it continually, sustaining the house in her mind just as it supports her sense of self. Goffman argues that if a setting is crucial for the performance of self, characters 'must terminate their performance when they leave it. It is only in exceptional circumstances that the setting, in a sense, follows along with the performers'; Ishiguro's examples are, like Goffman's, exceptional 'dream-like processions' (1956: 13).

V

Hailsham and Darlington Hall seem fixed in and to memorialize very specific periods in their and their occupants' history. Hoffman's hotel, a more public edifice, hosts many histories, both personal and national. As Gustav remarks (to Ryder hoping to contribute to history) with a pride that echoes Stevens's of Darlington, 'There have been events here of great historic interest over the years' (*U* 5). The lobby of the building, which has all the baffling qualities of Kafka's Hotel Occidental, establishes the disorienting atmosphere of the novel, set in what appears to be a composite of post-war European cities:

> The ceiling was low and had a definite sag, creating a slightly claustrophobic mood, and despite the sunshine outside the light was gloomy. Only near the reception desk was there a bright streak of sun on the wall, illuminating an area of dark wood panelling and a rack of magazines in German, French and English. (*U* 3)

This gloomy space captures perfectly the claustrophobia that infiltrates every aspect of this emotionally oppressive and cognitively disconcerting work, burdened with ominous pressures both personal and professional. At other points, Ryder finds himself rehearsing in cramped 'cubicles', a 'hut' for practice so small that he finds his 'back virtually touching the wall behind me' (*U* 356). The lobby is a peculiarly non-descript place, one which, as Siegfried Kracauer comments, 'accommodates all who go there to meet no one. It is the setting for those who neither seek nor find the one who is always sought' (1997: 53). Kracauer's enigmatic description, while perhaps a little bombastic and theological, nevertheless captures something of the plight of a man who inadvertently finds himself on an ill-defined mission of mercy in the midst of memories that time has veiled, remembering finally his hopes for reunion with parents whose visit came many years prior. Like *The Buried Giant*'s warren, an assortment of dwellings 'dug into the hillside, connecting one to the other by underground passages and covered corridors', Ryder's host city is an intricately interconnected matrix of buildings rooted in some odd rhizomatic way to the hotel (*BG* 4). One evening, Ryder, Boris and Sophie drive for some considerable distance away from the hotel for a celebration before Ryder recalls that 'the house adjoined the hotel' (*U* 277). Later, Ryder leaves Boris in a café, but, after much time and much distance passes through a doorway, only to recognize 'the room where I had earlier left Boris' (*U* 204). Time and space dilate and contract, things recede and loom simultaneously, in a series of architextural paradoxes which make orientation impossible for reader and the near homophone of Ryder. Space, like a mobius strip, returns the perplexed and increasingly fatigued traveller to a collapsed point of beginning and end.

The hotel is under constant renovation by Hoffman, who has a passion for redesigning the many guest rooms. Despite Ryder's deep and genuine satisfaction with his allocated room, which brings back those fond emotions of a fragile homeliness long lost, Hoffman feels that Ryder would be happier in a different room:

> There have even been times when I've become – ha ha! – some would say *obsessed*, yes, obsessed, with one room or another. Once I see the potential of a particular room, I spend many days thinking about it, and then I take the greatest care in having it renovated to match my vision as closely as possible. I am not always successful, but on a number of occasions the results, after much work, have come close to what I pictured in my head, and of course, that is very satisfying. But then – perhaps it's some sort of defect in my nature – no sooner have I completed the renovation of one room to my satisfaction, I am seized by the potential of another. ... Let me be frank, Mr Ryder. Your coming has put the room you're now occupying under its first true test ... I have a good mind to have it demolished in its present form. (*U* 120–1)

Ryder initially resists, assuring Hoffman that he has a 'lot of affection' for the space, until he is shamed at Hoffman's suggestion that he has a 'peculiar attachment' for the space (once more undone by his own pride). This passage is important thematically in a novel that interrogates a modern music so complex that it alienates, serves its own function or the 'vision' of its composer. Like Brodsky, Ryder and Christoff with music, Hoffman is wilfully indifferent to the use of the room or the happiness of its occupant; his concern for the 'unique characteristics' of space over its use mirrors the aestheticism which has infiltrated the novel's cultural landscape. Perhaps a hotel with functional dull rooms *is* boring for the long-term resident and employee, such as Hoffman, but it might be more suited to the utilitarian needs of the transient visitor. Hoffman is a facsimile of Ryder in the restricted space of the hotel; as Ryder moves with a shifting, vagrant passion from city to city, quickly losing interest in partially completed projects in favour of the allure of the new, so Hoffman is drawn irresistibly to the next challenge. As Carlos Garrido Castellano notes, 'The comforting role played by Ryder is limited to the five days he spends in the unnamed city of the novel. After this, the next awaits' (2020: 245). The hotel is a direct structural metaphor, Ishiguro's 'material manifestation' for the novel.

Ishiguro's most explicit comment on the failures of architecture in *The Unconsoled* takes him back to the council estates of his social work days, when we accompany Ryder and Boris as they seek out their old social housing apartment so that Boris can find his favourite football player, the much vaunted 'number nine':

> We were standing on the outer rim of a vast concrete basin. Some distance away, at the centre of the basin, was the artificial lake, its kidney shape making it resemble some gigantic version of the kind of vulgar swimming pool Hollywood stars were once reputed to own. I could not help admiring the way the lake – indeed the whole estate – proudly announced its artificiality. There was no trace of grass anywhere. Even the thin trees dotted around the concrete slopes had all been encased in steel pots and cut precisely into the paving. Looking down on the whole scene, completely encircling us, were the countless identical windows of the high-rise housing blocks. I noticed there was a subtle curve to the front of each block, making possible the seamless circular effect reminiscent of a sports stadium. But for all the apartments now surrounding us – at least four hundred, I guessed – there were hardly any people to be seen. I could make out a few figures walking briskly on the other side of the lake – a man with a dog, a woman with a pram – but there was clearly something about the atmosphere that kept people indoors. (*U* 210)

A dystopian vision, but a familiar sight in the post-war period of modernization and reconstruction across both Europe and Japan, which witnessed a celebration of the state-of-the-art 'artificiality' of new architectural technologies. Much social housing in the post-war period was designed with good intentions, to relieve the poverty of the working classes and to provide spaces that would accommodate their needs (construed functionally). We might think here of Thamesmead (Thamesmead West is a semicircle and may have influenced Ishiguro's vision), Robin Hood Gardens or Park Hill. However, this period in British architecture, more specifically the period between 1945 and 1960, is 'widely thought to have been a failure', even a 'disaster', as Adrian Forty notes (1995: 25). Troublingly, the 'failure of post-war British architecture has been linked exclusively with state-commissioned works – and not just social housing schemes, but schemes like the South Bank, and the British Library – denounced even before it is finished' (Forty 1995: 27). Designed around the requirements of a community that would have little need to leave the confines of the 'vast concrete basin', the prison-yard-like environment discourages forays outside, aside from the 'few figures' hurrying 'home'. Partly this is the failure of the strictly utilitarian ideology of functionalism; as Forty remarks, 'questions about the nature of the experience to be had from architecture, if they took place at all, occurred entirely at the level of the satisfaction of the user's needs' (1995: 33). That is to say that 'the architects of the welfare state' focused on the 'delivery of specific utilitarian functions', as opposed to 'public productions about the nature of private experience, to which certain uses, like a concert hall, or a hospital, might be attached' (Forty 1993: 33). It is in such a space that Boris, Sophie and Ryder lived, and here that their relationship disintegrated in conflict, isolation, excessive work and implied alcoholism. Nature is eradicated with 'no trace of grass anywhere', the organic obliterated in favour of the joyous expression of the synthetic. Like Etsuko's Japanese apartment block, each space here is identical, lacking even a gesture towards individual character. If Hoffman's obsession with uniqueness is problematic as an ethos, so this other extreme which flattens out difference and assumes identical needs for all inhabitants is equally misguided.

Despite this modernist outlier, Ryder's city also seems to be a traditional medieval walled city, albeit with the wall in a slightly unusual and grossly impractical location. During one particularly frustrating episode, while attempting to get to the concert hall for the main event, Ryder encounters the wall which divides the city, realizing to his growing annoyance that 'there was no way to get past' (*U* 387). An inexplicable and insurmountable barrier between oneself and one's goal is precisely the kind of obstacle one might encounter in an anxiety dream (or between oneself and one's *locus amoenus*) while also gesturing obliquely towards the very real nightmare of post-war Europe and the Berlin Wall. As with the bombings of Hiroshima and Nagasaki, Ishiguro avoids too direct an approach, preferring rather to indicate, to gesture towards the socio-historical conditions. Another building of central importance to the city and its artistic and political divisions is also very explicitly 'medieval'. On his way with Boris to the council estate, Ryder is accosted by two journalists intent on an interview; they take him on a long journey (insulting him openly all the while), eventually arriving at the Sattler building:

> When at last I felt reasonably recovered, I moved a few steps away from the building in order to get a view of it ... I found myself looking at a tall cylinder of white brickwork, windowless apart from a single vertical slit near the top.

It was as though a single turret had been removed from a medieval castle and transplanted here on top of the hill. (*U* 182)

The central fortification in the walled city, the building is also the symbolic centre of the city and novel's dilemma. While complementary fortifications, Sattler (phallic high tower with its arrow-slit enabling a view over the city) and the wall are also diametrically opposed, one extensive horizontally one vertically. Underprepared for what seems an impromptu interview, Ryder is initially unaware that his being photographed here will damage his reputation. At one point, he asks the photographer to 'explain the precise nature of this setting' (*U* 182). Later, in what Ishiguro has called a 'backward projection of judgement', Ryder is accused of provocatively 'standing in front of the Sattler monument! Smiling like that!', he thinks back and remembers that, although now appearing a 'miscalculation', he had chosen the setting because it represented 'the most telling way of sending out an appropriate signal' to the town (*U* 371). Although in hindsight claiming agency, Ryder is not initially aware of the 'distinctively political art of Architecture' (Ruskin 2000: 2). Ryder's reputation is already in decline at this point, and the patience and respect with which he has been treated is giving way to anger, frustration, indifference. This catastrophic error of judgment prompts accusations that he, as others in the city have done before, has gone 'too far'. As Pederson tells Ryder, it's 'not in this city's nature to embrace the extremes of Sattler. He holds an attraction for certain people *precisely because* he's so distant' (*U* 375). Sattler's monument's distinctiveness is typical of grand architectural vision. As Marc Augé remarks, 'Architectural works are singularities, expressing the vision of an individual author'; however, as he goes on, great buildings are also 'emancipated from local particularism', which in the case of Ryder's host city serves to exacerbate the already present arrythmia between the various sects (2008: xv–xvi). The Sattler monument is a Babelesque tower of folly, non-functional, purely aesthetic, a product of ego, and like the text's other example of *Verticality*, far too avant-garde.

For the city's divided populous, the ostentatious Sattler building stands as a monument to diffidence, roads not taken. In this way, it is another material manifestation of the concerns that preoccupy each of Ishiguro's out-of-touch narrators. Attempting to explain to Ryder the symbolism of the architecture, Pederson relates an anecdote about someone who misses a 'pivotal point' because they are a little 'timid', and who starts to think back

> let us say, [to] a moment when some woman tried to seduce him. Of course, he didn't allow it, he was much too proper. Or perhaps it was cowardice. Perhaps he was too young, who knows? He wonders if he'd taken another path then, if he'd been just a little more confident about … about love and passion. You know how it is, Mr Ryder. You know the way old men dream sometimes, wondering how it would have been if some key moment had gone another way. Well it can also be like that for a town, for a community. Every

now and then, it looks back, looks back at its history and asks itself: 'What if? What might we have become by now if we'd only ...' Ah, if we'd only what, Mr Ryder? Allowed Max Sattler to take us where he wished? Would we now be something else altogether? (*U* 374)

Intriguingly, as we see in a great many of Ishiguro's fictions, the metaphor of the path recurs. The Sattler building is the monument to Stevens's rejection of Miss Kenton's advances; Ono's decision to devote his time and talents to propaganda; Etsuko's move to England and the subsequent suicide of Keiko; Kathy's lost opportunities for love with Tommy; Axl and Beatrice's failure of one another and their son. Each lets moments pass that can never be recaptured, whether because of timidity, youth or cowardice. Pederson uncovers the city's foundational rift, here: Some wanted to follow Sattler and regret that missed opportunity; others, more cautious, are happy to have not been potentially misguided. We return once more (but changed, of course) to Robert Frost, 'Yet knowing how way leads on to way, / I doubted if I should ever come back' (2002: 219). The subjunctive mood infiltrates and seeds the texts with uncertainty, the narratives, the memories recalled. This building sits provocatively at the heart of Ishiguro's writing project, an architectural materialization of an architextural oeuvre as intricately interconnected as Hoffman's hotel. No matter which text, the setting, characters or genre, we always return to the same question: 'Would we now be something else altogether?' However, like the Peace Park statue and its memorial, mimetic and indexical failures, this structure (a pointing finger) simply stands as a futile testament to mistakes made that are, tragically, being repeated multiply in the novel during the present of narration.

VI

Despite modifications, renovations, ongoing repair, all buildings tend to ruin over time. Buildings gesture towards a permanence of both dwelling and edifice which they cannot maintain, at least in the material sense. In cases of war, the backdrop of all of Ishiguro's works (he is, finally, a war writer), rapid ruin is precipitated by violent destruction. Banks, searching for his kidnapped parents in a war zone, moving through a wasteland of debris, construes the devastated domestic landscape as the remnants of a single building: 'I often had the impression we were moving through not a slum district, but some vast, ruined mansion with endless rooms' (*WWO* 241). Banks's image evokes thoughts of community, desolate and ravaged by war; the district, an extended family home of sorts (the book is interested in the idea of a global community). There is nonetheless some perverse beauty in the squalor of ruin; as Ruskin writes, 'The picturesque is ... sought in ruin, and supposed to consist in decay' (2000: 193). Banks discerns beauty in the obliterated wastes of China, observing somewhat insensitively one 'fine afternoon' that the 'sun was beating down on the ruins of Chapei' (*WWO* 276). Ruins are indeed picturesque, romantic in some cases in such a way that acts as an attraction to a wilful child; Ono is told by his father that artists 'live in squalor and poverty', a lifestyle that tempts them to become 'weak-willed and depraved' (the entire narrative is Ono's defence against the suggestion that he is 'weak-willed') (*AFW* 46). Ono chooses to live in the decadent bohemian squalor of Mori-san's villa during his aestheticist phase: although 'two or three rooms [are] in a condition to suggest the splendour the villa must once have possessed', it is now 'in a state of considerable dilapidation … room after room of torn papering, tatami floors so worn that in several places there was a danger of falling right through if one trod carelessly' (*AFW* 137–8). Intent on capturing the floating world, Ono and his cohort have little concern for luxury – the crumbling villa is the ideal space for the function: If one is given to moral ruin in the pursuit of transient pleasure, a ruined villa deteriorating in real time would seem to be the perfect setting.

Another ruined villa appears in *The Buried Giant*, a novel that takes place in Britain after the fall of Rome, a historical moment which lingers once more in trace in the architextural landscape of Ishiguro's most overtly symbolic work, a 'fable', as Robert Eaglestone argues in a recent essay. As they begin their hopelessly optimistic journey to reunite with a son long dead (they will unknowingly be reunited in death, their journey successful still) in a psycho-geographical space addled with forgetfulness, Axl and Beatrice are forced to take shelter in a ruined Roman villa during a storm:

> The villa must have been splendid enough in Roman days, but now only a small section was standing. Once magnificent floors lay exposed to the elements, disfigured by stagnant puddles, weeds and grass sprouting though the faded tiles. The remains of walls, in places only ankle high, revealed the old layout of the rooms (*BG* 35–6)

Gesturing back towards Ono's 'splendour' and the ruined Japanese house, this description borrows much from the former. The ghostly outline of the building remains, for now, its rooms skeletally traced in time-eroded lines, three dimensions collapsed by the fourth into two. In the inevitable process of reclaiming both material and space, nature (Mr Cardinal's benevolent 'Mother') insistently pushes through the tiles with a slow certainty. Sylvia Plath's meditation on 'Mushrooms' comes to mind: 'Even the paving. / Our hammers, our rams, / Earless and eyeless, / Perfectly voiceless, / Widen the crannies, / Shoulder through holes' (2008: 139). Reminding us of the collapse of the great Roman Empire, the retreat from Britain and the eventual division and dissolution, the villa's failure to stand pays testament to the impermanence of even the most magnificent structure and the empires which enable them. As Augé suggests, ruins memorialize 'the impossibility of imagining completely what they would have represented to those who saw them before they crumbled'

(2008: xvii). We might here invoke Ozymandias's ironic imperative to 'Look on my Works, ye Mighty, and despair!' (Shelley 2009: 198). Despair we might, at our own impermanence, the inevitable decay to which we and our legacies succumb. As Augé goes on, ruins 'speak not of history but of time, pure time' (2008: xvii). In one way, such despair offers a kind of consolation to Ishiguro's narrators, determined as they are to ensure that their once pristine but now challenged legacies remain untarnished. Ishiguro suggests that such legacies are themselves transient, ephemeral, unimportant.

It transpires that the ruin is the childhood home of the boatman who seems to be the novel's oral narrator. He recalls that he 'didn't know just how splendid [the villa once was] for it was all I knew' (*BG* 45). While a testament to the destructive power of time, the house is yet another gesture towards the many wars that linger so persistently in Ishiguro's worlds, a witness to 'days of war, when many others like it were burnt to the ground and are no more now than a mound or two beneath grass and heather' (*BG* 45). Like the symbolic titular giant, buildings succumb to and merge with their landscape; the earth, like a canvass, dust-sheeting, or even pages, is overlaid onto and crudely limns the shape of the underlying form. Just as Banks and Ryder's unreliable memories are prompted by uncannily familiar spaces, the boatman's ruined memory-house stirs recollection in Axl's mind:

> It's just the ruin here. For a moment it was as if I was the one remembering things here ... When the man speaks of wars and burning houses, it's almost as if something comes back to me. From the days before I knew you [Beatrice] it must be. (*BG* 45)

Like Boris and Banks, Axl seems to find here a familiar structure. Axl's recall is troubled by the mist that has caused a universal amnesia, of course. But in a country torn by wars, in which every life is lived in the shadow of conflict past, present and future, these memories are also universal, capturing shared moments of divisions which unite in their similarity. If, as Bachelard suggests, buildings sustain memories, then for Ishiguro's narrators, typified by the fragmentary nature of their memories, the ruined building is the symbol par excellence of his writing; the memories evoked are as vague, gestural, partial, insecure and fragile as a once-splendid structure in decay.

Buildings and ruins can be repurposed, whether knowingly or unknowingly. In *The Buried Giant*, much of the action occurs in a monastery which might not always have served such ostensibly spiritual purposes. Wistan hypothesizes to his prodigy Edwin that 'not long ago, the place was surely no monastery, but a hillfort, and one well made to fight off foes' (*BG* 153). Ono also sees Morisan's villa, in its past, as a kind of hillfort: 'It would have been no easy task for hostile visitors to gain entry once that heavy gate had swung shut' (*AFW* 137). Wistan gives a remarkably detailed account of the building's past, commenting on its Saxon heritage: 'This fort was once in Saxon hands, for I see about it many signs of my kin perhaps invisible to you' (*BG* 153). Another kind of recognition of a space now lost but retained in trace, Wistan is sensitive to the semiology of architecture. The monks, Wistan feels, know little how 'this was once a place of slaughter and burning', they 'come inside this tower for its quiet and seclusion' (*BG* 210). Wistan encourages Edwin, his protégé, to see the trace of the original building behind the present façade (its memory); in so doing, he reveals and rekindles a past that the dragon has misted. Wistan hopes that Edwin will feel that this history is his and will follow in Wistan's vengeful wake when the death of Querig ushers in new wars and generations of ultimately futile conflict. Ishiguro's persistent interest in the theme of haunting, lingering, is at work in these buildings, too. Ruined buildings are also ghosts of a sort; as Jeanette Bicknell notes, there 'is a continuum between architectural ghosts and ruins … Ghosts, appropriately enough, are less corporeal. They can be appreciated only after an act of imaginative reconstruction' (2014: 436). Buildings die, too, along with the dream-memories which they sustain (and which reciprocally sustain them). Nevertheless, in the absence of the structure, there remains some essence, some emanation of the building that haunts its own 'piles of rubble', as Combray does. It is this trace that Wistan finds in the monastery. It is just such a spectre that he hopes to raise (to disinter), rather than exorcise.

We are all temporary occupants and must soon vacate our oneiric house, as Kathy must leave Hailsham, Stevens Darlington. Although such a loss may first appear to be deeply unwelcome, even traumatic, it might also make way for more suitable accommodation. The oneiric home is, after all, the purely ideational abode of a child long lost:

> Sometimes the house of the future is better built, lighter and larger than all the houses of the past, so that the image of the dream house is opposed to that of the childhood home. Late in life, with indomitable courage, we continue to say that we are going to do what we have not yet done: we are going to build a house. (Bachelard 1994: 61)

Banks has a similar realization when he re-encounters his lost childhood home (misrecognized as he misrecognizes Akira): 'We would probably not turn it back exactly to what it was then. For one thing, as I remember it, there were many things we were unhappy about' (*WWO* 193–4). In this moment, Banks the adult assumes a mature perspective unavailable during his childhood, when he still had a family, however dysfunctional it transpired. In retrospect, he adopts the role of parent, considering adding an office for his mother, a workshop for his father, as if they were the children (in this reading he becomes his own grandfather). The building prompts aspirational, hopeful fantasies of the reunification of a family that is, finally, irrecoverably dissolved. Like Sophie, Kathy and Boris, Banks imagines that things will 'go better' if only a suitable space can be found. Unfortunately, for all of Ishiguro's characters, home remains a dream lost in remembered fantasies of ideal family life. That is to say, there are no homes in Ishiguro's novels, each space simply a temporary stopping point from which characters optimistically imagine moving to more suitable accommodations that we the reader can see are utterly absent from the desolate architext.

Ishiguro and his narrators can only gesture towards homes that can never be, perhaps because 'the real houses of memory, the houses to which we return in dreams, the houses that are rich in unalterable oneirism, do not readily lend themselves to description' (Bachelard 1994: 13). Tuan offers another suggestion; 'The child', he proposes, 'knows the world more sensuously than the adult. This is one reason why the adult cannot go home again' (2018: 185). But they do have the home of the text, uniquely built to sustain each. One might also wonder whether Kathy's refusal to rebel, Stevens's decision to serve misguided masters, represent refusals to be homeless; they would each be homeless *only* if they turned, now, from their paths, from the perversion of dwelling that has come to be home for them. In these novelistic explorations of architexture, 'imagination, memory and perception exchange functions. The image is created through cooperation between real and unreal, with the help of the functions of the real and the unreal' (Bachelard 1994: 59). Tuan argues that 'an architect has an intuitive grasp, a tacit understanding, of the rhythms of a culture', that he 'seeks to give these symbolic form'; we might conclude that Ishiguro is indeed an architect of peculiar skill (2018: 164). The homes for which his characters long exist only outside of the architext that they inhabit and which inhabits their narratives. Each sustains the other in a tension between dwelling and vagrancy, in the tacit knowledge that neither can exist, dwell, be at home elsewhere. They are each, finally, one another's home.

Notes

1 Institutions, but his characters are not simply institutionalized, because that implies the possibility of experience before and after the institution.
2 Although it is tempting here to invoke the uncanny (homely/unhomely), that is not an overly useful analytic tool for Ishiguro's writing (even his most uncanny *PVH* and *NLMG*) because it threatens to introduce an unhelpful Freudian element to his psychological investigations.
3 Japanese architecture had a comparable, perhaps even more pervasive, influence on American architecture at the turn of the twentieth century, as Kevin Nute argues of Charles and Henry Greene's work in California, 'probably the best-known Japanese-influenced American domestic architecture' (1994: 170).
4 In *An Artist of the Floating World*, there are a number of spaces that serve a similar function to Sachiko's cottage. Mrs Kawakami's is a remnant of the past in the midst of a burgeoning modern future, acting for Ono as Sachiko's cottage does for Etsuko, as a material symbol of a spirit past. Some essence lingers not simply of a past but of the past selves sustained by the space.

5 Oddly, in a novel that has to do with losing touch with one's mother, Ishiguro nods towards Randy Newman's song 'Mama Told Me Not to Come', which has the line 'The smell of stale perfume' (1967).
6 At another point, he recognizes 'the remains of the old family car my father had driven for many years', but this car was in Worcestershire (as were his friends Fiona and George who appear in the novel) (*U* 260).

Chapter 5

SPACE

Ishiguro's literary appropriation of the symbolism of architectural and domestic space crosses the threshold into the world beyond the built. As he artfully erects a 'complex architecture' to simultaneously give form to and house ideas, his literary edifices each sit in carefully crafted landscapes (*The Guardian*, 2016). *The Buried Giant*'s hive-like warren could 'loom out of the greenery' only in post-Roman Britain; Darlington in a traditionally English (mythic) countryside; Hailsham in (morally) bleak post-war Britain. As he revealed to Tim Adams (returning once more to a familiar metaphor), 'Wherever Kathy went in England I would paint it like it was Norfolk on a grey day', 'an antidote to [the] heritage England' we see in *The Remains of the Day* (2005). Ishiguro's characters are attuned to the etiquette of their environments; *The Unconsoled*'s Miss Collins responds incredulously to Brodsky's suggested location for a long delayed and much anticipated reconciliatory rendezvous, asking, 'Did you say the *cemetery*? ... A restaurant, a café, perhaps some gardens or a lake. But you propose a cemetery!' (*U* 314). Intriguingly, each proposed space has an aligned series of possible or 'conventional' functions, slipping along a spectrum of enclosed/formal to open/informal. Whole counties breed associations, most poignantly Norfolk, which, for the clones in *Never Let Me Go*, becomes the repository of all things lost, even themselves, because of what Sebastian Groes has called a 'wildly misconstrued analogy' (2011: 219). Miss Emily's casual reference to it as a 'lost corner' (a place itself lost) leads to Kathy H. and her peers thinking of it as England's 'lost corner', where 'all the lost property found in the country ended up' (a found place where things lost washup, a line of barbed wire to snare the litter on the breeze').[1] Constitutionally lost like all of Ishiguro's most typical characters, Kathy pre-empts accusations of being 'daft' by reminding us that, for the spatially and emotionally cloistered students, any 'place beyond Hailsham was like a fantasy land; we had only the haziest notions of the world outside and about what was and wasn't possible there'; 'For all our map lessons,' she later recalls, 'we had no real idea at that point about distances and how easy or hard it was to visit a particular place' (*NLMG* 66). Surprisingly for so cosmopolitan a writer, his spatially and platially naïve characters are remarkably poor in world, desperately attempting to negotiate changing place, space and time yet perpetually, unconsolably spatiotemporally disoriented.

Space and place have become areas of intense interest to the humanities during the past half-century, due in part *to* but also informing the advent *of* the Anthropocene and the 'environmental turn', as human place encroaches ever further into and irrevocably maps over natural space. Henry Lefebvre (*The Production of Space*, 1974), Yi-Fu Tuan (*Space and Place*, 1977), Edward W. Soja (*Postmodern Geographies*, 1989) and Jeff Malpas (*Place and Experience*, 1999) have sought to demonstrate that 'the spatiality of our lives, the human geographies in which we live [have] the same scope and critical significance as the historical and social dimensions of our lives' (Borch 2002: 113). Space's centrality to human being, perhaps more human *community*, is self-evident: 'Everything in society', Soja proposes, 'is spatially and historically constituted. There are no spheres, realms, systems, perspectives, rationalities, relations, ideologies, identities, etc. that are aspatial' (2002: 116). Space and place are not the same thing; intricate terminological and philosophical debates about their differences continue. For Edward Casey, place has become the 'impoverished second cousin of Time and Space', physical space usurped by cosmic in a space-age imaginary (1994: xiv). Malpas suggests that 'space' traditionally seems 'to be tied, first and foremost, to a quite general notion of dimensionality' while retaining a range of 'common uses' 'not restricted to *physical* extension or location' (2018: 26). Place, on the other hand, is to a degree more phenomenological: '*integral to the very structure and possibility of experience*' (Malpas 2018: 31, original emphasis). Tuan is a little more direct in associating space with openness (uncharted) and chaos (conflict), place with closure (boundaries) and order (values): 'Enclosed and humanized space is place. Compared to space, place is a calm center of established values' (2018: 54). Possibly the difference resolves merely to presence – observed space imbued with meaning (the application of a schemata) becomes place. Again, for Tuan, place is idiosyncratically human, as it is for Heidegger who, as Rafael Winkler summarizes, 'distinguishes the human from the animal [by] the ability to construct a world' (2007: 522). Place, that is to say, is 'wherein the sort of being that is characteristically human [Heidegger's *dasein*] has its ground' (Malpas 2018: 32). One implication of this view is that space becomes a radical impossibility if apperception is sufficient cause for the formation of place from landscape's raw material. It is in this way that world (place, culture) comes to supervene upon earth (space, geography) at the instant of constitutive apprehension.

The imposition of physical and ideological borders enables the differentiation of the culturally undifferentiated singular space of the earth into meaningful human places. Moving from space to place, or place to place, always involves a kind of transgression, a 'going across' of lines etched physically or ideationally on terrain, cartographically and psychically transcribed (a topographical to neurological ekphrasis). Crossings occupy Ishiguro's characters, figuratively in his cyclical return to 'turning points' which represent personal or interpersonal boundaries transgressed (or a failure to transgress self-imposed boundaries, to accept proffered affection, for example), and literally as his characters coordinate themselves in unfamiliar space (Kathy crosses the wired boundary of Hailsham only to repeatedly re-encounter the barrier in the open country). Perhaps the clearest indication of Ishiguro's enduring interest in space, and what Sean Matthews and Sebastian Groes identify as a 'hesitancy with regard to the function of *place*', is his recurring fascination with travel (through space), more specifically travel away from home (place) (2009: 3). We encounter characters negotiating the psychological ruins of the collapsed illusions of dwelling, revelatory moments where the veil of mist evaporates, and intimate place dissolves into inhospitable space, though not because meaning is entirely evacuated but because the meaning attributed to the space is different to that imagined. Stevens undertakes a motoring journey from Darlington, attempting to recover and rebuild it ideationally around the disruptive material occupation of Mr Farraday (it is no coincidence that his recovery project manifests as retreat into England); Kathy's narrative describes her departure from Hailsham and her subsequent car trips between various recovery centres as she attempts in these impersonal institutional spaces to retrace (recover) the ideational intimate place of her childhood imaginary; Axl and Beatrice abandon (or are evicted from) the warren to begin their arduous final walk to what they imagine will be the more embracing place of their son's village (Beatrice is on a journey towards her son's now-mythic resting place); Etsuko manages (and Sachiko hopes) to travel geographically far from post-war Japan but, nonetheless, remains emotionally and psychologically anchored to the past while finding herself 'so pleased' to arrive in an England 'just the way I always imagined England would be' (because, of course, it is the imaginary England of its author); Banks travels far from China across oceans to London, but takes with him the at once comforting and unsettling space of his abruptly attenuated childhood, confessing later that all 'these years I've lived in England, I've never really felt at home there. The International Settlement. That will always be my home' (*WWO* 256). As they are bound to the 'oneiric house', they are bound also to 'oneiric' place, psychic traces traced onto terrain. As Arthur J. Mason's Kathrine passionately declares in his rediscovered novel, *The August Passage*, they would take England with them, in their blood and their very hearts ... They would transport it with them, wherever they went' (Ishiguro 1984: 12). However, their journeys are necessitated by the collapse of the illusion of place; they are not simply uncoordinated but ontologically disoriented, dissevered from but searching for place in the order of space, their quest perpetually deferred in an irresolvable category error. A Lacanian reading might suggest that they are looking in the symbolic for the pre-symbolic from which they are irredeemably alienated.

Kathy, Stevens, Axl and Beatrice are astute observers of the landscapes through which they travel (the first-person narrator has much responsibility). Each is finely calibrated to different systems of meaning whose significance is determined by their novel's unique concerns. Kathy, 'driving on a long weaving road across marshland, or maybe past rows of furrowed fields', moves in predetermined vectors between care centres, noting features of a futureless landscape made not for or by her kind; Stevens, ostensibly 'motoring for the pleasure of it', draws attention to the unique and quaint charms of his ideal England after its political demise; for Beatrice and Axl, a knowledge of the landscape's features is essential for survival, the space full of hidden danger, and lacking built structure, the landmarks are natural as opposed to constructed. Yugin Teo comments that 'characters have hidden past relationships with these geographical spaces' in which they find themselves, which is particularly true of *A Pale View of Hills* and *The Buried Giant* (2014: 17). Chu-Chueh Cheng has noted (specifically of his Japanese novels) that Ishiguro often 'minimizes geographical specifics'; this is perhaps because his landscapes are not representative of any 'real country' but rather manifest expressions of his characters' emotional states (Kelman 2019; Cheng 2010: 28). These journeys then are ideational, gestural, not simply, maybe not even spatial.

Indeed, for our protagonists, travel through space is also figured as travel through time. Perhaps this is because, as Tuan remarks, 'physical movement across space [can] generate similar temporal illusions' (2018: 125). Factually, travel through space is always travel through time, time as a construct nothing more than the record of planetary motion. But, in this sense, movement through time is always forward, whereas the 'distant view need not call forth the idea of future time; the view could be our backward glance and the vanishing road the path we have already trodden. Both the past and the future can be evoked by the distant scene' (Tuan 2018: 124). Joseph Conrad problematically exploits this spatiotemporal co-equality in *Heart of Darkness* (1899), his science-fiction-time-travel narrative in which Marlow and Co travel along the river Congo into the heart of Africa *as if* they were travelling back through the eons to mankind's' 'primitive' heart. Ishiguro's characters abandon homes that never were to move geographically towards an imaginary past-present-future singularity of radical recuperative possibility. Wojciech Drąg observes a similar pattern, suggesting that Ishiguro's narrators are motivated by the loss of something 'constructed in retrospect as the locus of meaning' in a present 'infused with a sense of lack' (2014: 1). Traversing space with the sole intention of moving back through time, Stevens, Kathy and Tommy, Beatrice and Axl, Etsuko and Ono come to realize that, in journeying to the reconstructed past, time still passes, and things let go tend not to return. This is the power of the figurative imperative to never let go: release is final.

Texts themselves are also semiotic terrains which give rise to affective and cognitive features, encounters with openness, blankness. Like landscape, a text unfolds in both space and time, has coordinates, recedes into a distant horizon promising the potential familiarity of place, if only for a visit. As David James notes, reading 'itself [is] a *voyage* punctuated by discovery and qualification' (2008: 24). Indeed, for Tuan, it is a 'function of literary art ... to give visibility to intimate experiences, including those of place' (2018: 162). 'Open space', though, is imposing precisely because it 'has no fixed pattern of established human meaning; it is like a blank sheet on which meaning may be imposed' (Tuan 2018: 54).² J. and N. Duncan observe affinities between place and text (adopting an arachnological vocabulary inflected with a Derridean jouissance), noting that texts 'have a web-like complexity, characterised by a ceaseless play of infinitely unstable meanings. This picture is interesting not only from a literary standpoint, but also because it resembles landscapes in many respects' (quoted in Ebbatson 2013: 6). Texts are complexes of signification; landscapes are complexes of signification. Language also comes to inflect our situatedness in place directly because, as Simon Pugh suggests, 'Our experience of landscape … is determined by descriptive language which modifies, even constitutes ways of seeing landscape' (1990: 3). Space is semiosis. Or, rather, space becomes place after the act of semiosis, the attribution and interpretation of (human) meaning. The land is a geological/archaeological record of the past, or even various pasts, a text (or texts) awaiting the careful excavation and interpretation of earth-eroded meanings (but is this once more to privilege the historical, the material?). Much like language which evolves but carries traces of its etymological past, 'every new phase in history reuses and transforms the older structures, in this way creating inextricable and dynamic palimpsests' (Renes 2015: 414). The word palimpsest has been a mainstay of the deconstructionist paradigm for decades now, a gesture towards the layered traces of meaning sustained by (inter)textuality. In the case of the multilayered earth, of geological space and the overlapping ideational places that it enables, the metaphor is supremely apt. As Peter Herring observes in a summation that might equally be applied to a work of literature, 'while landscape constantly changes it yet retains as timedepth the increasingly fragmentary chronicles of previous change' (2012: 486). Reading is an act of meaning attribution, converting space to place while uncovering stratified yet intermixed traces of places in space. Timedepth is a peculiarly apt description of the deceptive superficiality of Ishiguro's taut textual surfaces.

In this chapter, I accompany Ishiguro's itinerant characters into their private gardens, through the public park, over the hills, across streams and marshes to the 'glistening line that was the sea', the final point for Axl and Beatrice, Stevens and, by implication, Kathy, Tommy and Ruth on their wistful visit to the beached boat which promises but fails to inspire fantasies of unbounded oceanic escape (in any other novel of this kind, we might be permitted such optimism). The chapter is a journey, one which maps onto those taken by Ishiguro's narrators. Like those, it is the final territory traversed in this study. As Malpas has suggested, and I have argued in the previous chapter, there is an intimate bidirectional influence between what is inside and what is outside (what David Foster Wallace might call 'The Porousness of Certain Borders'), one that is inherently and deeply human: 'The stuff of our "inner" lives is thus to be found in the "outer" places in which we dwell, while those same places "without" are incorporate "within" us' (2018: 6). Ernst Bloch agrees that we 'take on the form of our surroundings. Not only does the man [sic] make his world, but the world makes the man [sic]' (1997: 43). Making the internal external is key to Ishiguro's expressionist project; as Brian W. Shaffer has commented, it is the 'quietly anguished interior landscape upon which the most compelling drama [of Ishiguro's novels] is being enacted' (2001: 2). The landscapes explored by Ishiguro's characters can exist only for them; they manifest and represent not objective space but rather subjective emotional place. As Ishiguro remarked, he conjures 'landscapes of the imagination, landscapes that somehow express various themes' (Swaim 2008: 96). Part of the role of the author, more particularly the 'British writer', according to Ishiguro, is that 'they have to use their imaginations to create completely imaginary landscapes' (Oe 1991: 121). Each character's 'imaginary landscape' is finely calibrated to the past and present of narrative and narrator, in what can only be described as a euphoric surrender to the pathetic fallacy. Once more, the landscape is not 'real' but merely a gesture towards a recalled and reimagined real. Ishiguro needs to know only 'the fictional landscape in which my novel takes place very well. That's the landscape I have to research, not any actual chunk of history or real country' (Kelman 2019). As he constructs unique buildings for his characters, so he develops for each a bespoke landscape, intended only for them. However, these spaces are no less hostile for the care taken in their design. Importantly, just as the same person cannot enter through the same door twice, there is no return from a journey for one fundamentally altered by its revelations, whether that be the reader or the heroine.

I

Stepping over the domestic threshold from inside to outside often begins with the private garden. Intermediary, intimate yet outdoor, gardens constitute continuations of the home space, 'where the "products of a network of social, physical and symbolic orderings of private living space" are collected or embodied. Above all, they are "scenes of intense personalization"' (Longstaffe-Gowan 1993: 48 quoted in Kimber 2004: 264). Gardens are also aspirational ideations: *Nocturne*'s young cellist Tibor visualizes musical epiphany as a 'garden I'd not yet entered. There it was, in the distance. There were things in the way. But for the first time, there it was. A garden I'd never seen before' (*N* 202). Perhaps like the novel Ishiguro saw 'tantalisingly, in [his] imagination', Tibor's garden is another conjectural space of possibility, a *locus amoenus*, but one which, like traditional chivalric walled gardens, recedes into an indefinite distance populated with dynamic obstacles (*The Guardian*, 2016). These 'things in the way' of self-realization might be Stevens learning to banter, the foreboding Great Plain, past political allegiances, childhood's lingering traumas or the literal wall which confounds hapless Ryder's ill-fated plans to return harmony to his aesthetically divided city. Harmony is crucial to gardens both as a function of the design and the emotions which they evoke. As Kimber notes, 'The experience of being in a garden contributes to a balanced life' (2004: 266).

It is no coincidence that many moments of great importance (turning points) for Ishiguro's characters take place in the setting of private and public gardens. We might think of Banks, imagining his filial reconciliation as 'a magnificent ceremony held in Jessfield Park' (*WWO* 111). Unfortunately for our hero, as Richard King observes, the fantasy must remain unrealized because of Banks's 'blindness to the evidence of larger realities' (2012: 271). Gardens and parks offer a private yet neutral space, facilitating at least the promise of harmony, especially after a period of personal or national conflict. Public parks create, certainly for Banks, an idealized sense of wider community, a place for personal consolations which, in turn, gesture towards national compensations.

Stevens's fateful (first and) final meeting with Mrs Benn takes place in the Rose Garden Hotel (combining two of his symbolic centres), not a garden as such but provocatively named (perhaps again a gesture towards the *Roman de la Rose*, or even the White House's Rose Garden in the novel's context of growing US influence). Stevens has much hope for this space, imagining that here he and Miss Kenton/Mrs Benn (she oscillates between the two identities as do Mrs Dalloway and Clarissa) might find some lost or evasive harmony, not simply reminiscing about their shared memories but travelling back through time to open doors left closed (the one behind which Miss Kenton sobs (even, in Ishiguro's overlapping sketches, the one behind which Sophie sobs, or Kathy dances)) in the intimate space of old acquaintance. As Lilian R. Furst observes in a tellingly topographic rhetoric, 'Miss Kenton has become an integral part of his landscape' (2007: 548). In their final (brief) encounter, despite the uncharacteristic emotional intimacy and informality of their conversation, they resort to reassuring spatial metaphors, Miss Kenton telling Stevens that 'my life does not stretch out emptily before me', to which he replies, 'I know I'm not awaited by emptiness' (*RD* 236–7). By implication, emptiness is undifferentiated space, 'open'; instead, each assures the other in a reciprocal self-protection that they will return to the familiar comforts of shared meanings in place. Lord Darlington, for all his faults, 'chose a certain path in life, it proved to be a misguided one', and Stevens realizes that he now must choose his. The closure facilitated by the meeting is not that for which Stevens wished; despite his readings of her apparently despairing letters, it seems Mrs Benn is not 'so alone and desolate' as he previously hoped, and has no desire to undertake the spatiotemporal return journey to Darlington by his side. Yet, in the poignant failure of Stevens's recuperative mission arises a moment of profound catharsis which allows him to chart a path away from the past, if only back to Darlington to adapt for the challenges that remain. We and he have foreseen his future in his father's senescence-curtailed career, but Stevens took his professional duties more seriously even than his father, and has himself no heirs.

However, the Darlington Hall that he left only days before has now become an altogether difference place, a fact revealed to him or emerging forcefully from deep in his psyche, as he travels further away from the building into the surrounding English landscape. Problematically, if Darlington is not quite

Darlington, the coordinate that is Miss Kenton is not quite Miss Kenton (because it is Mrs Benn). In this sense, he is utterly and irredeemably lost, triangulating himself between two points he takes to be cardinal, fixed, but which turn out to be transitory – Miss Kenton who is no longer Miss Kenton, and Darlington which is no longer Darlington. One might consider Stevens's journey an outright failure precisely because he travelled to a 'part of his landscape' which had ceased to exist many years prior and must return to a place with a completely different meaning; where once the house and name were a source of great pride, his repeated denials of acquaintance with his one-time master along his journey force him to confront the shame the name now connotes, and with which he and his life's labour are irremediably associated/tainted. Having traversed an 'interwar British landscape [that] concealed shameful implications', Stevens returns, or someone like Stevens returns from his motoring trip radically altered, in the at-once despairing and freeing certainty that a road not taken can never be taken (Whitehead 2011: 75). Troublingly, if his tragic flaw is his willingness to follow others' dubious paths, having made his great escape from American occupation in a borrowed car, he prepares to participate in the Americanization of the English country house, returning to 'an employer who treats the stately home as a theme park' (Lewis 2000: 99). Darlington Hall is now Farraday Land, Stevens a full-costume historical re-enactment for the gratification of his master and the entertainment of his master's guests.

Though private and, to a degree, segregated from the public realm, gardens are no less affected by world events and, as such, operate as micro-instantiations of national crises. Stevens and Kenton's relationship, and as such their final meeting, is determined entirely by interwar politics, anti-Semitism, fascism. Stevens's literary ancestor Masuji Ono thinks fondly of the garden to his grand house, designed by Akira Sugimura, observing in the late afternoon sun that his 'garden has recovered well [from] all its suffering during the war' (*AFW* 35). The word 'suffering' is an interesting choice for a garden and its insensate occupants, gesturing obliquely towards 'those who had suffered' in the war, to borrow Etsuko's phrase (*PVH* 13). Ono derives deep satisfaction from the 'splendidly harmonious' garden, which conveys a 'natural rambling feeling, with barely a hint of artificial design' (*AFW* 35). Managed with sufficient skill to create an illusion of the natural world, Ono's garden approximates an idealized and harmonious natural space, but one imbued with the significance of place in the aura of the house. Being a continuation of the family home, domestic conflict is inevitable. In one seemingly innocuous scene, he and his daughter Noriko disagree about his trimming of the shrubs, when she accuses Ono of 'meddling where it's not required', suggesting that he has 'unbalanced' the garden (*AFW* 106). This reminds us of Congressman Lewis telling Darlington's conference attendees that they are amateurs '*meddling* in large affairs that affect the globe' (*RD* 102). Clearly, Noriko has more in mind than the shrubs or bamboo in accusing Ono of disturbing the cherished harmony that he finds in the 'garden'. Intimate and enclosed, the private garden becomes the battle ground over a series of deeply rooted familial conflicts (planted and nurtured in the right conditions), and both parties are aware that the shrubbery is merely camouflage for the true subject of their talk. Troublingly for Ono, his past actions infiltrate the tranquil garden like an invasive (foreign) weed. As Cynthia Wong comments, everyday 'life for Ono is fraught with tension, especially with those of the younger generation', such as Noriko (Ono assumes), who hold him accountable for 'unbalancing' the nation (2005: 44). The garden acts as a metaphor that enables Noriko to express indirectly her resentment, one of which she may herself be unaware, or unwilling to discuss without subterfuge.

Ishiguro's use of gardens as a metaphor to examine conflict by proxy first appears in one of his earliest published stories, 'Summer after the War' (1983), which, as Shaffer remarks, was written between Ishiguro's first and second novels and 'clearly anticipates' *An Artist of the Floating World* (2009: 10). In the aftermath of a typhoon, the child narrator Ichiro reflects with peculiar sensitivity on the 'leaves and broken branches' that 'lay scattered everywhere'; 'I thought of the war,' he recalls, 'of the destruction and waste I had seen throughout my earliest years' (1983: 121).³ However, 'Within a few days, the garden had been tidied [and] ceased to hold much resemblance to that defeated place I had glimpsed on the night of my arrival' (1983: 121). If, as I argue in Chapter 2, toys are on a (micro) scale that enable the child to make some sense of – and to have some illusory agency over – the adult world, gardens foster a similar fantasy of (macro) control. In this instance, the destruction of the garden and its recovery allows Ichiro to envisage the end of war, the nation's recovery, the return to harmony, acting as a therapeutic intermediary between young Ichiro and the adult world which currently eludes but ultimately awaits him. This sense of hope flourishes in gardens, as Kenneth I. Helphand argues, 'They are a connection to home, they embody hope'; more, although these may be 'commonplace themes', the 'meaning of each is magnified in wartime' (2010: 13). Harmonious managed private spaces attain deeper meaning in the national disharmony of war, offering at least the temporary illusion of sanctuary, much like Banks and Ryder's fondly recalled playrooms. We see an implication that the grandfather is responsible for 'the younger generation's bewilderment and misery', in which young Ichiro and Noriko find themselves having to re-establish personal and, by implication, national balance amidst the 'destruction and waste' of their parents' legacies (Cheng 2010: 27). We might detect a more direct allusion to Hoffman's game of leaf piling here, too, as a metaphor for preventing or recovering from conflict, in which tidying the garden somehow prevents the city from exploding 'into a million pieces' (*U* 97).

The landscaped gardens of Darlington are also used as a metaphor to make sense of war and its causes. Attempting ineptly to convey carnal knowledge to Mr Cardinal (despite claiming some merit for assisting in 'large affairs', he fails in this trivial task), Stevens refers euphemistically to 'the glories of nature'. Presumably, Ishiguro has in mind a possible model for Stevens in Peter Sellers's 'Chance', or 'Chauncey Gardner' as he comes to be known in Hal Ashby's interpretation of Jerzy Kosiński's *Being There* (1979). Gardner is, in fact, a gardener, but his comments on gardening are taken to be deeply insightful metaphors for the US economy, so that he seems, at film's (stunning) end, to be on the brink of presidential nomination. Cardinal, though, takes literally Stevens's metaphor, remarking earnestly that 'we are all much too complacent about the great wonders that surround us', before meditating optimistically on the harmony of nature:

> Treaties and boundaries and reparations and occupations. But Mother Nature just carries on her own sweet way ... I wonder if it wouldn't have been better if the Almighty had created us all as- well-as sort of plants. You know, firmly embedded in the soil. Then none of this rot about wars and boundaries would have come up in the first place. (*RD* 108)

Complacency, we recall, is the title of Ono's first work of propaganda. There is an accidental wisdom in Cardinal's awareness that a mechanical capacity to traverse space necessitates boundaries, which in turn facilitate territorial aggression. The odd capitalization of both Mother Nature and the Almighty ironically collapses the pagan and the Christian, a theological disharmony which itself resulted in the deaths of many over the centuries (a conflict at the heart of *BG*). Aptly named after the points of the compass (alongside the theological connotation), Cardinal is peculiarly insightful in his apprehension of the spatial and platial causes of conflict; in the most fundamental estimation, wars are fought over land (space) and ideology (place). Cardinal is also hopelessly naïve in his belief in the sweetness of nature. To be static is to be vulnerable, unable to evade danger, to protect oneself, to be subject precisely to the threat of 'rot' latent in Cardinal's rhetoric. As we see in 'Summer after the War', nature wreaks devastation and is not as 'sweet' or benign as this managed landscape portrays. Darlington Hall's gardens are used to interrogate the idea that human beings and human concerns are somehow outside of nature while also gesturing towards conflict's corporeal conditions. Ishiguro demonstrates too, repeatedly, that roots are not exclusively material; to be embedded in the soil of one's place as, if not more, ideological. As Rupert Brooke eulogizes of the war-dead colonizing friendly fields post-mortem, 'there's some corner of a foreign field / That is forever England', in 'that rich earth a richer dust concealed' (2010: 139).

In *The Unconsoled*, the 'Sternberg Garden' offers the possibility of reconciliation between Miss Collins and Mr Brodsky, a renewed harmony upon which the city's hopes rely. The garden is a neutral space, public (safe, after Brodsky's previous abuse mentioned by Parkhurst) yet private (sustaining personal intimacy). Miss Collins recalls a day in the distant past that might have led to peace, meditating that, instead of returning to her apartment knowing Brodsky was following her forlornly, she should have 'gone into the Sternberg Garden'; 'even if for a while they had wandered about the shrubs in silence', she thinks, 'sooner or later they would have started to talk. And sooner or later he would have given her the flowers' (perhaps she should have bought the flowers herself) (*U* 323). Her apartment is dauntingly privately intimate, the garden publicly intimate. Later in the novel, they do have a meeting in the garden, one with much expectation, on them but also the space:

> Essentially a concreted square no larger than a supermarket car park, it seemed to exist primarily for horticultural interest, rather than to provide beauty or comfort to the neighbourhood. There was no grass or trees, simply rows of flower beds, and at this point in the day the square was a sun-trap with no obvious sign of shade anywhere. But Miss Collins, looking around at the flowers and ferns, clapped her hands in delight. Brodsky, closing the iron gate carefully after him, looked at the garden without enthusiasm, but seemed to take satisfaction from the fact that, aside from the apartment windows overlooking them, they had complete privacy. (*U* 323–4)

It is crucial for Brodsky that he makes the public space into something like an intimate private garden, hence his closing the gate so carefully. This gesture towards enclosure has the desired effect on both he and Miss Collins, because the 'awkwardness [between them] evaporated entirely' (*U* 324). Miss Collins is enamoured with the managed horticultural beauty of the space, but for Brodsky (who can compare only to the car park), it fails in its role of providing 'comfort to the neighbourhood'. Collins knows Brodsky well: 'You've never liked gardens like these', she remarks. 'You despise all this harnessing of nature … No, you'd prefer something wilder. But you see, it's only with careful control and planning some of these species can survive at all' (*U* 324). Collins pre-empts the catastrophic failure of Brodsky's rehabilitative concert performance, during which he 'uncovers' the 'peculiar life-forms hiding just under the shell' of the Mullery piece (*U* 492). A garden is carefully orchestrated, a harmonious environment protected somewhat from nature; Brodsky, though, is seduced by wilder forms. In this way the inevitable failure of his final performance is gestured towards via the symbolism of this scene in the public park.

Gardens and parks are artificial, more inside/private than outside/public spaces. They are, that is to say, social space partitioned into an illusion of meaningful domestic place. At stake in Ishiguro's gardens is harmony, accord; Stevens, Ono and Brodsky seek reconciliation, but in the public domain (this is the first time that Stevens has ever encountered Miss Kenton outside of Darlington, and it is only outside that he can finally recognize her changed status). But, in each encounter, the gardens, rather than enabling affinities to bloom, become micro-instantiations of the wider disharmony between the characters and those that provide the historical context for the novels. Gardens also enable characters to find a language, a rhetoric, a metaphor for the deeply rooted insidious and often unspoken conflicts which have come to divide them. If Tibor imagines a garden of delights as reward for surmounting certain obstacles, these examples show us that those obstacles are often insurmountable, that ostensibly neutral space becomes, in the tension of profoundly held interpersonal sentiment, precisely the painfully intimate place which necessitated separation, drifting apart. In this sense, place is indeed oneiric, psychically traced, portable.

II

Beyond private gardens and public parks lies the ostensibly undifferentiated space of the open country. Blank space, however, is not simply dormant, awaiting the ideological/cultural attribution of meaning. Indeed, place emerges phenomenologically from space in the constitutive dynamic between body and environment. Distance acquires meaning as a measure of bodies in motion, the size and constitution of the body determining 'how easy or hard it [is] to visit a particular place', to borrow Kathy's words. This view is particularly apposite for Beatrice, disabled through age and struggling to traverse the barren terrain, until she is carried across the final threshold, but not by Axl who is also compromised by senescence. Infirmity contracts worlds, as Elaine Scarry observes, 'in the very old and sick people, the world may exist only in a circle of two or three feet out from themselves' (1987: 32). Or Ruth, previously the dynamic core of her group, after her donations on a short walk traversing space becomes exhausting, 'her shoulders rising and falling with her breathing' so that Kathy and Tommy realize in the intimacy of that precise moment 'just how frail she was' (*NLMG* 218). As Deborah Lilley remarks of the clones, their 'experience of nature – whether the internal nature of their own bodies, or of the landscapes that they explore – are necessarily compromised for them' (2016: 67). Maurice Merleau-Ponty argues that space is actively organized by the body: 'In so far as I have hands, feet, a body, I sustain around me intentions which are not dependent on my decisions and which affect my surroundings in a way that I do not choose' (1962: 440). Tuan shares this view, proposing that 'the human being, by mere presence, imposes a schema on space' (2018: 36). Drew Leder agrees that 'the body [is the] very medium whereby our world comes into being. It is via my sensorimotor powers that I encounter a world charged with meaning and organized into significant gestalts' (1990: 15). Malpas goes further, insisting that place is that '*on which* the notion of subjectivity is founded' because place enables distance and, therefore, differentiation between objects/subjects (beings in and for themselves) (2018: 34). Space forms around the perceiving subject/object and, in that sense, is a perpetually immanent, virtual, contingent state of potentiality. It is not simply the body, however, which alters one's perception of topography; cultural perspectives and political allegiances also terraform objective topographical space into subjective place.

Space's susceptibility to the psychology of the perceiver is eminently demonstrated in Stevens's journey. He is enamoured with *The Wonder of*

England, his narrative a travelogue, but one which once more evidences his inability to see the bigger picture in which his story fits, because of his preoccupation with identifying on his trip what Lord Darlington refers to as the 'traditions of our country' (*RD* 123). As Lewis remarks, his journey is one into 'his English sense of self', as opposed to a crossing of terrain, or an opportunity to reflect on his nation's changing status (2000: 78). Darlington Hall stands resolutely, or certainly seems initially to do so, at the centre of Stevens's 'traditional' England, while England, in turn, occupies the 'calm center of established values' (Darlington Hall is Britain in microcosm amidst a sea of change). Perhaps central to 'the values embodied' by this countryside is Britain's 'essentially decent heart' of which Ishiguro speaks so frequently (*Financial Times*, 2016). We find Stevens at a vital moment, venturing boldly (and bodily) beyond the familiarity of his home range for the first time in a life as restricted as that of Hailsham's residents. Although at first recognizing the environment immediately adjacent to the great house:

> eventually the surroundings grew unrecognizable and I knew I had gone beyond all previous boundaries. I have heard people describe the moment, when setting sail in a ship, when one finally loses sight of the land. I imagine the experience of unease mixed with exhilaration often described in connection with this moment is very similar to what I felt in the Ford as the surroundings grew strange around me. This occurred just after I took a turning and found myself on a road curving around the edge of a hill. I could sense the steep drop to my left, though I could not see it due to the trees and thick foliage that lined the roadside. The feeling swept over me that I had truly left Darlington Hall behind, and I must confess I did feel a slight sense of alarm – a sense aggravated by the feeling that I was perhaps not on the correct road at all, but speeding off in totally the wrong direction into a wilderness. (*RD* 26)

David Spurr writes of the typically 'English' belief that 'the culture of an ordered English tradition emanates from the center outward, from noble house to tamed wilderness' (2012: 21). Poor in world, Stevens has travelled only a few miles in his American automobile before he introduces his grandiose metaphor of oceanic exploration. This too is idiosyncratically British; David Lowenthal and Hugh Prince remark, 'That theirs is a "little land" ... the English often remain unaware until they confront the unnerving bigness of abroad' (1964: 310). Nonetheless, the metaphor of a sea voyage reinforces the idea that Darlington Hall and its gardens stand as a metaphor for the British Isles, and that Stevens really is travelling into the refigured post-war world. Stevens's tendency to exaggerate his achievements (international tension alleviated through polished silver) renders him more complicit, in spirit at least, in his master's misguided political interventions. Stevens's experience of the world beyond Darlington Hall is merely vicarious – He has overheard conversations about travel by his master's worldly guests and maps this overheard (Stevens is an incorrigibly undignified eavesdropper, after all) knowledge onto his own journey. Although he claims to have 'truly' left Darlington behind, we know that it is with him, he with it. The landscape with its precipitous but occluded precarity, Stevens's sense that he may not be on the 'correct road', symbolic of his own sense that he and Darlington navigated (or drove and navigated) a treacherous road. To pursue the metaphor, Darlington ventured too close to the edge, Stevens always hanging back, survived through his own lack of commitment (if Stevens found himself in post-war Japan, questions of ritual suicide may arise).

A short while later, following the advice of a (caricature of a) characterful local on a bench (he seeks advice from another local on a bench at novel's end), he takes time to reflect on the beauty and 'greatness' of the English landscape's rolling hills. Ishiguro again draws our attention to ageing and the physicality of movement, the local cautioning Stevens that 'you got to have a good pair of legs and a good pair of lungs to go up there. Me, I haven't got neither, so I stay down here' (*RD* 27). Determined to correct the local's 'foolish ... insinuation' about his infirmity, Stevens accepts the challenge and finds himself overlooking an idyllic vista, which, as Monika Gehlawat observes, 'fulfils our more or less conventional expectations by being almost too picture-perfect', because it, like Ishiguro's Japan, is purely imaginary, constructed of images (2013: 495). Stevens ponders:

> I have seen in encyclopedias and the *National Geographic Magazine* breathtaking photographs of sights from various corners of the globe; magnificent canyons and waterfalls, raggedly beautiful mountains. It has never, of course, been my privilege to have seen such things at first hand, but I will nevertheless hazard this with some confidence: the English landscape at its finest – such as I saw it this morning – possesses a quality that the landscapes of other nations, however more superficially dramatic, inevitably fail to possess. It is, I believe, a quality that will mark out the English landscape to any objective observer as the most deeply satisfying in the world ...
>
> [it is] the very lack of obvious drama or spectacle that sets the beauty of our land apart. What is pertinent is the calmness of that beauty, its sense of restraint. It is as though the land knows of its own beauty, of its own greatness, and feels no need to shout it. In comparison, the sorts of sights offered in such places as Africa and America, though undoubtedly very exciting, would, I am sure, strike the objective viewer as inferior on account of their unseemly demonstrativeness. (*RD* 28–9)

Stevens's Anglocentrism is not unusual; as Tuan notes, people everywhere 'tend to regard their own homeland as the center of the world' (2018: 149). In admitting his ignorance but 'hazarding' with 'confidence' on the objective aesthetic superiority of the English landscape, Stevens echoes British diplomat T. B. Macaulay's infamous 'Minute on Indian Education' (1835), in which, despite confessing that he has 'no knowledge of either Sanscrit or Arabic', he concludes 'that a single shelf of a good European library was worth the whole native literature of India and Arabia' (in Krishna Dutta 2003: 198). The passage is also attuned both to space and the relationship between space and its inhabitants. Stevens has in mind his ambiguous position in regard to Mr Farraday's unseemly banter, the challenges posed by this development to his aspirations for dignity, professional prestige and his self-image. Stevens implies that Mr Farraday's brashness re-creates the brashness of America's 'exciting' topography while also reading himself both in and into the 'calmness' and 'restraint' of the English landscape. Stevens draws encouragement in this uniquely nurturing Englishness, beginning 'for the first time to adopt a frame of mind appropriate for the journey before me' (*RD* 26). Yugin Teo also comments that his 'portrait of England' and its charms has 'more to do with the mythical idea of England' and is 'little more than a performance of an identity or myth' (2014: 28). Stevens is enchanted by 'charming sights', frequently remarking on the 'charm' of Salisbury and the other towns and cities he visits. This restrained charm is not to be found in what he figures as a kind of untamed 'wilderness' that might feature on the cover of a glossy magazine. The same 'charm' is noticed by two Swiss guests in 'Malvern Hills', who observe that the softly undulating hills 'have a charm all their own because they are gentle and friendly' (*N* 98). But this charm, like the 'quaint' that so angers Ono, is derogatory, reminding us of the somewhat patronizing moment during Lord Darlington's fateful conference when Congressman Lewis suggests that the British 'would actually be charming' if they stopped interfering in politics. That is to say, they could be harmless, gentle, innocuous like the placid landscape.

But the countryside can be disconcerting for one accustomed to 'glittering cities like London', as is *A Pale View of Hill*'s Niki (Adams 2005). Niki visits her mother for a short while after the funeral of her sister Keiko, but their mother Etsuko observes that her 'country house and the quiet that surrounds it made [Niki] restless, and before long I could see she was anxious to return to her life in London' (*PVH* 9). Niki disputes the distinction between country (natural) and city (artificial) implicit in Etsuko's description of her house as being in the 'countryside', telling her mother that hers 'was not the real countryside, just a residential version to cater for the wealthy people who lived here' (*PVH* 47). Indeed, as Prince and Lowenthal observe, even in the early twentieth century, there were 'few blanks on the map of England; almost everywhere is a *place*, with a meaning and a character of its own' (1964: 310). Of course, Niki is not unsettled by the space but by her mother's claustrophobic guilt-inflected mourning. In order to explore England as (inhospitable) space, Ishiguro needs to imagine what the nation might have looked like during the medieval period. To 'spark' his imagination, he takes inspiration from an earlier text, *Sir Gawain and the Green Knight*, which, like the novel it inspires, contemplates 'the problems of becoming oriented within ideological, theological, and geographic space' (Vernon and Miller 2018: 71).

> In that fragment (of *Sir Gawain and the Green Knight*), which is literally about one stanza, there's a mini-description of the landscape that he crosses, and then he gets to the castle and the story continues.
> What really sparked my imagination as far as *The Buried Giant* was concerned was that tiny little description of the country he was crossing. It sounds like such a weird place. Britain in those days was really rough. There weren't any inns or anything like that where he could stay, so he had to sleep on rocks in the pouring rain ... I thought, 'This is a rather interesting landscape' ... So that helped form the fictional landscape in which *The Buried Giant* took place. (Rukeysa 2015)

Landscape provided the first inspiration for the narrative (usually, as I mention in Chapter 4, it is the idea which comes first, the setting after). However, it is not simply the evocatively 'weird' (the opposite of familiar, homely) space that inspired the author, but more the idea that Gawain had to traverse this uncivilized wilderness. Necessarily, the possibilities for the novel's plot were restricted by the space (this landscape could hardly support a country house novel, a dystopian fiction). Yet, like many of Ishiguro's works, *The Buried Giant* is a road narrative, but rather than a 'motoring' journey, this is undertaken by foot (and occasionally horse). Axl and Beatrice are more closely in contact with the natural environment than Stevens or Kathy, who only intermittently venture from the security of their vehicles and, as such, are never really *in* the landscape in quite the same way (they are visitors, in transit). Ishiguro is a little inconsistent in his portrayal, suggesting in the opening that one 'would have searched a long time for the sort of winding lane or tranquil meadow for which England later became celebrated', only to remark later that the view from a window 'may not have differed so greatly from one to be had from the high windows of an English country house today' (*BG* 3; 87). It is, of course, an ideational space, like his 'imaginary' Japan, his 'mythic' England, and so is no more hostage to the 'real' than its inspiration.

The Buried Giant charts the foundations of an idea of Britain as place emerging from the cultural vacuum of the Roman retreat, when we see once more the 'island as it existed before nations' (Vernon and Miller 2018: 69). Necessarily, the process of nation-building takes many centuries and involves countless conflicts, as various nascent groups tussle not simply for military supremacy, but for the right to determine precisely what kind of place their emergent nation will be. In this sense, all wars are culture wars. It is not only the villas and roads, the material remnants of a once great empire that lie in ruin, but the very concept of 'Roman Britain' erodes in lived memory as the maps are redrawn, or maps of place recede to reveal, once more, blank space. George Steiner sees 'a seminal relationship between European humanity and its landscape' because 'that landscape has been moulded, humanised by feet and hands' as 'in no other part of the globe'; the 'cartography of Europe', he continues, 'arises from the capacities, the perceived horizons of human feet.

European men and women have walked their maps' (2016). Axl and Beatrice are among the first to begin the process of reconnoitring and in this way investing with meaning the space of medieval Britain. The novel takes its title from the giant buried beneath 'The Great Plain', a landmark for the ancient Britons which Axl and Beatrice must cross on their way to their son's village: 'The path goes over where the giant is buried. To one who doesn't know it, it's an ordinary hill' (*BG* 33). Maybe it is yet another wrong path. As the narrator remarks, demonstrating an awareness that neither space nor place are absolute, one might take this 'meaningful space', or place, as simply 'ordinary' space, depending on whether or not the observer is initiated into the culture for which the space is allotted significance. One reading of the novel is that it is interested in the construction of place, the imposition of meaning(s) on an otherwise undifferentiated landscape with its hidden timedepth. In killing the dragon, sickly as she is, Wistan acts as a proxy for Saint George in the formative event of England's birth. History, in this sense, is little more than the transformation of barren open space into culturally and ideologically meaningful place through event. *The Buried Giant* charts the foundations of the England onto which is overlaid Darlington, Hailsham. These moments described, inscribed in the medieval landscape constitute the timedepth for his later works: Stevens, Kathy and Banks walk over the buried bones of Querig, Gawain, Wistan, Beatrice, Axl; Darlington and Hailsham rest on, take root in, the great plain, nourished by the 'richer dust' of the past's buried giants.

III

The landscape of *The Buried Giant* has the 'remarkable ... degree of variety' that Lowenthal and Prince see as 'preeminently characteristic' of England (1964: 309). In the opening passage, the narrator describes 'miles of desolate [a word Stevens associates with Mrs Benn's marriage], uncultivated land; here and there rough-hewn paths over craggy hills or bleak moorland', sparsely populated with 'castles containing music' and monasteries 'steeped in learning' (*BG* 3). Cowed with the burden of age, Axl and Beatrice must traverse this space in a journey that is, once more, both in space and time. The first obstacle is the Great Plain 'where the giant is buried' (*BG* 33). It is interesting that Ishiguro introduces his central conceit so early in the novel, and that it plays no significant role later in the story (presumably after the death of Querig the giant rises, shaking off earth and age ('like dew' to invoke Shelley) once more to ravish the land). The plain is appropriately treacherous, 'covered in heather and gorse, never more than knee high, and only occasionally did a tree come into view – some solitary, crone-like specimen, bowed by endless gales' (*BG* 34). The narrator's despairing description (free indirect discourse as the oral storyteller imagines Axl and Beatrice's emotions) embodies the scene's and character's growing trepidation. The anthropomorphic tree emerges in a landscape unconducive to life, stunted by its rootedness to place, its inability to move, the necessity to passively adapt to an inescapable hostile environment. We might think back to Mr Cardinal's suggestion that life would be better if persons were 'firmly embedded in the soil': presumably, that depends on the nature of the soil, whether it is the carefully managed garden of an English country house in which Stevens germinates, or the untamed wilderness of medieval Britain from which Wistan or Edwin emerges battle-ready. Inspired by *Sir Gawain*, Ishiguro evokes the tortured terrain of another revisionist Arthurian romance, which sees Robert Browning's Childe Roland 'pledged to the plain', enduring the 'starv'd ignoble nature' in which 'nothing throve' (1989: 95). 'Gawain's first reverie', his own dramatic monologue, is remarkably similar in its ominous tone, Gawain asking, 'Those dark windows. For what purpose did God place them on this mountain path before me?' (*BG* 221). Moving inevitably towards his own death in Browning's suicide narrative (in many ways and for many characters in *BG*, suicide is inevitable, longed for), Roland later encounters 'some palsied oak', kin to Ishiguro's 'crone-like specimen' (1989: 98). Like Browning's, Ishiguro's post-Roman geography is suffused with memories of war and death; the marshy dead land drenched in the mixed blood of battles past is a personification of the quiet despair of one knowingly moving towards a final boundary with a simultaneous sense of dread and desire. In crossing the inhospitable land, Roland, Axl and Beatrice move through mindscapes rendered material, mapped onto landscape to be traversed physically and mentally.

Certain natural features in this otherwise undifferentiated space accumulate deep communal meaning. One such is 'the old thorn', a 'local beauty spot' that grows near the warren. Another thorn features prominently in the final scenes with Querig, one which draws us back by association to the warren in much the same way that corridors connect the apparently disparate domains of Hoffman's hotel (Ishiguro's recurring characters also perform this portal function in his novels, uniting them in one matrix of interconnected themes). Querig's pit, 'like a drained pond', has at its centre 'a solitary hawthorn bush sprouting incongruously through the stone' (*BG* 309–10). Life emerging, taking precarious hold in the most unlikely terrain. Perhaps Ishiguro has in mind William Wordsworth's poem 'The Thorn', in which the titular shrub is a 'mass of knotted joints, / A wretched thing forlorn', which nonetheless becomes a landmark, a symbolic anchor, on which many local myths become ensnared like the litter on Kathy's barbed wire (2008: 59). Even such an unassuming specimen as this can, in certain circumstances, become a companion, as it does for both Wordsworth's 'wretched woman' (tellingly mourning a dead child) and the dying dragon cursed by Merlin. Awaiting her death at the hands of Wistan (a cowboy/knight/samurai), Querig seems to seek final consolation in 'the only other thing alive in the pit', leading Axl to speculate that it 'had become a source of great comfort to her, and that even now, in her mind's eye, she was reaching for it' (*BG* 320). This moment of anticipated victory is one not of triumph but pathetic spectacle, Querig 'alone and desolate' to borrow Stevens's phrase, Beatrice remarks with sympathy that she is sickly, 'no more than a fleshy thread' (*BG* 310). As Roland stumbles on the object of his quest, 'Dotard, a-dozing at the very nonce, / After a life spent training', Beatrice asks, 'Can this really be her?' (*BG* 310). Querig's spilt blood nourishes the thorn, a natural feature which will outlast but memorialize the fateful occasion. Roots do not simply grow on the land, rather they draw from it (much like language), and, in so doing, pull the hidden past into the present: memory, history is formed in this very moment. Roots consume and recycle that which has been buried, drawing deeply from what Gawain calls 'an old burial ground', seemingly a 'pleasant copse in the springtime. Dig its soil, and not far beneath the daisies and buttercups come the dead' (*BG* 186). The trees, the hawthorns, are both bent and cowed by the inclemency of exposure to weather, and by the polluted soil in which they are embedded. We can say the same of Axl, Wistan, Beatrice, Gawain; loosely rooted, mobile yet anchored to place, they are assailed also by the winds of history, of conflicting ideologies and ancient animosities while also drawing their nourishment, or poison, from the polluted ground, posing once more Eliot's question, made more resonant by the hawthorn erupting from rock, 'What are the roots that clutch, what branches grow / Out of this stony rubbish?' (2004: 61). Eliot, of course, is referring to the detritus of Western culture, from which only a 'dead tree' emerges, offering no shelter.

Sometimes, though, forests grow from such unpromising land. Forests and their rich symbolism open up more possibilities than altered terrain and have been a mainstay of literature, more specifically folk literature, for millennia. As Marco Post observes, the 'forest in the West-European fairy tale recurrently has the function of a *limen* to the Otherworld, which is to say a conventional landmark which signifies the boundary between the mundane and the banal on the one hand and the magical and fantastic on the other' (2014: 69). Ishiguro's woods are often used to convey a fear of the unknown, the unseen (told and not told, seen and not seen), the partially obscured. In *The Buried Giant*, we are told that for the inhabitants the 'woodland … would have stirred a sense of foreboding' (*BG* 87). Becoming frailer as the novel and her journey towards death progresses as she traverses the textscape, Beatrice fears returning to 'Merlin's wood'; 'let's not go back to that wood', she pleads with Axl, 'for I'm sure some evil lingers there' (*BG* 296). Woods are enclosed, wild, obstructing vision, hiding the potential danger of predation. Ogres too occupy these woods, possibly literal but equally likely explanatory narratives for dangers as yet unknown. In *Never Let Me Go*, the woods loom threateningly just off-screen: 'There were all kinds of horrible stories about the woods … a boy had had a big row with his friends and run off beyond the Hailsham boundaries. His body had been found two days later, up in those woods, tied to a tree with the hands and feet chopped off' (*NLMG* 50). As I suggest in Chapter 2, this nightmare is soon to become reality, the fantasy identical to the clone's future. Coincidentally, commenting on the figure of the 'doner' in the Russian folk tale (a figurative made literal here), Vladimir Propp remarks that the 'donor is encountered accidentally, most often in the forest (in a hut), or else in a field, on the roadway, in the street' (2009). Woods, like Frost's 'yellow wood' in which 'two roads diverged', encourage thoughts of partings, separation. On their visit to the abandoned boat, Kathy, Tommy and Ruth encounter a small wood, Kathy 'led the way to where the woods began, but then, faced with three distinct paths through the trees, had to stop to consult the sheet of directions I'd brought with me' (*NLMG* 84). Paths again. At this point they have already metaphorically entered alone the woods in their lives, experienced the brutality portended by their earlier fears of dismemberment. One might, as does Cheng, see some meaningful friendship, consolation here, the idea that 'they remain indivisible as they cling to one another in a futureless world' (2010: 49). However, it is no coincidence that the three travellers, inextricably alone despite proximity's illusory comradery, encounter three paths. Through the terrible individuality of their experiences, they have been irredeemably divided, their life-paths diverging long before this symbolic temptation to let one another go.

Yet, once again, they come to a barrier that reminds them of 'the wire mesh boundary with the garden' at Hailsham (*NLMG* 47). For many years, their world was limited by barbed wire. These are fences, yes, but also a symbolic gesture towards their lacerated futures: to leave Hailsham is to cross a brutal visceral barrier, one which very literally cuts through the soft permeable membrane of the body. Organs in this sense, torn flesh, are a kind of offering, a price to be paid to leave Hailsham and the inhuman(e) world which enables it. Indeed, the novel ends with just such a (much discussed) provocation, as Kathy stands before 'acres of ploughed earth' and a barbed wire fence:

> All along the fence, especially along the lower line of wire, all sorts of rubbish had caught and tangled. It was like the debris you get on a sea-shore: the wind must have carried some of it for miles and miles before finally coming up against these trees and these two lines of wire ... if I waited long enough, a tiny figure would appear on the horizon across the field, and gradually get larger until I'd see it was Tommy, and he'd wave, maybe even call. (*NLMG* 281–2)

It is not by chance that Kathy envisages freedom as being situated beyond the barbed wire. Here, we clearly see that the landscape acts for Kathy as a continuation of the grounds of Hailsham; beyond, past this final barbed wire, is free space, and it is this heaven in which she imagines Tommy, after his great (corporeal) escape. Perhaps though, as Tommy speculates, 'There are more donations, plenty of them, on the other side of that [figurative and literal] line', just 'no more recovery centres, no carers, no friends' (*NLMG* 274). Kathy recalls that at the cottages 'we'd evolved this system where we called for particular favourite scenes to be played again – like, for instance, the moment the American jumps over the barbed wire on his bike in The Great Escape. There'd be a chant of: "Rewind! Rewind!" until someone got the remote and we'd see the portion again, sometimes three, four times' (*NLMG* 97). With a terrible poignancy, Kathy is unaware as to why this moment of cinema history comes to mind as the first example, not of escape but simply a scene from life after 'home'. Oddly, this inability to relate art to life manifests in her reading of *Daniel Deronda*, as John Mullan has commented (in a watery metaphor): 'The fact that the novel is about a man who tries to discover his true parentage, about the hunger to know your origins, never breaks surface' (2009: 106). A sensitive reading might suggest that these two instances of art are radically alien: the post-human clones have nothing to do with human parenting, or nothing to do with human wars. A less sensitive reading might see a constitutional failure to relate one's experiences to art, one that may evidence the profound otherness upon which their brutal treatment is predicated. One might conclude further that if they had produced art that conveyed a sense of their souls, their 'humanity', then universal deferral might have followed; it is the failure of their art to do so that results in Hailsham's closure and the end of a movement towards their emancipation. That is to say, the experiment was unsuccessful because it revealed the clones' fundamental lack of humanity. Or, perhaps as Shameem Black argues, the novel 'makes a case for an ethics offering a very different approach to art and empathy that relies on the recognition of the inhuman' (2009: 786). Regardless, the power of the final scene is not simply attributable to the fact that Kathy cannot traverse a material demarcation. Even were she able to cross this polyvalent boundary (as she does elsewhere), she'd find herself not in the free space that her imagination presents, but simply in another variety of place that is not hers. As Rosemarie Garland-Thomson notes, they do not 'know how to interact with nonclones or to use public space in any way' (2017). The final tragedy for Kathy and the clones is that space is always imbued with meanings formed in the oneiric space of childhood, and that, as a result, there is no escape, not over the barbed wire or across the ocean in a broken-down trawler.

IV

Water plays a vital role in Ishiguro's topographical poetics, featuring recurrently in the form of rivers, marshes, lakes and the sea. These bodies of water, the 'pond, river, or well', are, as Post remarks, like forests, 'limen', portals to some imagined 'Otherworld' (2014: 69). In one of their final encounters in *Never Let Me Go*, during one of Kathy's visits, Tommy conjures an image which invests the novel's title with more depth than the shallow pop song that so moves Kathy and Madame:

> I keep thinking about this river somewhere, with the water moving really fast. And these two people in the water, trying to hold onto each other, holding on as hard as they can, but in the end it's just too much. The current's too strong. They've got to let go, drift apart. That's how I think it is with us. It's a shame,

> Kath, because we've loved each other all our lives. But in the end, we can't stay together forever. (*NLMG* 277)

Tommy is merely suggesting that he and Kathy cannot, ultimately, remain together: they, like us all, must one day let go, and be let go. Despite the illusion that they can 'cling to one another in a futureless world', they are profoundly alone, already adrift (Cheng 2010: 49). Tommy takes recourse to a metaphor that derives its power from the irresistible physical force of rushing water. The forces that assail the clones are history, personal and national, other people, loneliness and, of course, death. In some ways, the metaphor seems to be inaccurate; presumably the current would act with equal force on each, and the final destination would be the same (completion). Drifting apart also feels incongruous in this context of rushing water – surely, they would be dragged apart, violently separated. But we know that they are not violently separated precisely because they offer no resistance; their fatal separation is indeed as passive, as undramatic as Tommy's metaphor implies. Tommy's conflation of two watery images, the idea of irresistible currents and slow drift, has a peculiar power to convey the subtle but inevitable forces which prise people apart over the course of a life, or simply act to erode the illusion that they were together in the first place.

Tommy is reconciled to their immanent parting in a way that Kathy is not, possibly because he has overcome more obstacles in his short life, and because he has already taken the first steps in his final journey. His mature acceptance finds illustration in the awful banality of his colloquialisms, although these also indicate an unwillingness or inability to face, and perhaps oppose, the (slings and arrows of the) realities of his fate. One might see something noble in such acquiescence. Possibly, though, Tommy has come to realize not that separation and the end of childhood love are inevitable at life's end, but that he and his friends were never meaningfully together, but were rather always radically, irredeemably alone in their identical but unique destinies. The many disagreements documented by Kathy evidence a desire to be together in the face of a deep aloneness. Tommy seems to be more aware than the others of the nature of their condition, an awareness expressed in his characteristic rages which, as Robert Eaglestone notes, 'come from deep inside him' but represent a 'conscious knowledge' that has no other means of expression (2017: 22). The novel's tragedy is encompassed in the misleading title: it is not the prospect of friends and lovers letting one another go which invests tragedy but rather the more urgent pain of never having had. Like Axl at the genuinely moving moment on the beach when he is compelled to relinquish Beatrice, the sadness attends his acknowledgement that love was never at stake, that the fear of a more despairing loneliness was the only thing which necessitated the shared illusion of togetherness. In other words, the idea that each had the other was nothing more than a shared mythos, a game. In the long term, their destination may be the same, but for now, Kathy is adrift from Ruth and Tommy, who share an experience that, for Kathy, lies in a future outside of her text. A less generous reading might suggest that Tommy, Ruth and Kathy have been playing at a love learned from films, television, books and pop songs (as Banks mimics his heroes), that, due to both youth and their status as clones, their curtailed possibility for longevity (aspirations to grow old together are, presumably, central to love) means that, in fact, they can have no conception of love. Love is future-oriented, clones are futureless. Like the trite song from which the title comes, Tommy gives voice to words which are ultimately vacuous. In this way, the love that is so absent reflects also the absence of souls that mean so much in their world.

A remarkably similar scenario to the one described by Tommy occurs when Axl and Beatrice find themselves having to travel a river 'swiftly to [their] son's village' because, as Axl tells a frail Beatrice in a suitable metaphor of distances, 'walking's beyond' them (*BG* 244). Finding no boat (the boat (perhaps the same boat that Tommy, Ruth and Kathy visit but cannot board) is saved for the climax), they are placed into coracle-like barrels by a kindly boatman. However, there being no single basket sufficiently large to accommodate both, they must go 'one to each basket' (*BG* 244). With some trepidation, Beatrice begs Axl 'let's not separate', 'let's not be parted', but Axl assures her that all will be well, despite having no more certainty than she (*BG* 244–5). During their journey along the river, slow but treacherous with marshy banks, they come across a boat, in which Axl finds a woman (the same old woman seems to haunt the couple) who he assumes to be assailed by hordes of pixies. Axl tries to save the woman before realizing, just in time, that his wife is in fact the target. Desperate to return to her side to defend Beatrice, he 'waded through the weeds, the broken bulrushes, the mud tugging at his feet' (*BG* 254). The woman tells Axl several times, 'leave her, stranger, leave her to us', to which Axl replies, bringing back *Never Let Me Go*, 'I'll never, never give her up' (*BG* 254). He manages to rescue her, but it is inevitably a temporary reprieve: This is simply the wrong time to let her go, but that moment must, as Tommy has warned us, come eventually. The river, slow, by turns deep and shallow, reed-obscured banks, cannot be the same fast-flowing river that Tommy imagines. The two are equally symbolic, but their landscapes and the characters give rise to features that are unique to their experience.

It is in Ishiguro's debut that a river features most prominently, polluted, eternally dark, running along the waste ground between Etsuko's modern building and Sachiko's dilapidated cottage. The river is haunted, at least for Mariko, by a ghostly figure that she refers to several times as the 'woman from across the river' (*PVH* 18). Mariko has been traumatized by a particular memory from her life in Tokyo after the war:

> There was a canal at the end and the woman was kneeling there, up to her elbows in water. A young woman, very thin. I knew something was wrong as soon as I saw her. You see, Etsuko, she turned round and smiled at Mariko.

> I knew something was wrong and Mariko must have done too because she stopped running. At first I thought the woman was blind, she had that kind of look, her eyes didn't seem to actually see anything. Well, she brought her arms out of the canal and showed us what she'd been holding under the water. It was a baby. I took hold of Mariko then and we came out of the alley. (*PVH* 74)

With a deep insensitivity, Sachiko later drowns Mariko's kittens in the river by the cottage. The act maps directly onto the previous incident (the desire for and terror of the eternal return). This however is only an example of the varieties of abuse and neglect which Mariko has experienced. As Cynthia Wong (in a watery and botanical metaphor) has noted, 'Mariko harbours deeply rooted resentments against her mother' (2005: 29). For Mariko, the river is identical with the canal of her Tokyo memory. As Sachiko flows into Etsuko, Mariko into Keiko, the two streams coalesce outside of time, outside of space, the river a physical manifestation of Mariko's enduring trauma and evidence of the inescapability of the meaningful places of our lives. Mariko ports the Tokyo canal to her new home. In this sense, the river is the symbolic centre of the novel, the externalization of the narrative, Etsuko's temporal vagrancy and the various traumas of war that flow through the characters' lives. Beatrice has a similarly morbid experience with water in Merlin's wood, looking into a clear pool she sees 'babes, and only a short way beneath the water's surface. I thought first they were smiling, and some waving, but when I went nearer I saw how they lay unmoving' (*BG* 296). Not waving, but drowning, as it were. Oddly, however, Mariko has no desire to leave the river, telling Etsuko that she does not 'want to go away'; she is drawn compulsively time and again to its apparently foreboding but for her comforting banks. As Lewis remarks, she 'is constantly running away from her mother to spend time alone by the river' (2000: 35). We know that she is not alone, here. In this bizarre inversion, Mariko becomes the ghost of the drowned child, haunting a limin that acts for her and, for Etsuko, as a portal into not one but multiple Otherworlds, of past, present and future. Indeed, perhaps the woman from 'across the river' is Etsuko, appearing ethereally from the past, an incarnation that doubles her presence in the recalled present of narration. Ishiguro is fascinated by memory's self-haunting, the inherently uncanny, gothic nature of recalls' self-doubling. This finds its way into landscape; as James remarks, Ishiguro furnishes 'everyday landscapes with powerful mnemonics' (2008: 96). One evening Etsuko searches for Mariko on the far side of the ominous river. Crossing the bridge, she recalls that the ground 'felt soft, almost marshy under my feet. Perhaps it is just my fancy that I felt a cold touch of unease there on that bank, a feeling not unlike premonition' (*PVH* 40). The river acts as a multidimensional conduit, collapsing persons, times and experiences: her premonition has to do with the later death of her own daughter, but that premonition is possibly added retrospectively, in the present of narration. This crossing is also the precise moment at which Etsuko *becomes* the ghostly woman from across the river that Mariko encounters repeatedly (this is why she recognizes Etsuko, even though, at that time, Etsuko had yet to return to haunt Mariko), in a text which overlays its various time signatures and psychic timedepths.

Lakes are less common features in Ishiguro's landscapes: There is that in *The Buried Giant* surrounded by Ogres visible to Edwin but invisible to Wistan; that in Merlin's wood, the kidney-shaped lake at the centre of Ryder's housing estate; and Mortimer's Pond in *The Remains of the Day*. Like the gardens of Darlington, Mortimer Pond offers tranquillity, 'an atmosphere of great calm' conducive to reflection. Stevens, typically, decides to sit and look on at the spectacle, with the excuse that his 'footwear is not such as to permit me easily to walk around the perimeter – I can see even from where I now sit the path disappearing into areas of deep mud – but I will say that such is the charm of this spot that on first arriving, I was sorely tempted to do just that. Only the thought of the possible catastrophes that might befall such an expedition' (*RD* 120–1). Once again, Stevens resorts to his sole criteria of aesthetic judgment: the charming. The pond is constructed, not natural at all. It is perfectly appropriate then that Stevens finds in this garden-like place the harmonious calm which has eluded him. Once more sitting on a bench, he reflects that the 'tranquillity of the present setting ... has enabled me to ponder all the more thoroughly these thoughts which have entered my mind over this past half-hour or so' (*RD* 121). James suggests that Stevens's memories are 'sparked by topographical features discovered unexpectedly in enclaves that seem at first serene' (2008: 96). However, this calm comes at the expense of avoiding a more troubled path; he both literally and figuratively refuses to take the path less trodden, because it is marshy, muddy, and he is ill equipped in his borrowed lounge suit. Confronted with resistance, that is to say, he balks, decides rather to surrender to convenience. We might think back to the situation of the Jewish maids that Stevens was asked to let go, a request to which he acquiesced without challenge in an attempt to avoid 'catastrophes' which actually arose through inaction. His experience at the lake, his pondering only so far, echoes his unwillingness to venture further into the murkier implications of his own and his master's past.

Marshes perform a similar function in *Never Let Me Go*. Kathy, Tommy and Ruth travel together to visit a much-mythologized boat, 'just sitting there, stranded in the marshes' (*NLMG* 268–70). It is not clear why the boat holds such a fascination, not just for our heroes but for the wider clone community. It is, after all, a common site around any coast. The friends themselves have no real idea of the appeal, although they do recognize that the trip brings them together for one final reunion. It too is 'stranded', of course, unable to escape its certain fate. Picturesque as it is, Lilley argues that 'the pastoral is used to manage and to explore the tensions between appearances and reality that gradually emerge as the purposes of Hailsham and the characters' lives becomes clear' (2016: 61). Perhaps on some irretrievably geologically rooted level, some buried ambition, the boat in the marshland represents or gestures towards at least the possibility of freedom, even if not for them. Or, perhaps it speaks of the 'unwanted freedom' that Mark Currie sees as so central to a novel which, to an extent, revels in rapture (2009: 92). However, they can get only so close:

> Not so long ago, the woods must have extended further, because you could see here and there ghostly dead trunks poking out of the soil, most of them broken off only a few feet up. And beyond the dead trunks, maybe sixty yards away, was the boat, sitting beached in the marshes under the weak sun ... We were surrounded by silence and when we started to move towards the boat, you could hear the squelch under our shoes. Before long I noticed my feet sinking beneath the tufts of grass, and called out: 'Okay, this is as far as we can go'. (*NLMG* 218–19)

Echoing Stevens, not only does Kathy realize that her ailing companions cannot physically traverse so treacherous a barrier, she acts as something of a guardian, reinforcing boundaries. We see here the process of growth and decay, those rooted trees now themselves reabsorbed into the soil which once supported them. Beyond lies the sea, freedom, even an image of openness and possibility, hinted at on the earlier search for Ruth's possible when they entered a gallery in which 'the paintings too – mostly oils in deep blues and greens – had sea themes' (*NLMG* 160). Seeing the marshes, Kathy 'heard Tommy say behind me: "Maybe this is what Hailsham looks like now. Do you think?" ' (*NLMG* 220). Ruth replies, pragmatically, that 'it wouldn't turn into marshland just because it's closed', to which Tommy responds, again both telling and not telling, that 'this is pretty close to the picture in my head. Except there's no boat, of course' (*NLMG* 220-1). In his memory, Tommy refigures the landscape of Hailsham as the marsh, and in this symbolic reimagining, there can be no boat, even one that fails to inspire fantasies of escape. There is an optimism in his ability to see Hailsham in a distant future, and the woods that surrounded it and which caused such fear becoming little more than 'dead trunks'. But this is also a metaphor of the tragedy of the clones, so utterly anchored to Hailsham, in their marshy landscape of quiet despair, that escape is not even part of their imaginative world. One might, though, see some oblique philosophical consolation here in the environmental evolution, a suggestion that their own passing, however premature, participates still in the inevitable cyclicality of fecundity and decay. But this would be a rather transparent fantasy.

Stevens's journey, at once more and less eventful than he had anticipated, also concludes by the seaside: There is no further to go on an island nation. Appropriately, his journey ends at early evening, as he sits with 'a good view ... of the sun setting over the sea, and though there is still plenty of daylight left – it has been a splendid day – I can see, here and there, lights starting to come on all along the shore' (*RD* 231). Sitting on a bench on a pier after his final meeting with Miss Kenton, he reminisces and, remarkably similarly to the Mortimer Pond scene, has a moment of almost epiphanic clarity enabled by the space:

> What can we ever gain in forever looking back and blaming ourselves if our lives have not turned out quite as we might have wished? The hard reality is, surely that for the likes of you and I there is little choice other than to leave our fate, ultimately, in the hands of those great gentlemen at the hub of this world what employ our services. What is the point in worrying oneself too much about what one could or could not have done to control the course one's life took? Surely it is enough that the likes of you and I at least try to make our small contribution count for something true and worthy. And if some of us are prepared to sacrifice much in life in order to pursue such aspirations, surely that is in itself, whatever the outcome, cause for pride and contentment. (*RD* 244)

As with his recognition that any possibility for an intimate personal relationship with Miss Kenton is truly past, he recognizes his professional failures, but once more abrogates responsibility for the 'course one's life took'. As Cheng argues, he is reassured by the words of a fellow butler on the peer 'that he is one of the collective we, and if he ever erred he did not err alone' (2010: 45). Like Mortimer Pond, he refuses the opportunity to tread more treacherous moral ground. Watching the strangers on the pier become friends, he very poignantly, though unwittingly, reveals his most profound failing when he observes that 'it is curious how people can build such warmth among themselves so swiftly' (*RD* 245). With the absurdity of Prufrock standing existentially alone on the seashore, Stevens thinks of 'the mermaids singing, each to each', concluding with his forebear that 'I do not think that they will sing to me' (Eliot 2004: 16). We might find in his curiosity about people and their relationships a renewed hope – he no longer sits and ponders his troubled past, but instead is outward-looking, attentive to his environment. Now that his past is finally left behind, he thinks of the outside world; his spatial journey then has been therapeutic, enabling him to free himself from the timelessness of Darlington. He has, that is to say, travelled into a future that holds possibility, by travelling through space to a lost past. But the assumption of that loss enables him to chart a new journey, a return to Darlington not as it was in the past but as it is in the present and as it will be in the future. The return journey then will not be undertaken by the Stevens we know to the Darlington Hall that he knows.

These often one-way journeys enable Ishiguro's characters the time and space they need to contemplate and, in some cases, to come to terms with their changing personal and political landscapes. Sometimes, as with Stevens, they are forced to recognize that 'what might have been is an abstraction / Remaining a perpetual possibility / Only in a world of speculation' (Eliot 2004: 171). Space acts to facilitate often profound realizations, in some cases offering a kind of harmony, even if that involves acknowledging an existential aloneness. One might see a hostility in Ishiguro's despairing rendering of homeless characters adrift in spaces which leave them bereft of family, of intimate and comforting place. However, they are singularly at home, uniquely oriented in their bespoke textscapes. Each textual terrain is constructed only for them, and although they cannot recognize their meta-home, their meta-place, from the outside they at least appear to be in the single spaces which can support their being. In this sense, their lostness, their homelessness transpires at home, in place, although they can never see themselves as such, entrenched as they are in their own personal emotional wildernesses. Tragically, these carefully designed spaces are indeed wilfully hostile, discomforting, unconsoling.

Notes

1 This is reminiscent of Colson Whitehead's inspiration for *The Underground Railroad*: 'You know, I think when you're a kid and you first hear about it in school or whatever, you imagine a literal subway beneath the earth. And then you find out that it's not a literal subway, and you get a bit upset. And so the book took off from that childhood notion.' Interview with David Bianculli, *NPR*, 8 November 2016.
2 A more ecologically minded study might take issue with the perceived blankness of space in the absence of human habitation.
3 Intended originally to be the narrator of *An Artist of the Floating World*. The story contains the seeds of many later reworkings, including Boris and his grandfather's battles with thugs.

Conclusion: The Remains of the ...

This study is little more than an imprecise, partial gesture towards a series of profound, ineffable gestures, ones that have elicited global critical and popular acclaim, a knighthood, numerous literary prizes and, perhaps, the greatest accolade of all, the Nobel Prize for Literature. The latter, of course, is never really or simply a literary award, but a laurel bestowed on those perceived to 'have conferred the greatest benefit to humankind'. Aspiring to the title of 'great butler', Stevens would envy the certainty of Ishiguro's greatness, seeing in it the consolation that one has not, as Ishiguro might say, 'backed a wrong, shameful, even evil cause, and wasted one's best years and talents to it' (*The Guardian*, 2016). Ishiguro himself might laugh at the suggestion that he is a 'great novelist', as he did in an interview with Cody Delistraty, asking incredulously 'What the hell is a great novelist?' (2015). Despite such modesty, few authors are greeted, or are greeted with and *sustain*, the degree of international critical and popular acclaim that Ishiguro has inspired from his first novel in 1982 and, very likely, the much-anticipated *Klara and the Sun* (forthcoming). His success can be attributed to his sensitivity to the terrible but mundane pains of the human condition, of ageing, acting on misguided beliefs, failures to love and be loved. Regardless of the great variety of themes, settings, periods and characters, his works always touch on these, the simple regrets that colour our individual, intimate and public lives.

Ishiguro is the first British recipient of the Nobel Prize since Doris Lessing in 2007, although it seems absurd to refer to Ishiguro as a 'British' author, as it does to describe his novels as Japanese, or British, or Medieval, or to try to place them in traditions or genres. Part of the wide appeal of Ishiguro's writing is its seeming vagrancy, its unrootedness, its cosmopolitanism. This feeling comes from the form itself; the novel, as Lukacs suggest, 'is, like no other, an expression of ... transcendental homelessness' (1971: 41). Homelessness is a pervasive mood in Ishiguro's fictional and lived world(s); as he told Kenzaburo Oe, he thinks of himself as 'a homeless writer', 'neither a very English Englishman [or] a very Japanese Japanese either' (1991: 115). He is an émigré, an immigrant, the archetype of the 'transnational' writer working in a global literary tradition. Ishiguro has spoken in many interviews about his own literary influences, including, as Cynthia Wong notes, 'Anton Chekov, Fydor Dostoyevsky, and Franz Kafka', as well as his admiration for Gabriel Garcia Marquez (*One Hundred Years of Solitude* is certainly important to *The Buried Giant*), Mario Vargas Losa, Milan Kundera, Samuel Beckett and Henry James. He has also invoked film as an influence on his writing, notably Yasujirō Ozu, Akira Kurosawa, Andrei Tarkovsky, Francis Ford Coppola and even Quentin Tarantino. Most apparent in this list of writers and directors is Ishiguro's interest in world culture, one that perhaps reflects, or at least is informed by, the author's own somewhat itinerant status.

While not interested in the 'New Sincerity' so typical of the contemporary and pointedly post-postmodern period in which we find ourselves, Ishiguro's fictions do advance the modernist and postmodernist aesthetic by investing formal and narratological innovation with a renewed concern for a global humanism or, as Rebecca Walkowitz sees it, 'critical cosmopolitanism' (2006). In an interview given shortly after being made Noble Laureate, Ishiguro remarked on the capacity of the arts to unite the world, even to establish panhuman values:

> This is a very weird time in the world, we've sort of lost faith in our political system, we've lost faith in our leaders, we're not quite sure of our values, and I just hope that my winning the Nobel prize contributes something that engenders good will and peace … It reminds us of how international the world is, and we all have to contribute things from our different corners of the world. (Ellis-Peterson and Flood 2017)

This inclusive use of 'our' and 'us' both designates and constructs a global cultural in-group. Of course, this group is self-selecting, a community of readers united by a joy in the possibilities, consolatory or redemptive, of writing. But there is also a sense of duty, here, responsibility, in the idea that artists '*have* to contribute', echoing perhaps 'Cellist's Eloise's sense that the artist or connoisseur is on a vital 'mission', one that Ryder attempts and fails. Ishiguro holds the arts in high esteem, assuming the great responsibility of contributing to, as Stevens might say, 'the course of history' and having, as Ono might say, a 'position of large influence' (*AFW* 139). But there is also a very deliberate suggestion that the arts should be traditional, distinct, not homogenous – the works that come from the 'different corners of the world' (which rhetorical inaccuracy reminds us of Stevens's 'different corners of the globe') need to share something of that world but also to represent difference. We might return here to Deleuze and Guattari's fascination with the 'armature' model of architecture which 'holds heterogeneities together without their ceasing to be heterogeneous' (2005: 329). For Ishiguro, the arts are the armature of global culture, connecting, uniting, but supporting difference. As I have written elsewhere (Sloane 2018), Ishiguro is very wary of the homogenization of world culture.

I have attempted to give some expression to or to uncover the armature of Ishiguro's own gestural poetics, his repurposing of literary tradition, his interest in imagination, art, architecture and space. Through each of these means, Ishiguro simultaneously moves towards and recedes from the real, the world of sense. Necessarily, this attempt is gestural. His texts provide an outline of aspects of the human condition that cannot be approached directly, because the noumenal 'essence of world' which is the true subject of the texts 'can only be indicated' (Heidegger 2011: 108). Ishiguro's fictions offer trivial details, insignificant anecdotes, from which the shape or even location of the undisclosable thingness of the work emerges while it itself evades the grasp. It is impossible, that is to say, to speak directly of the thingness of Ishiguro's novels. In this gestural world, 'Everything is seen as many-sided ... things appear as isolated and yet connected, as full of value and yet totally devoid of it' (Lukacs 1971: 75). It is precisely this phenomenon that disturbs his narrators: Stevens cannot get to the thingness of great butlering, of dignity; Kathy cannot get to the heart of her life at Hailsham; Axl and Beatrice are utterly unable to determine whether they are together through love, habit or despair. Each is too close to the superfice of their subject. On the surface, the stories are simple, the dilemmas trivial. But underneath live 'strange life forms', to quote Ryder, riven with ambiguity, simultaneously replete and void of meanings. In this sense, his fictions are fundamentally attuned to the dilemmas of existentialism, the fear of meaninglessness, of bad faith, but a desire to attribute some meaning because, in its absence, a loneliness far worse awaits.

If this book has managed to say anything at all about Ishiguro's poetics, to crystalize the diaphanous, then it is a failed enterprise, one unattuned to its subject's singular qualities. The beauty of Ishiguro's writing is its surface's deceitful sheen which inevitably eludes the mind's grasp, while other, more unsettling possibilities emerge in perpetual immanence from the text's hidden depths. Ishiguro's fictions work through sleight of hand, the reader misled as to where the action is occurring by narrators who are themselves variously misled and misleading. Like his most poignant characters and their belated efforts at recuperative consolation, it is only after the reading experience has ended, sometimes many hours or even years after, that the reader realizes that some moment of great import was overlooked, thought trivial. Naturally, much here has been missed; in focusing on those details that appeared most salient, or which were presented as most salient by conspiratorial interlocutors whose rhetoric involves appeals to the like-minded, the fellow butler, carer, traveller, perhaps I have overlooked some terribly trivial detail that will, inevitably, come to haunt me. It is that very haunting that distinguishes Ishiguro's fictions for both character and reader. If his characters often despair at being misremembered, there is in his fictions a fear of being taken literally, being mistaken for a 'traditional social realist' (Gaby Wood 2017). In many interviews Ishiguro exhibits an anxiety about the reception of his fictions, a fear that somehow they will be misread, misunderstood, taken as trivial realist narratives. Such a possibility arises because his writing is so deceptively simple, his stories so apparently straightforward. He is, though, most delicately experimental a writer, concerned with uncovering those utterly trivial but utterly profound moments that come to define lives while our attention is distracted. The only way to really capture the essence of Ishiguro's writing is to continually edit, revise, update, modify. Once more then, this work in hand is transient, subject to revision as new details, new works arise. And on this note, we await the publication of *Klara and the Sun* to see whether it encourages a return to the previous texts to discover turning points missed, errors of critical judgment. But, criticism like life is iterative, and these things can emerge only in hindsight. We must simply wait, then, for history to unfold and to accept its judgments.

REFERENCES

Primary works

Ishiguro, Kazuo (1983), 'The Summer after the War', in *Granta: Best of Young British Novelists*, vol. 7, printed and published for the proprietor by King, Sell, & Railtor.
Ishiguro, Kazuo (1993), *The Remains of the Day*, London: Faber.
Ishiguro, Kazuo (2005a), *A Pale View of Hills*, London: Faber.
Ishiguro, Kazuo (2005b), *When We Were Orphans*, London: Faber.
Ishiguro, Kazuo (2006), *Never Let Me Go*, London: Faber.
Ishiguro, Kazuo (2010), *Nocturnes*, London: Faber.
Ishiguro, Kazuo (2013a), *The Unconsoled*, London: Faber.
Ishiguro, Kazuo (2013b), *An Artist of the Floating World*, London: Faber.
Ishiguro, Kazuo (2015), *The Buried Giant*, London: Faber.

Secondary works

Adams, Tim (2005), 'For Me, England Is a Mythical Place', *The Guardian*, 20 February.
Adorno, Theodor (1991), *The Culture Industry*, London: Routledge.
Adorno, Theodor (1997a), *Prisms*, trans. Samuel and Shierry Weber, Cambridge, MA: MIT Press.
Adorno, Theodor (1997b), 'Functionalism Today', in Neil Leach (ed.), *Rethinking Architecture: A Reader in Cultural Theory*, 5–19, London: Routledge.
Aitkenhead, Decca (2009), 'The G2 Interview: Kazuo Ishiguro', *The Guardian*, 27 April.
Allot, Miriam (1959), *Novelists on the Novel*, London: Routledge and Kegan Paul.
Anderson, Richard C. et al. (1978), 'Schemata as Scaffolding for the Representation of Information in Connected Discourse', *American Educational Research Journal*, 15(3): 433–40.
Antliff, Mark (2002), 'Fascism, Modernism, and Modernity', *Art Bulletin*, 84(1): 148–69.
Arendt, Hannah (1971), 'Thinking and Moral Considerations: A Lecture', *Social Research*, 38(3): 417–46.
Ashbery, J. (1974), 'Self-Portrait in a Convex Mirror', *Poetry*, 124(5): 247–61, www.jstor.org/stable/20596528 (retrieved 6 June 2020).
Atkinson, Rob (1995), 'How the Butler Was Made to Do It: The Perverted Professionalism of *The Remains of the Day*', *Yale Law Journal*, 105(1): 177–220.
Auden, W. H. (1995), *Auden: Poems*, New York: Alfred A. Knopf.
Augé, Marc (2008), *Non-Places: An Introduction to Supermodernity*, London: Verso.
Bachelard, Gaston (1994), *The Poetics of Space*, Boston, MA: Beacon Press.

Baddeley, Alan (1992), 'What Is Autobiographical Memory', in Martin A. Conway, David C. Rubin, Hans Spinnler and Willem A. Wagenaar (eds), *Theoretical Perspectives on Autobiographical Memory*, 13–29, Netherlands: Springer.

Badiou, Alain with Nicholas Truong (2012), *In Praise of Love*, trans. Peter Bush, London: Serpent's Tail.

Baillie, Justine, and Sean Matthews (2009), 'History, Memory, and the Construction of Gender in *A Pale View of Hills*', in Sean Matthews, Sebastian Groes and Kazuo Ishiguro (eds), *Kazuo Ishiguro: Contemporary Critical Perspectives*, 45–56, New York: Continuum.

Ballard, J. G. (2014), *The Atrocity Exhibition*, London: Fourth Estate.

Barth, John (1980), *Lost in the Funhouse: Fiction for Print, Tape, Live Voice*, New York: Bantam Books.

Barth, John (1984), *The Friday Book: Essays and Other Non-Fiction*, London: John Hopkins University Press.

Barthes, Roland (1982), 'The Reality Effect', in Tzvetan R. Todorov and R. Carte (trans.), *French Literary Theory Today: A Reader*, 11–17, Cambridge: Cambridge University Press.

Barthes, Roland (1990), *S/Z*, trans. Richard Miller, Oxford: Blackwell.

Barthes, Roland (2000), 'French Toys', *Mythologies*, London: Vintage.

Bataille, Georges (1997), 'Museum', in Neil Leach (ed.), *Rethinking Architecture: A Reader in Cultural Theory*, 20–3, London: Routledge.

Beckett, Samuel (2006), *The Complete Dramatic Works*, London: Faber and Faber.

Bedggood, Daniel (2017), 'Kazuo Ishiguro: Alternate Histories', in James Acheson (ed.), *The Contemporary British Novel Since 2000*, 109–18, Edinburgh: Edinburgh University Press.

Beedham, Matthew (2010), *The Novels of Kazuo Ishiguro*, London: Palgrave Macmillan.

Bell, Clive (1914), *Art*, New York: Stokes.

Bennett, Andrew (2009), *Ignorance: Agnoiology and Literature*, Manchester: Manchester University Press.

Bennett, Caroline (2011), '"Cemetaries Are No Places for Young People": Children and Trauma in the Early Novels of Kazuo Ishiguro', in Sebastian Groes and Barry Lewis (eds), *Kazuo Ishiguro: New Critical Visions of the Novels*, 82–94, London: Palgrave Macmillan.

Berberich, Christine (2007), *The Image of the English Gentleman in Twentieth-Century Literature*, Hampshire: Ashgate.

Berryman, John (2014), *The Heart Is Strange: New Selected Poems*, ed. Daniel Swift, New York: Farrar, Straus and Giroux.

Bicknell, Jeanette (2014), 'Architectural Ghosts', *Journal of Aesthetics and Art Criticism*, 72(4): 435–41.

Bigsby, Christopher (2008), 'In Conversation with Kazuo Ishiguro', in Brian W. Shaffer and Cynthia Wong (eds), *Conversations with Kazuo Ishiguro*, 15–26, Jackson, MI: University Press of Mississippi.

Bishop, Claire (2004), 'Antagonism and Relational Aesthetics', *October*, 110: 51–79.

Bix, Herbert P. (1982), 'Rethinking "Emperor-System Fascism": Ruptures and Continuities in Modem Japanese History', *Bulletin of Concerned Asian Scholars*, 14(2): 2–19.

Black, Shameem (2009), 'Ishiguro's Inhuman Aesthetics', *Modern Fiction Studies*, 55(4): 785–807.

Blanchot, Maurice (1995), *The Work of Fire*, trans. Charlotte Mandell, Stanford, CA: Stanford University Press.

Bloch, Ernst (1997), 'Formative Education, Engineering Form, Ornament', in Neil Leach (ed.), *Rethinking Architecture: A Reader in Cultural Theory*, 43–50, London: Routledge.

Bloom, Harold (1994), *The Western Canon: The Books and School of the Ages*, New York: Harcourt Brace.

Borch, Christian (2002), 'Interview with Edward W. Soja: Thirdspace, Postmetropolis, and Social Theory', *Distinktion: Journal of Social Theory*, 3:1: 113–20.

Bourdieu, Pierre (1996), *The Rules of Art Genesis and Structure of The Literary Field*, Cambridge, MA: Polity.

Bourriaud, Nicolas (2002), *Relational Aesthetics*, Dijon: Les Presses du Reel.

Brecht, Bertolt (1978), *On Theatre*, trans. John Willett, London: Methuen.

Brink, Andre (1998), *The Novel: Language and Narrative from Cervantes to Calvino*, Basingstoke: Macmillan.

Brooke, Rupert (2010), *Collected Poems*, intro. by Lorna Beckett, Cambridge: Oleander Press.

Browning, Robert (1989), *Selected Poems*, ed. Daniel Karlin, London: Penguin.

Cain, Sian (2015), 'Writer's Indignation: Kazuo Ishiguro Rejects Claims of Genre Snobbery', *The Guardian*, 8 March.

Carey, John (2000), 'Few Novels Extend the Possibilities of Fiction. This One Does': Review of When We Were Orphans, *Sunday Times*, 2 April.

Carey, John (1992), *The Intellectuals and the Masses: Pride and Prejudice among the Literary Intelligentsia, 1880–1939*, London: Faber and Faber.

Carrier, David (2003), 'Remembering the Past: Art Museums as Memory Theaters', *Journal of Aesthetics and Art Criticism*, 61(1): 61–5.

Carroll, R. (2012), *Rereading Heterosexuality: Feminism, Queer Theory and Contemporary Fiction*, Edinburgh: Edinburgh University Press.

Carver, Raymond (2003), *What We Talk about When We Talk about Love*, London: Vintage.

Casey, Edward (1994), *Getting Back into Place*, Bloomington: Indiana University Press.

Castellano, Carlos Garrido (2020), 'Ryder Meets Bourriaud. Kazuo Ishiguro's *The Unconsoled* and the Contradictions of "Creative Capitalism"', *Critique: Studies in Contemporary Fiction*, 61(2): 236–47.

Chang, Elysha (2015), 'A Language That Conceals: An Interview with Kazuo Ishiguro, Author of *The Buried Giant*', *Electric Literature*, 27 March, https://electricliterature.com/a-language-that-conceals-an-interview-with-kazuo-ishiguro-author-of-the-buried-giant/.

Chaudhuri, Amit (1995), 'Unlike Kafka', *London Review of Books*, 17(11), 8 June.

Cheeke, Stephen (2008), *Writing for Art: The Aesthetics of Ekphrasis*, Manchester: Manchester University Press.

Chen, Ken (2015), 'Kazuo Ishiguro: My Own Private Japan', *The Margins*, 7 April.

Cheng, Chu-Chueh (2010), *The Margin without Centre*, Oxford: Peter Lang.

Chira, Susan (1989), 'Book Review Desk', *New York Times*, 8 October, p. 3, column 1.

Conway, Martin A. (1996), 'Failures of Autobiographical Remembering', in Douglas Herrmann, Cathy McEvoy, Christopher Hertzog, Paula Hertel and Marcia K. Johnson (eds), *Basic and Applied Memory Research: Theory in Context*, vol. 1, 295–315, Mahwah, NJ: Lawrence Erlbaum Associates.

Cooke, Rachel (2011), 'Kazuo Ishiguro Is Never Letting Go', *Evening Standard*, 3 February.
Currie, Mark (2009), 'Controlling Time: *Never Let Me Go*', in Sean Matthews, Sebastian Groes and Kazuo Ishiguro (eds), *Kazuo Ishiguro: Contemporary Critical Perspectives*, 91–103, New York: Continuum.
Dannenbaum, Jed, Carroll Hodge and Doe Mayer (2010), *Creative Filmmaking from the Inside Out: Five Keys to the Art of Making Inspired Movies and Television*, New York: Simon and Schuster.
Dean, Dominic (2019), 'Violent Authenticity: The Politics of Objects and Images in Ishiguro', *Textual Practice*, doi:10.1080/0950236X.2019.1651762.
Deleuze, Gilles, and Felix Guattari (2005), *A Thousand Plateaus: Capitalism and Schizophrenia*, trans. Brian Massumi, London: University of Minnesota Press.
Delistraty, Cody (2015), 'Lost Toys and Flying Machines: A Talk with Kazuo Ishiguro', *New Yorker*, 20 March.
Derrida, Jacques (1993), *Aporias*, trans. Thomas Dutoit, Stanford, CA: Stanford University Press.
Descartes, Rene (2017), *Meditations on First Philosophy, with Selections from the Objections and Replies*, 2nd ed., ed. John Cottingham, Cambridge: Cambridge University Press.
Dickens, Charles (2003), *Hard Times*, ed. Kate Flint, London: Penguin.
Doran, D'Arcy. (2016), 'How Working with Homeless People Gave Kazuo Ishiguro an Education in Human Nature', *Huck Magazine*, 20 January.
Drąg, Wojciech (2014), *Revisiting Loss: Memory, Trauma and Nostalgia in the Novels of Kazuo Ishiguro*, Newcastle upon Tyne: Cambridge Scholars Publishing.
Duncan, J., and N. Duncan (1988), '(Re)Reading the Landscape', *Space and Society*, 6(2): 117–26.
Dutta, Krishna (2003), *Calcutta: A Cultural and Literary History*, Oxford: Signal Books.
Eaglestone, Robert (2017), *The Broken Voice: Reading Post-Holocaust Literature*, Oxford: Oxford University Press.
Eaglestone, Robert (2018), 'The Past', in Daniel O'Gorman and Robert Eaglestone (eds), *The Routledge Companion to Twenty-First Century Literary Fiction*, 311–20, London: Routledge.
Earhart, H. Byron (2011), 'War and Peace', in *Mount Fuji: Icon of Japan*, Columbia: University of South Carolina Press.
Ebbatson, Roger (2013), *Landscape and Literature 1830–1914: Nature, Text, Aura*, Basingstoke: Palgrave Macmillan, https://ebookcentral-proquest-com.proxy.library.lincoln.ac.uk/lib/ulinc/detail.action?docID=1209504.
Eliot, T. S. (2004), *The Complete Poems and Plays*, London: Faber and Faber.
Ellis-Peterson, Hannah, and Alison Flood (2017), 'Kazuo Ishiguro Wins the Nobel Prize in Literature 2017', *The Guardian*, 6 October.
Ennis, Stephen (2016), 'Taking Note of the Kazuo Ishiguro Archive', *The Ransom Center Magazine*, 15 June.
Fanon, Frantz (1963), *The Wretched of The Earth*, preface by Jean-Paul Sartre, trans. Constance Farrington, New York: Grove Press.
Farrant, Marc (2020), 'Literary Endgames: The Post-Literary, Postcritique, and the Death of/in Contemporary Literature', *Critique: Studies in Contemporary Fiction*, 61(2): 144–56.

Ferris, Ina (1983), 'Realism and the Discord of Ending: The Example of Thackeray', *Nineteenth-Century Fiction*, 38(3): 289–303.
Finn, Richard B. (1992), *Winners in Peace: MacArthur, Yoshida, and Postwar Japan*, Berkeley: University of California Press.
Fleming, Tom (2009), 'Heartbreak in Five Movements', *The Observer*, 10 May.
Forty, A. (1995), 'Being or Nothingness: Private Experience and Public Architecture in Post-War Britain', *Architectural History*, 38: 25–35.
Foster, Roger (2013), 'Adorno on Kafka: Interpreting the Grimace on the Face of Truth', *New German Critique*, 118: 175–98.
Freedman, Ralph (1969), 'Refractory Visions: The Contours of Literary Expressionism', *Contemporary Literature*, 10(1): 54–74.
Frost, Robert (2002), *Robert Frost's Poems*, New York: St. Martin's.
Furst, Lilian R. (2007), 'Memory's Fragile Power in Kazuo Ishiguro's "Remains of the Day" and W. G. Sebald's "Max Ferber"', *Contemporary Literature*, 48(4): 530–53.
Gadamer, Hans-Georg (1977), *Philosophical Hermeneutics*, trans. and ed. David E. Linge, Berkeley: University of California Press.
Gadamer, Hans-Georg (1997), 'The Ontological Foundation of the Occasional and the Decorative', in Neil Leach (ed.), *Rethinking Architecture: A Reader in Cultural Theory*, 125–37, London: Routledge.
Garland-Thomson, R. (2017), 'Eugenic World Building and Disability: The Strange World of Kazuo Ishiguro's *Never Let Me Go*', *Journal of Medical Humanities*, 38: 133–45.
Gasché, Rodolphe (2005), 'The Felicities of Paradox: Blanchot on the Null-Space of Literature', in Carolyn Bailey Gill (ed.), *Maurice Blanchot: The Demand of Writing*, 34–69, London: Routledge.
Gehlawat, Monika (2013), 'Myth and Mimetic Failure in "The Remains of the Day"', *Contemporary Literature*, 54(3): 491–519.
Genova, P. (1997), 'Japonisme and Decadence: Painting the Prose of a Rebours', *Romantic Review*, 88(2): 267–90.
Goffman, Erving (1956), *The Presentation of Self in Everyday Life*, Edinburgh: University of Edinburgh Social Sciences Research Centre.
Gould, Thomas (2018), *Silence in Modern Literature and Philosophy: Beckett, Barthes, Nancy, Stevens*, Cham: Palgrave Macmillan.
Griffiths, Ruth (2002), *A Study of Imagination in Early Childhood and Its Function in Mental Development*, Abingdon: Routledge.
Groes, Sebastian (2011), 'Something of a Lost Corner: Kazuo Ishiguro's Landscapes of Memory and East Anglia', in Sebastian Groes and Barry Lewis (eds), *Kazuo Ishiguro: New Critical Visions of the Novels*, 211–24, London: Palgrave Macmillan.
Groes, Sebastian, and Paul Daniel-Veyret (2009), 'Like the Gateway to Another World: Kazuo Ishiguro's Screenwriting', in Sean Matthews and Sebastian Groes (eds), *Kazuo Ishiguro*, 32–44, New York: Continuum.
Guppy, Shusha (1986), 'Alain Robbe-Grillet, The Art of Fiction 91', *Paris Review*, Spring.
Hagglund, David (2017), 'Kazuo Ishiguro, the 2017 Nobel Prize Winner in Literature', *New Yorker*, 5 October.
Hammer, Louis (1981), 'Architecture and the Poetry of Space', *Journal of Aesthetics and Art Criticism*, 39(4): 381–8.

Harvey, Samantha C. (2013), *Transatlantic Transcendentalism: Coleridge, Emerson, and Nature*, Edinburgh: Edinburgh University Press.
Heidegger, Martin (2011), *Basic Writings*, ed. David Farell Krell, London: Routledge.
Helphand, Kenneth I. (2010), 'Gardens and War', *SiteLINES: A Journal of Place*, 5(2): 11–13.
Hensher, Philip (2000), 'It's the Way He Tells It…', *The Guardian*, 19 March.
Herring, Peter (2012), 'The Past Informs the Future; Landscape Archaeology and Historic Landscape Characterisation in the UK', in S. J. Kluiving and E. B. Guttmann-Bond (eds), *Landscape Archaeology between Art and Science: From a Multi- to an Interdisciplinary Approach*, 485–502, Amsterdam: Amsterdam University Press.
Hitchens, Christopher (2009), 'Fade to Black', *New York Times*, 1 October.
Hofweber, Thomas (2017), 'Conceptual Idealism without Ontological Idealism: Why Idealism Is True after All', in Tyron Goldschmidt and Kenneth L. Pearce (eds), *Idealism: New Essays in Metaphysics*, 121–41, Oxford: Oxford University Press.
Holmes, Frederick M. (2005), 'Realism, Dreams and the Unconscious in the Novels of Kazuo Ishiguro', in James Acheson and Sarah C. E. Ross (eds), *The Contemporary British Novel Since 1980*, 11–23, New York: Palgrave Macmillan.
Hudson, Cheryl (2007), 'American Popular Culture and Anti-Americanism', in Brendan O'Connor (ed.), *Anti-Americanism: Causes and Sources*, 239–62, Santa Barbara: Greenwoood.
Hume, David (1874), *A Treatise on Human Nature, Being an Attempt to Introduce the Experimental Method of Reasoning into Moral Subjects* and *Dialogues Concerning Natural Religion*, vol. I, ed. T. H. Green and T. H. Grose, London: Longmans, Green.
Hunnewell, Susannah (2008), 'Kazuo Ishiguro: The Art of Fiction No. 196', *Paris Review*, 184.
Ingarden, Roman (1961), 'Aesthetic Experience and Aesthetic Object', *Philosophy and Phenomenological Research*, 21(3): 289–313.
Ishiguro, Kazuo (1984), *The August Passage: A Profile of Arthur J. Mason*, unpublished manuscript, held by the Harry Ransom Center, The University of Texas at Austin.
Ishiguro, Kazuo (2005a), 'I Remain Fascinated by Memory', *Spiegel International*, 5 October, https://www.spiegel.de/international/spiegel-interview-with-kazuo-ishiguro-i-remain-fascinated-by-memory-a-378173.html
Ishiguro, Kazuo (2005b), 'An Interview with Kazuo Ishiguro', *Readers Read*, https://www.readersread.com/features/interview-with-kazuo-ishiguro-100120051.
Ishiguro, Kazuo (2009), 'I'm Sorry I Can't Say More: An Interview with Kazuo Ishiguro', in Sean Matthews and Sebastian Groes (eds), *Kazuo Ishiguro*, 114–25, New York: Continuum.
Ishiguro, Kazuo (2014), 'How I Wrote *The Remains of the Day* in Four Weeks', *The Guardian*, 6 December.
Ishiguro, Kazuo (2015), 'Kazuo Ishiguro Interview', *Geek's Guide to the Galaxy*, 6 April.
Ishiguro, Kazuo (2016), 'Thatcher's London and the Role of the Artist in a Time of Political Change', *The Guardian*, 24 June.
Ishiguro, Kazuo (2016), 'Kazuo Ishiguro on His Fears for Britain after Brexit', *Financial Times*, July.
Ishiguro, Kazuo (2017), 'Exclusive Interview', *NHK World – Japan*, 8 December.
Iwata, Miki (2008), 'Records and Recollections in "Krapp's Last Tape"', *Journal of Irish Studies*, 23: 34–43.

Iyer, Pico (1995), 'The Butler Didn't Do It Again', *Times Literary Supplement*, 28 April.
James, David (2008), *Contemporary British Fiction and the Artistry of Space: Style, Landscape, Perception*, New York: Continuum.
James, David (2009), 'Artifice and Absorption: The Modesty of *The Remains of the Day*', in Sean Matthews and Sebastian Groes (eds), *Kazuo Ishiguro*, 54–66, New York: Continuum.
James, David (2012), *Modernist Futures: Innovation and Inheritance in the Contemporary Novel*, New York: Cambridge University Press.
James, David (2019), *Discrepant Solace: Contemporary Literature and the Work of Consolation*, Oxford: Oxford University Press.
Jessica C. E., Gienow-Hecht (2006), 'Always Blame the Americans: Anti-Americanism in Europe in the Twentieth Century Author', *American Historical Review*, 111(4): 1067–91.
Jordison, Sam (2015), 'The Unconsoled Deals in Destruction and Disappointment', *The Guardian*, 27 January.
Kania, Andrew, and Theodore Gracyk (eds) (2011), The Routledge Companion to Philosophy and Music, New York: Taylor and Francis.
Kant, Immanuel (2001), *Prolegomena to Any Future Metaphysics That Will Be Able to Come Forward as Science, with Kant's Letter to Marcus Herz February 27, 1772*, 2nd ed., trans. Paul Carus, revised by James W. Ellington, Indianapolis: Hackett Publishing.
Kearney, Richard (1984), 'Dialogue with Jacques Derrida', in *Dialogues with Contemporary Continental Thinkers: The Phenomenological Heritage*, 105–26, Manchester: Manchester University Press.
Kellogg, Caroline (2017), 'British Writer Kazuo Ishiguro Is a Rarity and Now a Nobel Laureate', *New York Times*, 5 October.
Kelman, Susanne (2019), 'Ishiguro in Toronto', *Brick*, 14 February.
Kermode, Frank (2000), *The Sense of an Ending: Studies in the Theory of Fiction*, Oxford: Oxford University Press.
Kierkegaard, Søren (1967), *Soren Kierkegaard's Journals and Papers*, vol. 3, ed. Edna Hatlestad Hong, Minneapolis: Indiana University Press.
Kimber, Clarissa T. (2004), 'Gardens and Dwelling: People in Vernacular Gardens', *Geographical Review*, 94(3): 263–83.
King, Richard (2012), ' "But Perhaps I Did Not Understand Enough": Kazuo Ishiguro and Dreams of Republican Shanghai', in Richard King, Cody Poulton and Katsuhiko Endo (eds), *Sino-Japanese Transculturation*, 261–74, New York: Lexington Books.
Koshiro, Yukiko (2001), 'Japan's World and World War II', *Diplomatic History*, 25(3): 425–41.
Kracauer, Seigfried (1997), 'The Hotel Lobby', in Neil Leach (ed.), *Rethinking Architecture: A Reader in Cultural Theory*, 51–9, London: Routledge.
Leavis, Q. D. (1985), *Collected Essays*, ed. G. Singh, Cambridge: Cambridge University Press.
Leder, Drew (1990), *The Absent Body*, Chicago: University of Chicago Press.
Lefebvre, Henri (2019), *Rhythmanalysis*, New York: Bloomsbury.
Leonard, Kevin Allen (1990), ' "Is That What We Fought for?" Japanese Americans and Racism in California, the Impact of World War II', *Western Historical Quarterly*, 21(4): 463–82.

Levenson, Michael (2011), 'Modernism In and Out of War', in *Modernism*, 219–66, New Haven: Yale University Press.

Lewis, Barry (2000), *Kazuo Ishiguro*, Manchester: Manchester University Press.

Lilley, Deborah (2016), 'Unsettling Environments: New Pastorals in Kazuo Ishiguro's *Never Let Me Go* and Sarah Hall's *The Carhullan Army*', *Green Letters*, 20(1): 60–71.

Lippet, Noriko Mizuta (1980), *Reality and Fiction in Modern Japanese Literature*, New York: Routledge.

Lodge, David ([1977] 2015), *The Modes of Modern Writing: Metaphor, Metonymy, and the Typology of Modern Literature*, New York: Bloomsbury.

Lowenthal, David, and Hugh C. Prince (1964), 'The English Landscape', *Geographical Review*, 54(3): 309–46.

Lukacs, Georg (1969), *The Meaning of Contemporary Realism*, trans. John and Necke Mander, London: Merlin.

Lukacs, Georg (1971), *The Theory of the Novel*, trans. Anna Bostock, London: Merlin Press.

Lyon, John (2009), 'War, Politics, and Disappearing Poetry: Auden, Yeats, Empson', in Tim Kendall (ed.), *The Oxford Handbook of English and Irish War Poetry*, 279–98, Oxford: Oxford University Press.

Machinal, Helene (2009), '*When We Were Orphans*: Narration and Detection in the Case of Christopher Banks', in Sean Matthews and Sebastian Groes (eds), *Kazuo Ishiguro*, 79–90, New York: Continuum.

Malpas, Jeff (2018), *Place and Experience: A Philosophical Topography*, London: Routledge.

Marinetti, Filippo Tommaso (2006), *Critical Writings*, ed. Gunter Berghaus, trans. Doug Thompson, New York: Farrar, Straus and Giroux.

Marx, Karl, and Friedrich Engels (2008), *The Communist Manifesto*, Auckland: Floating Press.

Mason, Gregory, and Kazuo Ishiguro (1989), 'An Interview with Kazuo Ishiguro', *Contemporary Literature*, 30(3): 335–47.

Matthews, Sean, and Sebastian Groes (2009), 'Introduction', in Sean Matthews and Sebastian Groes (eds), *Kazuo Ishiguro*, 1–8, New York: Continuum.

McCaffery, Larry (2012), 'A Conversation with David Foster Wallace', in Stephen J. Burn (ed.), *Conversations with David Foster Wallace*, Jackson: University Press of Mississippi.

McCombe, John P. (2002), 'The End of (Anthony) Eden: Ishiguro's "The Remains of the Day" and Midcentury Anglo-American Tensions', *Twentieth Century Literature*, 48(1): 77–99.

McKeon, Michael (1985), 'Generic Transformation and Social Change: Rethinking the Rise of the Novel', *Cultural Critique*, 1: 159–81.

McNeil, Peter (1992), 'Myths of Modernism: Japanese Architecture, Interior Design and the West, c. 1920–1940', *Journal of Design History*, 5(4): 281–94.

Merleau-Ponty, Maurice (1962), *The Phenomenology of Perception*, trans. Colin Smith, London: Routledge and Kegan Paul.

Mishima, Yukio (1977), *The Sailor Who Fell from Grace with the Sea*, trans. John Nathan, Harmondsworth: Penguin.

Molino, Michael R. (2012) 'Traumatic Memory and Narrative Isolation in Ishiguro's *A Pale View of Hills*', *Critique: Studies in Contemporary Fiction*, 53(4): 322–36.

Mullan, John (2009), 'On First Reading *Never Let Me Go*', in Sean Matthews and Sebastian Groes (eds), *Kazuo Ishiguro*, 104–13, New York: Continuum.
Nancy, Jean-Luc (1993), *The Birth to Presence*, trans. Brian Holmes and others, Stanford, CA: Stanford University Press.
Nicholls, Peter (1995), *Modernisms*, New York: Springer.
The Nobel Prize in Literature (2017), NobelPrize.org, Nobel Media AB 2020, 29 April 2020.
Nute, Kevin (1994), 'Frank Lloyd Wright and Japanese Architecture: A Study in Inspiration', *Journal of Design History*, 7(3): 169–85.
Oe, Kenzaburo, and Kazuo Ishiguro (1991), 'The Novelist in Today's World: A Conversation', *Boundary 2*, 18(3): 109–22.
Ortega y Gasset, José (1972), *The Dehumanization of Art and Other Essays on Art, Culture, and Literature*, Princeton, NJ: Princeton University Press.
Paller, Ken A., and Donna J. Bridge (2012), 'Neural Correlates of Reactivation and Retrieval-Induced Distortion', *Journal of Neuroscience*, 32(35): 12144–51.
Patea, Viorica (2012), *Short Story Theories: A Twenty-First Century Perspective*, Amsterdam: Rodopi.
Pater, Walter (1994), 'The Poems of William Morris', in Henri Dorra (ed.), *Symbolist Art Theories: An Anthology*, 26–30, London: University of California Press.
Petras, James (1994), 'Cultural Imperialism in Late 20th Century', *Economic and Political Weekly*, 29(32): 2070–3.
Plath, Sylvia (2008), *Collected Poems*, ed. Ted Hughes, New York: Harper Collins.
Post, Marco R. S. (2014), 'Perilous Wanderings through the Enchanted Forest: The Influence of the Fairy-Tale Tradition on Mirkwood in Tolkien's "The Hobbit"', *Mythlore*, 33(125): 67–84.
Potter, Rachel (2012), 'Modernism and Politics', in Rachel Potter (ed.), *Modernist Literature*, 177–210, Edinburgh: Edinburgh University Press.
Propp, Vladimir (2009), *Morphology of the Folktale*, Austin: University of Texas Press.
Proust, Marcel (1943), *Remembrance of Things Past: Swann's way*, London: Chatto and Windus.
Pugh, Simon (1990), 'Introduction', in Simon Pugh (ed.), *Reading Landscape: Country-City-Capital*, Manchester: Manchester University Press.
Punch Magazine (2017), 'Kazuo Ishiguro: A Writer of the Floating World', 30 September.
Purton, V. (1993), 'The Reader in a Floating World: The Novels of Kazuo Ishiguro', in N. Page and P. Preston (eds), *The Literature of Place*, 170–9, London: Palgrave Macmillan.
Query, Patrick R. (2015), '*Never Let Me Go* and the Horizons of the Novel', *Critique: Studies in Contemporary Fiction*, 56(2): 155–72.
Rader, Melvin (1967), 'Art and History', *Journal of Aesthetics and Art Criticism*, 26(2): 157–68.
Reitano, Natalie (2007), 'The Good Wound: Memory and Community in The Unconsoled', *Texas Studies in Literature and Language*, 49(4): 361–86.
Renes, Johannes (2015), 'Layered Landscapes: A Problematic Theme in Historic Landscape Research', in Johannes Renes et al. (eds), *Landscape Biographies*, 403–22, Amsterdam: Amsterdam University Press.
Richards, Linda (2000), 'The January Interview: Kazuo Ishiguro', *January Magazine*, October.

Robinson, Richard (2009), '"To Give a Name, Is That Still to Give?" Footballers and Film Actors in The Unconsoled', in Sean Matthews and Sebastian Groes (eds), *Kazuo Ishiguro*, 67–78, New York: Continuum.

Rorty, Richard (2009), *Philosophy and the Mirror of Nature: Thirtieth Anniversary Edition*, with a new introduction by Michael Williams and a new afterword by David Bromwich, Princeton: Princeton University Press.

Ross, Michael, and Anne E. Wilson (2003), 'Autobiographical Memory and Conceptions of Self: Getting Better All the Time', *Current Directions in Psychological Science*, 12(2): 66–9.

Rose, Charlie (1995), 'Interview with Kazuo Ishiguro', https://charlierose.com/videos/18999.

Roth, Philp (1961), 'Writing American Fiction', *Commentary*, March.

Rukeysa, Rebecca (2015), 'Kazuo Ishiguro: Mythic Retreat', *Guernica*, 1 May.

Rushdie, Salman (2012), 'Rereading the Remains of the Day by Kazuo Ishiguro', *The Guardian*, 17 August.

Ruskin, John (2000), *The Seven Lamps of Architecture*, New York: Dover.

Russell, Bertrand (2009), *The Basic Writings of Bertrand Russell*, ed. Robert E. Egner and Lester E Dennon, London: Routledge.

Rymer, Thomas (1693), 'A Short View of Tragedy'.

Salmon, Arthur L. (1925), 'Conservatism and Modernism in Music', *Musical Times*, 66(983): 20–1.

Scarry, Elaine (1987), *The Body in Pain: The Making and Unmaking of the World*, Oxford: Oxford University Press.

Schopenhauer, Arthur (1909), *The World as Will and Idea*, vol. 1, trans. R. B. Haldane and J. Kemp, London: Kegan Paul.

Segal, J. (2016), *Art and Politics: Between Purity and Propaganda*, Amsterdam: Amsterdam University Press.

Seiler, Claire (2016), 'Fictions of the Human in Postwar Japan', in Allan Hepburn (ed.), *Around 1945: Literature, Citizenship, Rights*, Montreal: McGill-Queen's University Press.

Shaffer, Brian W. (2009), 'Ishiguro's Short Fiction', in Sean Matthews and Sebastian Groes (eds), *Kazuo Ishiguro*, 9–19, New York: Continuum.

Shaffer, Brian W., and Kazuo Ishiguro (2001), 'An Interview with Kazuo Ishiguro', *Contemporary Literature*, 42(1): 1–14.

Shakespeare, William (2008), *Hamlet*, ed. G. R. Hibbard, Oxford: Oxford University Press.

Shelley, Mary (2008), *Frankenstein, or, The Modern Prometheus*, Oxford: Oxford University Press.

Shelley, Percy Bysshe (2009), *The Major Works, Including Poetry, Prose, and Drama*, ed. Zachary Leader and Michael O'Neil, Oxford: Oxford University Press.

Shibata, Motoyuki, and Motoko Sugano (2009), 'Strange Reads: Kazuo Ishiguro's *A Pale View of Hills* and *An Artist of the Floating World* in Japan', in Sean Matthews and Sebastian Groes (eds), *Kazuo Ishiguro*, 20–31, New York: Continuum.

Simmel, Georg (1997), 'Bridge and Door', in Neil Leach (ed.), *Rethinking Architecture: A Reader in Cultural Theory*, 64–9, London: Routledge.

Simon, Scott (2015), 'The Persistence – and Impermanence – of Memory in "The Buried Giant"', *NPR*, 28 February, http://www.npr.org/2015/02/28/389530345/the-persistence-and-impermanence-of-memory-in-the-buried-giant.

Sini, Carlo, and Thomas Behr (2011), 'The Beyond of Language', *Annali d'Italianistica*, 29: 123–30.
Slattery, Mary Francis (1972), 'What Is Literary Realism?', *Journal of Aesthetics and Art Criticism*, 31(1): 55–62.
Sloane, P. (2018), 'Literatures of Resistance under US "Cultural Siege": Kazuo Ishiguro's Narratives of Occupation', *Critique: Studies in Contemporary Fiction*, 59(2): 154–67.
Spurr, David (2012), 'An End to Dwelling: Architectural and Literary Modernisms', in David Spurr (ed.), *Architecture and Modern Literature*, 50–72, Ann Arbor: University of Michigan Press.
Stacy, Ivan (2019), 'Looking Out Into the Fog: Narrative, Historical Responsibility, and the Problem of Freedom in Kazuo Ishiguro's *The Buried Giant*', *Textual Practice*, doi: 10.1080/0950236X.2019.1652677.
Steiner, George (2016), 'The Idea of Europe', *Open Democracy*, 22 June.
Sterne, Laurence (1760), *The Life and Opinions of Tristram Shandy, Gentleman*, vols I and II, York: A. Ward.
Stewart, Jack F. (1985), 'Color in *To the Lighthouse*', *Twentieth Century Literature*, 31(4): 438–58.
Su, John J. (2002), 'Refiguring National Character: The Remains of the British Estate Novel', *Modern Fiction Studies*, 48(3): 552–80.
Swaim, Dom (2008), 'Dom Swaim Interviews Kazuo Ishiguro', in Brian W. Shaffer and Cynthia Wong (eds), *Conversations with Kazuo Ishiguro*, 89–109, Jackson: University Press of Mississippi.
Swift, Graham, and Kazuo Ishiguro (1989), 'Kazuo Ishiguro', *BOMB*, 29, special issue on new writing: 22–3.
Swift, Jonathan (2004), *Gulliver's Travels*, London: Collector's Library.
Szafraniac, Asja (2007), *Beckett, Derrida, and the Event of Literature*, Stanford, CA: Stanford University Press.
Tallis, Raymond (1988), *In Defence of Realism*, London: Edward Arnold.
Tayler, Christopher (2009), 'Scenes from an Italian Café', The Guardian, 16 May.
Teo, Yugin (2014), *Kazuo Ishiguro and Memory*, New York: Palgrave Macmillan.
Tisdale, Jennifer (2015), 'Kazuo Ishiguro's "Notes on Some Great Writers"', *Ransom Center Magazine*, 24 August.
Tolstoy, Leo N. ([1897] 1996), What Is Art?, trans. Aylmer Maude, Indianapolis: Hackett Publishing.
Tuan, Yi-Fu (2018), *Space and Place: The Perspective of Experience*, Minneapolis: University of Minnesota Press.
Vattimo, Gianni (1997), 'The End of Modernity, the End of the Project?', in Neil Leach (ed.), *Rethinking Architecture: A Reader in Cultural Theory*, 147–54, London: Routledge.
Vernon, Matthew, and Margaret A. Miller (2018), 'Navigating Wonder: The Medieval Geographies of Kazuo Ishiguro's *The Buried Giant*', *Arthuriana*, 28(4): 68–89.
Vonnegut, Kurt (2005), *A Man without a Country*, ed. Daniel Simon, New York: Seven Stories.
Walkowitz, Rebecca L. (2001), 'Kazuo Ishiguro's Floating Worlds', *ELH*, 68(4): 1049–76.
Walkowitz, Rebecca L. (2006), *Cosmopolitan Style: Modernism Beyond the Nation*, New York: Columbia University Press.
Wallace, David Foster (2009), *Girl with Curious Hair*, London: Abacus.

Wang, Ching-Chi (2008), *Homeless Strangers in the Novels of Kazuo Ishiguro: Floating Characters in a Floating World*, New York: Edwin Mellen.
Warren, J. R. (2017), 'Music Ethics Politics', *New Sound: International Journal of Music*, 50(2): 25–41.
Watt, Ian (1983), *The Rise of the Novel*, New York: Penguin.
White, Hayden (1992), *The Content of the Form: Narrative Discourse and Historical Representation*, Baltimore, MD: Johns Hopkins University Press.
Whitehead, Anne (2011), 'Writing with Care: Kazuo Ishiguro's "Never Let Me Go"', *Contemporary Literature*, 52(1): 54–83.
Wilde, Oscar (2005), *The Picture of Dorian Gray*, London: Penguin.
Winkler, Rafael (2007), 'Heidegger and the Question of Man's Poverty in World', *International Journal of Philosophical Studies*, 15(4): 521–39.
Wong, Cynthia (2005), *Kazuo Ishiguro*, Devon: Northcote House.
Wong, Cynthia with Grace Crummett (2008), 'A Conversation about Life and Art with Kazuo Ishiguro', in Brian W. Shaffer and Cynthia Wong (eds), *Conversations with Kazuo Ishiguro*, 204–20, Jackson: University Press of Mississippi.
Wood, Gaby (2017), 'Kazuo Ishiguro: "There Is a Slightly Chilly Aspect to Writing Fiction"', *The Telegraph*, 5 October.
Wood, James (2015), 'The Uses of Oblivion: Kazuo Ishiguro's "The Buried Giant"', *New Yorker*, 16 March.
Woodworth, R. S. (1906), 'Imageless Thought', *Journal of Philosophy, Psychology and Scientific Methods*, 3(26): 701–8.
Woolf, Virginia (1971), 'Mr Bennett and Mrs Brown', in *Collected Essays*, vol. 1, 319–37, London: Hogarth
Woolf, Virginia (1986), 'Modern Fiction', in Andrew McNeille (ed.), *The Essays of Virginia Woolf, Volume 4: 1925 to 1928*, London: Hogarth Press.
Woolf, Virginia (2003), *Mrs Dalloway*, afterward Anna South, London: CRW Publishing.
Woolf, Virginia (2015), *The Waves*, ed. David Bradshaw, Oxford: Oxford University Press.
Wordsworth, William (2008), 'The Thorn', in Stephen Gill (ed.), *The Major Works*, 59–65, Oxford: Oxford University Press.
Wright, Timothy (2014), 'No Homelike Place: The Lesson of History in Kazuo Ishiguro's "An Artist of the Floating World"', *Contemporary Literature*, 55(1): 58–88.
Wroe, Nicholas (2005), 'Living Memories', *The Guardian*, 19 February.
Zeitlin, Froma I. (2013), 'Figure: Ekphrasis', *Greece & Rome*, 60(1): 17–31.
Zola, Émile (1893), *The Experimental Novel and Other Essays*, trans. Belle M. Sherman, New York: Cassell Publishing.

INDEX

Adams, Tim 133
Adorno, Theodor 26, 48, 89
aesthetics 75–102
   ekphrastic transfiguration 77–8
   figurative painting 77
   influenced by Japanese art 83
   manipulability of memory 77
   modernism in 83
   relational 93
Aitkenhead, Decca 6
Antliff, Mark 82
architext 103–31
Artist of the Floating World, An (AFW)
   9, 19, 27, 83, 84, 90, 97, 100–1, 104,
   130 n.4, 141, 160 n.3
À rebours 83
Auden, W. H. 82
autobiographical memory 8–9
Axl (character) 1–3, 5, 9, 13–14,
   20–2, 35, 38, 42, 57, 101, 104,
   106–9, 126–8, 135–7, 144, 148–51,
   154–5, 163

Bachelard, Gaston 13, 49, 51, 73,
   105–7, 112
Back to the Future 102 n.9
Badiou, Alain 3
Baker, Chet 90
Ballard, J. G. 103
Banks (character) 7, 9, 11, 16, 18, 21–5,
   36, 38, 40, 43, 53, 55–62, 73, 76,
   79–81, 113–14, 119, 126–9, 135,
   139, 141, 149, 155
Barth, John 82
Barthes, Roland 19, 55–6,
   76
   'French Toys' 55
Bataille, Georges 78
Beatrice (character) 1–5, 9, 13–14,
   20–2, 35, 38, 42, 54, 57, 104, 106–8,
112, 126–8, 135–7, 144, 148–51,
154–6, 163
Beckett, Samuel 10, 162
Bedggood, Daniel 24, 117
Beedham, Matthew 16
Behr, Thomas 8
Being There 142
Bell, Clive 78
Bennett, Andrew 9–10
Berberich, Christine 117
Berryman, John 56
   'The Ball Poem' 56
Black, Shameem 80, 153
Blanchot, Maurice 11
Bloch, Ernst 137
Bloom, Harold 77
Boris (character) 25–6, 42, 44, 51–5,
   58, 60, 65–7, 94, 106, 118, 122–4,
   128–9, 160
Born, Georgina 94
Bourdieu, Pierre 15
Bourriaud, Nicolas 91–2, 97, 102 n.7
Brave New World 84
Bridgewater, Judy 89
Brink, Andre 31
Brooke, Rupert 142
Brynner, Yul 50
Buried Giant, The (BG) 4, 16, 18, 23, 32,
   78, 101 n.1, 104, 122, 127–8, 133,
   136, 148, 149, 151, 157

Cage, John 98
Carey, John 49, 96
Carrier, David 78
Carroll, Rachel 119
Carver, Raymond 11
Casey, Edward 134
Castellano, Carlos Garrido 81, 95, 97,
   102 n.7
Chaudhuri, Amit 101

Cheeke, Stephen 76
Cheng, Chu-Chueh 136, 159
childhood arts 62–7
childhood imagination 51–2
Christie Malry's Own Double Entry 40
Chronicles of Narnia, The 52
Colet, Louise 24
Conrad, Joseph 136
Cooke, Rachel 101
Coppola, Francis Ford 162
Crying of Lot 49, The 21

Daniel Deronda 153
Daniel-Veyret, Paul 60, 80
Dark City 119
Dean, Dominic 64
death 8
Deleuze, Gilles 76–7, 103
Delistraty, Cody 46 n.2, 161
Derrida, Jacques 8–9, 41
Descartes, Rene 48
Descombes, Vincent 39
Dickens, Charles 5, 23
dislocated PTSD narrative 47
doors 112–13
Dostoyevsky, Fydor 162
Drąg, Wojciech 136
Duncan, J. 137
Duncan, N. 137

Eaglestone, Robert 1, 4, 37, 127, 154
Earhart, H. Byron 86
Eastman, Julius 98
Eastwood, Clint 50
ekphrastic transfiguration 77–8
Eliot, George 23
Esthetique Relationelle 92
Etsuko (character) 9, 19, 22, 27, 29–30, 39, 44, 47, 50, 57, 61–3, 73, 78, 85, 88, 92, 109–12, 116, 124, 126, 130 n.4, 135–6, 140, 147, 155–7
Evans, Ray 89

Farrant, Marc 37
Ferris, Ina 20
figurative painting 77
Fleming, Tom 90
floating world 47

Frankenstein 13
Frost, Robert 126
Fry, Roger 32

Gadamer, Hans-Georg 6, 33
galleries role 70
games 52–7
  'Mother Hen Target Game' 56
  society as 60
Gardner, Tony 90
Garland-Thomson, Rosemarie 104, 153
Castellano, Carlos Garrido 123
Gasset, Ortega Y. 31, 82, 96
Gautier, Théophile 82
Gee, Maggie 17
Geek's Guide to the Galaxy, The 18
Gehlawat, Monika 146
gestures 15–46. *See also* modernism; realism
Glass Passions 98
Glass, Philip 98
Glynne, Jess 89
Goffman, Erving 116
Gould, Thomas 10
Great Expectations 21
Groes, Sebastian 47, 60, 75, 80, 81, 135
Guattari, Felix 76–7, 103
Gulliver's Travels 97

Hailsham, art in 69
Hamlet 5–6
Hard Times 5
Heart of Darkness 136
Heidegger, Martin 4, 6–7, 10–13, 87, 104
Helphand, Kenneth I. 141
Hensher, Philip 89, 105
Herring, Peter 137
Hitchens, Christopher 89
Hoffman (character) 22–4, 59–60, 66–7, 81, 89, 95, 99–100, 121–6, 141, 150
Hofweber, Thomas 10
Holmes, Frederick M. 25
homelessness 161
Houellebecq, Michel 46 n.6
Hume, David 48–9
  human nature 49

on imagination 48–50
   memory versus 49–50
Huxley, Aldous 84
Huysmann, J. K. 83

Ignorance: Agnoiology and Literature 9
imagination 47–73. *See also* games
   art in Hailsham 69
   childhood 51–2
   deferrals in 71
   distancing oneself from the world 48
   for Descartes 48
   as esemplastic 51
   for Hume 48–9
   human nature 49
   memory versus 49–50
   real world and thought relationship 71
   short-term distractive strategy 53
   as transformative 51
In Memory of W.B. Yeats 82
Ingarden, Roman 11
Ishiguro, Kazuo 3–6, 10, 50–1
   architectural anchors 109
   art in the art of 80
   conventional novels 15
   doors in the works of 113
   homeless characters 108
   idea of 'home' 80
   realist fascination, manipulation 21
   repurposing realism and modernism 16–17
   'tatami' in the novels of 19
   on tunnel memory 26
Iwata, Miki 34
Iyer, Pico 16

James, David 18, 20, 25, 31, 52, 89, 101, 136, 162
James, Henry 20
Johnson, B. S. 40

Kafka, Franz 101, 162
Kant, Immanuel 6
Kathy H. (character) 27, 44, 62–3, 109–12, 115, 130, 135, 155–6
Kazuo Ishiguro and Memory 8
Kent, Stacey 89
Kermode, Frank 16

Kierkegaard, Søren 39
Klara and the Sun 3, 161, 164
Koshiro, Yukiko 84
Kosiński, Jerzy 142
Kracauer, Siegfried 122
Krapp's Last Tape 33
Kubrick, Stanley 50
Kundera, Milan 162
Kurosawa, Akira 162

language 10
   modernism and 39
Ledoux, Henri 7
Lefebvre, Henri 29, 96–8, 134
Lewis, Barry 19, 39, 106, 115–16
Lewis, C. S. 52
Lightfoot, Marcus 90
literature, experimental approach to 23
Livingstone, Jay 89
Locke, John 10
Lord Darlington (character) 6, 13, 21–4, 34–5, 45, 60, 80, 98, 105–8, 114–16, 120–1, 129, 133, 135, 139–49, 157, 159
Losa, Mario Vargas 162
Lowenthal, David 145
Lukacs, Georg 15, 31, 33
Lyon, John 82

Macaulay, T. B. 146
Machinal, Helene 25
Madame Butterfly 63
Maddin, Guy 101 n.2
Magnificent 7, The 50
Malpas, Jeff 107, 134, 137
Mariko (character) 14 n.4, 44, 61–6, 77, 110, 155–7
Marquez, Gabriel Garcia 14 n.1
Masuji Ono (character) 4, 7, 9, 13, 16–24, 27, 29–30, 34–5, 38, 42, 47, 52, 55, 57, 60, 64, 76, 79, 83–7, 91–2, 95, 97, 106, 108–9, 115, 120, 126–30, 136, 140–3, 147, 162
Matsuda, Chishi (character) 83–8, 95
Matthews, Sean 47, 81, 135
McCormack, Eloise (character) 90
McFly, Marty 102 n.9
McKeon, Michael 15

McNeil, Peter 109
memory 8, 49–50
Middlemarch 23
Mishima, Yukio 5
Miss Kenton (character) 7, 20–5, 35, 41–2, 88–9, 113, 116–17, 126, 139–40, 143, 159
modernism 31–8
　forms of 32–3
　language in 39
　memory and 33–4
　perceptions 33
　silences 38–9
Moriyama, Seiji (character) 83, 87
Mullan, John 153

Nancy, Jean-Luc 10, 41
Never Ending Story 52
Never Let Me Go (NLMG) 3–4, 9, 23, 39, 61–2, 67, 72, 80, 89, 94, 101, 104, 119–21, 133, 151, 153, 155
Nguyen, Viet Thanh 17
Nietzsche, Friedrich 10
Night Pieces 89
Nocturnes (N) 15, 75, 89, 90, 94, 98, 138
Nute, Kevin 130 n.3

Oe, Kenzaburo 18
One Hundred Years of Solitude 14 n.1, 162
ongoing dissociative episode 47
Origin of the Work of Art, The 87
Ozu, Yasujirō 162

Pale King, The 40
Pale View of Hills, A (PVH) 9, 19, 27, 61–2, 83, 136, 147
Patea, Viorica 15
Pater, Walter 87
Picture of Dorian Gray, The 83
Place and Experience 134
poetics of home 107
Poetics of Space, The 107
Post, Marco 151
Postmodern Geographies 134
Potter, Rachel 81
Pound, Ezra 82

Presentation of Self in Everyday Life, The 116
Prince, Hugh 145
Production of Space, The 134
Proust, Marcel 34
Proyas, Alex 119
Puccini 63
Pugh, Simon 137
Pynchon, Thomas 21

quasi gothic dreamscape 47
Query, Patrick R. 41

Rader, Melvin 57, 76
realism 18–23
　in Ishiguro's works 16–19
　in Lodge's work 23
Reilly, Terry 98
Remains of the Day, The (RD) 9, 47, 87–8, 90, 98, 114, 133, 157
Rings of Saturn, The 23
Rise of the Novel, The 15
Robbe-Grillet, Alain 20, 50
Robinson, Richard 50
Rorty, Richard 49
Rose, Charlie 16
Roth, Philip 26
Rushdie, Salman 17
Russell, Bertrand 5
Ruth (character) 3, 37–43, 58–63, 68–71, 93, 137, 144, 152, 154–8
Ryder (character) 7, 13, 16, 21, 24–6, 30, 32, 41–4, 47, 50–7, 60, 65–7, 73, 76, 81, 88, 94–108, 112–26, 138, 141, 157, 162–3, 167

Sachiko (character) 27, 44, 62–3, 109–12, 155–6
Saddest Music in the World, The 80, 101 n.2
Sailor Who Fell from Grace with the Sea, The 5
Salmon, Arthur 82
Scarry, Elaine 144
Schopenhauer, Arthur 77, 93
Sebald, W. G. 23
Self Portrait in a Convex Mirror 63
Sellers, Peter 141

Shaffer, Brian W. 11, 21, 138
Shakespeare, William 5
Shelley, Mary 13
silences 38–9
Simmel, Georg 112
Sini, Carlo 8
Sir Gawain and the Green Knight 147
Slattery, Mary Francis 21
Soja, Edward W. 134
Songs after Dark 89
Space and Place 134
space 133–60
  forests 151
  gardens 143
  lakes 157
  landscape 148
  parks 143
  public space 143
  susceptibility to the psychology of perceiver 144
  timedepth 137
Spurr, David 103, 109, 115, 145
Stacy, Ivan 2
Steiner, George 148
Stevens (character) 4–12, 14, 16, 18, 20–30, 34–5, 38, 41–5, 48–9, 57, 60, 63, 73, 76, 83, 85, 88–91, 105–8, 113–17, 120–1, 126, 129, 130, 135–50, 157–63
Stewart, Jack F. 33
Su, John J. 114
Symons, Jane 45
Szafraniac, Asja 10

Tallis, Raymond 20
Tarantino, Quentin 162
Tarkovsky, Andrei 162
Tayler, Christopher 89
Teo, Yugin 7–8, 50, 76, 147
timedepth 137
Tolstoy, Leo 80

Tommy (character) 3, 7, 14 n.3, 34–5, 37–8, 42–4, 57, 60, 68–72, 101, 104, 120, 126, 136–7, 144, 152–8
Tony Gardner (character) 90, 142
Trial, The 101
Tuan, Yi-Fu 56, 59, 78, 103, 134, 136
2001: A Space Odyssey 50

Unconsoled, The (U) 7, 16, 18, 22, 24, 26, 39, 46 n.3, 50, 59, 65–6, 88, 91, 94, 96–7, 100–1, 104, 117, 123, 133, 142
Underground Railroad, The 160 n.1
Unsettled, Unconsoled 94

Vattimo, Gianni 79
Vaughan, Sarah 90
Verticality 99
Veyret, Paul-Daniel 75
Voice of Terror, The 73 n.1

Waits, Tom 88
Walkowitz, Rebecca 85, 162
Wallace, David Foster 40
Warren, Jeff 92
Waves, The 33
When We Were Orphans (WWO) 36, 53, 61, 79, 105
Whitehead, Anne 93
Whitehead, Colson 160 n.1
Wilde, Oscar 83
Wittgenstein, Ludwig 13
Wonder of England, The 45, 145
Wong, Cynthia 16, 38–9, 141, 156, 162
Wood, James 16, 18–20, 46
Woolf, Virginia 15, 24, 32–5
Wright, Timothy 108

Zola, Émile 18, 23–4

www.ingramcontent.com/pod-product-compliance
Lightning Source LLC
Chambersburg PA
CBHW061835300426
44115CB00013B/2386